The "Here and Now" of French Psychoanalysis

The "Here and Now" of French Psychoanalysis provides an overview of the living psychoanalytic landscape in France through the voice of experienced psychoanalysts who continue to transform the legacy of Freud, Lacan and others in their publications and clinical practice.

Rachel Boué-Widawsky interviews a wide range of practitioners, underscoring the specificities of French psychoanalysis and exploring how the French psycho-analytic community has responded theoretically and clinically to the global crisis of the COVID-19 pandemic and racial and gender issues. Mimicking the process of psychoanalytic dialogue, the interview format allows for a lively and engaging dis-cussion of each practitioner's theoretical background and their clinical approach. Boué-Widawsky includes leading individuals in the field as well as representatives of key institutions including La Maison de Solenn and the Centre Jean-Favreau.

The "Here and Now" of French Psychoanalysis presents an accessible intro-duction to this distinctive psychoanalytic landscape. It will be essential reading for psychoanalysts in practice and in training and for academics and students of psychoanalytic studies.

Rachel Boué-Widawsky, PhD, is a psychoanalyst in private practice in New York, on the faculty of IPTAR (Institute for Psychoanalytic Training and Research). She is editor of the Foreign Books Reviews of *JAPA* (*Journal of the American Psy-choanalytic Association*). She is also the author of numerous articles on French psychoanalysis and of several books in French on literary criticism.

"In this volume we get to hear the response of a diverse group of French and francophone psychoanalysts to current societal issues; a very interesting addition to this body of work."

Dana Birksted-Breen, L.ès L. PhD, *Distinguished Fellow and Training Psychoanalyst of the BPAS*

"The depth and complexity of contemporary French psychoanalytic thinking has often presented challenges to anglophone readers, because of insufficient translation and the often times demanding poetics of the French intellectual literary style. Here is an accessible, thought provoking and deeply personal window into the hearts and minds of leading figures in contemporary French analysis, one that will offer readers of all levels of experience an invaluable treasure chest of personal, historical, and clinical psychoanalytic resources that cannot help but entice, engage and expand one's thinking and understanding about oneself and one's clinical practice. To read this book is to encounter, challenge and enlarge one's assumptions and understandings about one's knowledge of psychoanalysis in the most imaginative and creative ways possible. It is a vital experience that should not be missed and for which readers will long be grateful."

Howard B. Levine, *Training-Analyst, Member of PINE, NYU Post-Doc, author of* Affect, Representation and Language: Between the Silence and the Cry; *editor of* The Freudian Matrix of André Green: Towards a Psychoanalysis for the Twenty-First Century *and* On The Destruction and Death Drives by André Green

"*The "Here and Now" of French Psychoanalysis, Conversations with Contemporary French Psychoanalysts* is an exciting book, a compilation of conversations with contemporary French psychoanalysts which brings to life the central themes and controversies in French psychoanalysis today. Dr. Boué-Widawsky's thoughtful interviews make French psychoanalysis accessible to the anglophone reader. Although it would be possible to use the book as a reference to learn about a specific author, my sense is that readers will be stimulated, as I was, to read it through and to engage with the lively and erudite conversations that it presents. The book is a pleasure to read as well as a useful introduction to French psychoanalysis."

Lucy LaFarge, M.D., *Editor in Chief*, The Psychoanalytic Quarterly, *Training Analyst at Columbia University Center for Psychoanalytic Training and Research, Clinical Professor of Psychiatry at Cornell Medical College*

"Separated more by failures of translation than differences in language per se, French and Anglo-American psychoanalytic histories have evolved relatively independent of each other. Rachel Boué-Widawsky's volume bridges this divide through a series of structured interviews with leading contemporary French psychoanalysts; a method that reveals the diversity of each personal journey as well as the foci and themes that distinguish French psychoanalysis as a distinct theoretical and clinical perspective. Her excellent introduction not only sets the scene for the interviews that follow but also provides a valuable resource for scholars and clinicians who wish to contrast, compare, and perhaps incorporate French psychoanalytic thinking into their own work."

Bonnie E. Litowitz, PhD, *Faculty, Chicago Psychoanalytic Institute;*
Japa Editor-in-Chief, Emerita; co-editor (with G. Gabbard
and P. Williams), The Textbook of Psychoanalysis

The "Here and Now" of French Psychoanalysis

Conversations with Contemporary Psychoanalysts

Rachel Boué-Widawsky

Translated by

Andrew Weller

Routledge
Taylor & Francis Group

LONDON AND NEW YORK

Designed cover image: Arman, L'heure de tous, (temps de tout le monde), 1985 © 2024 Artists Rights Society (ARS), New York/ ADAGP, Paris

First published 2025
by Routledge
4 Park Square, Milton Park, Abingdon, Oxon OX14 4RN

and by Routledge
605 Third Avenue, New York, NY 10158

Routledge is an imprint of the Taylor & Francis Group, an informa business

British Library Cataloguing-in-Publication Data
A catalogue record for this book is available from the British Library

ISBN: 978-1-032-37902-9 (hbk)
ISBN: 978-1-032-37901-2 (pbk)
ISBN: 978-1-003-34250-2 (ebk)

DOI: 10.4324/9781003342502

Typeset in Times New Roman
by KnowledgeWorks Global Ltd.

Contents

Notes on Contributors

Marilia Aisenstein, a philosopher by training, is a psychoanalyst and former president of the Paris Psychoanalytical Society (SPP). She has published more than 150 articles and four books in French, English and Spanish on the body, transference and counter-transference, psychosomatic illness and masochism. Her most recent book is titled *Desire, Pain and Thought: Primal Masochism and Psychoanalytic Theory* (Routledge, 2023).

Christine Anzieu-Premmereur is a psychiatrist and psychoanalyst in New York City who works in private practice with adults, children, parents and their babies. She is a member of the SPP but is also on the faculty of the Columbia Psychoanalytic Center for Training and Research and is Assistant Clinical Professor in Psychiatry at Columbia University. She is the chair of the International Psychoanalytical Association (IPA) Committee for Child and Adolescent Psychoanalysis (COCAP), and the cofounder, with Vaia Tsolas, of Pulsion Institute. She has recently published two book chapters, "The process of representation in early childhood" (in: H. B. Levine, G. S. Reed & D. Scarfone (Eds.), *Unrepresented States and the Construction of Meaning*, Routledge, 2013) and "Attacks on linking in parents of young disturbed children" (in: C. Bronstein & E. O'Shaughnessy (Eds.), *Attacks on Linking Revisted*, Routledge, 2017). She coedited, with Vaia Tsolas, *A Psychoanalytic Exploration of the Body in Today's World: On the Body* (Routledge, 2017) and *A Psychoanalytic Exploration of the Contemporary Search for Pleasure: The Turning of the Screw* (Routledge, 2023).

Danièle Brun (1938–2023) was a psychoanalyst, member of the Espace analytique, Professor Emeritus at Paris Diderot University (later Paris City University), and a former president of the Société Médecine et Psychanalyse. She wrote a number of important books for analytic thought, in particular *La Passion dans l'amitié*, *La Féminité retrouvée*, *Une part de soi dans la vie des autres*, *Mères majuscules* and *L'Empreinte du corps familial*.

Catherine Chabert is a psychoanalyst, a full member of the French Psychoanalytical Association and Professor Emeritus at Paris Descartes University. Her work is focused mainly on the feminine, masochism, melancholia and mania, but also on the transference and the psychoanalytic method. She has published many articles in national and international journals and several edited collections in the *Petite Bibliothèque de psychanalyse* (Paris, Presses Universitaires de France (PUF)). She has edited the *Traité de psychopathologie* in four volumes: *Les névroses, Narcissisme et dépression, Les psychoses, Psychopathologie des limites* (Dunod, (2008/2010)). She is the author of *Féminin mélancolique* (PUF, 2003), *L'amour de la différence* (PUF, 2011), *La jeune fille et le psychanalyste* (Dunod, 2015), *Maintenant, il faut se quitter* (PUF, 2017), *Les belles espérances. Le transfert et l'attente* (PUF, 2020), and her latest book is called *Se retrouver. Rencontres avec ...* (PUF, 2023).

Bernard Chervet is a psychiatrist by training, a training psychoanalyst at the SPP, and a former president of the SPP. He is a representative on the IPA Board and on the IPA Executive Committee, as well as the scientific director of the Congress of French-Speaking Psychoanalysts (CPLF). He founded the SPP Publications. He has published numerous articles in French and international journals and was awarded the Maurice Bouvet Prize in 2017 for his work as a whole. He wrote the keynote to the CPLF on the theme of "après-coup" and is the author of *Après-coup in Psychoanalysis: The Fulfilment of Desire and Thought* (2023, Routledge). He was a contributor to the IPA Inter-Regional Encyclopedic Dictionary (IRED).

Paul Denis, MD, is a psychiatrist, psychoanalyst and supervising analyst at the SPP. He is a former editor of the *Revue française de psychanalyse*. He has published many papers and a number of books including *Emprise et satisfaction. Les deux formants de la pulsion, Rives et dérives du contre-transfert, De l'exaltation, Œdipe médecin, Les phobies* and *Le narcissisme*.

Nicolas Evzonas (PhD in literature and PhD in psychoanalysis) is an associate professor at Paris City University. He is a Paris-based therapist, a training candidate at the French Psychoanalytical Association (APF) and the European consultant of the IPA Sexual and Gender Diversity Studies Committee. He has served as guest editor of *Studies in Gender and Sexuality, The Psychoanalytic Review* and *Psychoanalytic Inquiry*. He is the author of numerous papers on body experiences and a book in French on transference and countertransference, which will also be published in English by Routledge.

Alain Gibeault is a philosopher, clinical psychologist and psychoanalyst, a full member of the SPP, a former president of the European Federation of Psychoanalysis and former secretary of the IPA. His publications include *Chemins de la symbolisation* (PUF, 2010) (forthcoming in English) and a number of contributions to edited collections: D. Birksted-Breen, S. Flanders & A. Gibeault (Eds.), *Reading French Psychoanalysis* (Routledge, 2010); B. Reith (Ed.), *Initiating Psychoanalysis* (Routledge, 2012); B. Reith (Ed.), *Beginning Analysis. On the Processes of Initiating Psychoanalysis* (Routledge, 2018); F. Sacco & E. Robert (Eds.), *L'origine des représentations. Regards croisés sur l'art préhistorique* (Editions d'Ithaque, 2016).

René Kaës was born in 1936, has a doctorate in both Psychology and Letters and Humanities and is Professor Emeritus of the Universities. He is a psychoanalyst, group analyst and psychodramatist. His publications include *L'Appareil psychique groupal* (Dunod, 1976); *La polyphonie du rêve. L'espace onirique commun et partagé* (Dunod, 2002); *Linking, Alliances and Shared Spaces. Groups and the Psychoanalyst* (International Psychoanalysis Library, 2007); *Les alliances inconscientes* (Dunod, 2009); *Le malêtre* (Dunod, 2012); *L'Extension de la psychanalyse. Pour une métapsychologie de troisième type* (Dunod, 2015).

Laurence Kahn is a training and supervising analyst at the APF, of which she was president between 2008 and 2010. She is the author of numerous articles and several books including *Psychoanalysis, Apathy and the Postmodern Patient* (Routledge, 2018) and *What Nazism did to Psychoanalysis* (Routledge, 2022).

Vassilis Kapsambelis is a psychiatrist, psychoanalyst and full member of the SPP. He is the director of the *Revue française de psychanalyse* and a former director of the Psychoanalytic Centre of the Mental Health Association in the 13th district of Paris. He has made a number of contributions on psychoses and borderline states, and his latest book is *Le schizophrène en mal d'objet* (PUF, 2020).

Julia Kristeva is a writer and a psychoanalyst. Author of many acclaimed books, she is the first recipient of the Holberg Prize and of many other awards. As a psychoanalyst, she uses psychoanalytic theory in unique transformative ways to address societal and clinical issues.

Laurie Laufer is a psychoanalyst, professor and director of the Department of Psychoanalytic Studies of the Humanities, Sciences and Societies Institute (IHSS) at Paris City University. With Sandra Boehringer, she coedited *Après Les Aveux de la chair. Généalogie du sujet chez Michel Foucault* (EPEL, 2020). She is the author of *Murmures de l'art à la psychanalyse* (Hermann, 2021) and *Vers une psychanalyse émancipée. Renouer avec la subversion* (La Découverte, 2022). Her latest book, written with Serge Hefez, *Questions de genre*, was published by Editions d'Ithaque in 2022.

Clotilde Leguil is a psychoanalyst in Paris, and a member of both the École de la Cause freudienne and the World Association of Psychoanalysis. She graduated from the École normale supérieure with an *agrégation* and doctorate in philosophy and is currently a professor at the Department of Psychoanalysis at the University of Paris 8 Vincennes-Saint-Denis, where she specializes in contemporary French philosophy and the thought of Jacques Lacan. She is the author of several book essays, including *Céder n'est pas consentir. Une approche clinique et politique du consentement.* (PUF, 2021) and *L'ère du toxique. Essai sur le nouveau malaise dans la civilisation.* (PUF, 2023).

Sophie Mendelsohn practises psychoanalysis in Paris. She cofounded The Pantin Collective, which uses psychoanalytic tools to address issues arising from colonialism and postcolonialism, in particular racism and the intersections between gender and race, on which she has published numerous articles. With Livio Boni she coauthored *La vie psychique du racisme. 1. L'empire du démenti* (Paris, La Découverte, 2021). They also coordinated an edited collection titled *Psychanalyse du reste du monde. Géo-histoire d'une subversion.* (La Découverte, 2023).

Dominique Scarfone, MD, is Member Emeritus of the Montreal Psychoanalytic Society and Institute (French branch of the Canadian Psychoanalytic Society and Institute) and Honorary Professor of the Department of Psychology at Montreal University. His most recent book is titled, *The Reality of the Message: Psychoanalysis in the Wake of Jean Laplanche* (The Unconscious in Translation, 2023).

Alain Vanier, MD, PhD, is a psychoanalyst and psychiatrist practising in Paris, a member and former president of the Espace Analytique, a member of the Après-Coup Psychoanalytic Association and Honorary Professor of Paris City University. He is the author of numerous articles (including some in English) on psychoanalysis and culture and books (in English: *Lacan* (Other Press, 2000)).

Notes on the Author

Rachel Boué-Widawsky, PhD, is a psychoanalyst in private practice in New York. She is on the faculty and Chair of Admissions at the Institute for Psychoanalytic Training and Research (IPTAR) and Associate Clinical Professor of NYU Medical School. She is the Editor of the Foreign Books Reviews of the *Journal of the American Psychoanalytic Association* (*JAPA*).

Author of numerous articles on French psychoanalysis, her most recent contributions are "Perversion, Sublimation and Ethic" in *American Imago* (2024) and the chapters "Maternal eroticism or the necessary risk of madness" in *Eroticism* (2019) and "Maternal Eroticism and the journey of a concept in Julia Kristeva's work" in *The Philosophy of Julia Kristeva* (2020). She is also the author of several books in French on literary criticism.

Acknowledgements

This book is a tribute to the contributors' passion and dedication to psychoanalysis as a practice and as a thinking process. In this series of interviews, the writers gracefully and generously disclose the meanings and the meanderings of their personal and intellectual trajectories. Prior to this collective project, reading their works over the years, on the other side of the Atlantic, taught me how to build an inclusive and pluralistic psychoanalytic mind. I owe them my extended and continued education, and this book is a tribute to their thinking and legacy.

Andrew Weller's seminal role in the diffusion of French psychoanalysis in anglophone countries has to be underscored. Andrew has translated over 50 books since *The Work of the Negative* by André Green in 1999. It has been a privilege to experience his living memory of French psychoanalysis from a translational view point.

All my gratitude goes also to the Routledge editor, Susannah Frearson, whose support and trust in this project have been infallible through the various stages of publication.

Ashley D'Arcy my freelance copy editor deserves many thanks for the sharpness of her close reading.

I am also very grateful to my dear friend Xavier Luciani for taking the picture of Arman's sculpture for the cover of the book.

My special thanks go to Daniel, Elias and Sophie's sharp sense of humour in putting up with my passion for psychoanalysis!

Preface

The "Here and Now" of French Psychoanalysis: Conversations with Contemporary Psychoanalysts continues the discourse from two seminal publications on French psychoanalysis by Marion Oliner (1988) and by the editors Dana Birksted-Breen, Sara Flanders and Alain Gibeault (2010). Oliner delineated the theoretical specificities of French psychoanalysis in its historical, linguistic and cultural context whereas Birksted-Breen, Flanders and Gibeault, presented a panel of eminent authors, emblematic of French psychoanalytic tenets. *The "Here and Now" of French Psychoanalysis* takes a different perspective by exploring the diversity of French contemporary psychoanalysis stance in the current societal debates.

As a series of interviews, *"Here and Now"* provides a window into the contemporary psychoanalytic landscape in France through the voice of experienced psychoanalysts who continue, in transforming it, Freud's, Lacan's and/or others' legacies in their publications and clinical practice. It underscores the specificities of French psychoanalysis and explores how the psychoanalytic community has responded theoretically and clinically to global crises, such as the COVID-19 pandemic, the impact of climate change and racial and gender issues.

Despite its competitors or sometimes detractors—competition with psychopharmacology, prominence of neurosciences and cognitivism in research programs—French psychoanalysis has a unique presence in the French society. It is integrated into medical care in French hospitals and is part of the public discourse—psychoanalysts are invited onto radio and TV shows and asked to write in mainstream newspapers. In order to match that level of relevance and diffusion in French society, I decided to conduct interviews with prominent French psychoanalysts to capture the specific interface between the external and the internal reality that pure theoretical writing can't always reflect.

To remedy a lack of access to a broader understanding of contemporary French psychoanalysis—due to the scarcity of translations—interviews with French living analysts, reflecting on their theoretical background and their clinical practice, present personal vignettes of how French psychoanalysis situates itself within today's global psychoanalytic debates. In this context, these psychoanalysts from various theoretical backgrounds—from post Freudian, post Lacanian and the Psychosomatic School to new intersectional trends—present their theoretical and clinical views.

In "*Here and Now*", French psychoanalysts from different theoretical horizons have the opportunity to speak freely of themselves, of their theoretical views and clinical practice. Behind the label of "French psychoanalysis", *diversity* speaks for itself through the personal experiences, the singular voices and the styles of each author. However, their common denominator is an unmistakable vocational commitment to psychoanalysis through their private practice, their publications and institutional work. When reading these interviews, you won't only meet a practitioner or an author but also a person with their unpredictable biographical meanders that lead them to psychoanalysis. These personal narratives rightfully remind us that psychoanalysis is not a professional occupation like others reducible to a set of skills. It is a singular encounter, what Roland Barthes called a "*tuché*", between a biography, another modality of thinking and eventually, for some people, a vocation. These interviews shed a nuanced light on what makes a truthful psychoanalyst.

In addition to the diversity and the personal touch that these interviews candidly express, they also highlight the underpinnings and the tenets of what can still be labelled as French psychoanalysis with its historical intellectual and theoretical Freudian legacy. In that regard, it is important to take into consideration that French psychoanalysis did not develop under James Strachey's translation of Freud's work—the result of which will be examined in the Introduction.

My hope is that, through these interviews, anglophone readers will further the opportunity to encounter and to explore French psychoanalysis today in a manner that is linguistically and theoretically accessible.

While the purpose of the introduction is to provide the reader with a frame of reference to situate the broad outlines of contemporary French psychoanalysis, this volume of interviews aims to highlight the singularity of each of the authors from different theoretical backgrounds.

In order to preserve the fluid and original character of these interviews, which is enhanced by the dialogue format, the idea of highlighting one or two salient features of each author's thinking has been substituted for the traditional principle of an abstract.

Introduction

French psychoanalysis is the product of two inseparable legacies, those of Freud and Lacan. This dual heritage, highlighted by Dana Birsksted-Breen and Sara Sanders in their introduction to *Reading French Psychoanalysis* (Birksted-Breen, Sanders & Gibeault 2010), is certainly one of the most distinctive features of French psychoanalysis, which is indebted to two founding fathers. The great names of French psychoanalysis—Green, Aulagnier, Laplanche, Pontalis—were all students of Lacan, even if they all distanced themselves from him, each in their own way, as I shall explain below. All French psychoanalytical thought from 1950 to 1970 was influenced by Lacan, and French psychoanalysis today still bears the imprint of that period, whether it concerns the distinction between drives and instincts, desire and need, the notion of lack as a derivative of castration, the question of the intrapsychic Other, the symbolic role of the father or the notion of après-coup. Some of the authors in this volume (Anzieu-Premmereur, Vanier) bear witness in their writings to the intellectual ferment of that period, to which French psychoanalysis contributed.

The second specific aspect of French psychoanalysis lies in its attention to language/representation at the levels of both metapsychology and history. The influence of Lacan here, who, it should be remembered, as early as 1953, developed a theory of the unconscious and the psychical apparatus around the role of the signifier (Lacan 2006/1953), can be recognized here. But this interest can also be attributed to the paradoxical fact that, to this day, there is still no authoritative translation of Freud's works in French, since Laplanche's translation has been criticized by the majority of the psychoanalytical community.[1] In the absence of a unified edition of Freud's complete works, as exists in German, English, Spanish, Italian and Japanese, French psychoanalysis continues to cultivate its garden, to use the title of Marion M. Oliner's 1988 book, in a conceptual language reputed to be difficult to understand because it is idiosyncratic or of literary inspiration.[2] Nevertheless, this pitfall is also what gives French psychoanalysis its richness, depth and creativity. In fact, French psychoanalysis constantly renews its exegesis of Freud's texts, establishing new connections between the original texts and current clinical practice. So the lack of an officially recognized French standard edition is the source of an active reading of Freud, thereby avoiding, in my view, the ossification of concepts and thought.

A third distinctive aspect of French psychoanalysis, related to the previous one, is the manner in which psychoanalysis is transmitted through writing, seen as a process that is capable of reflecting the intricacies and complexity of psychic thought. For French psychoanalysts, inspired by *Jokes and their Relation to the Unconscious* (Freud 1905c) and Lacanian inventiveness, language and even style, reflect the vagaries of the work of the unconscious of the analysand and analyst alike. Thus, for French analysts, Oliner explains (1988, 71–77), contradiction, imprecision and obscurity are not considered incompatible with the writing of serious texts. In their view, they reflect the natural opacity of the psychical apparatus, which cannot be evoked by writing formatted by a methodology that claims to be scientific:[3] "Fruitful obscurity is worth more than a premature clarification" (Green, 1977, 140). If this validation, not to say sanctification, of convoluted writing is not without a chauvinist accent, it is above all rooted in a philosophical and linguistic tradition according to which the *word* is not the *thing*. Meaning is therefore essentially a matter of construction or interpretation. It emerges from the gap between the signifier and the signified, like an indecisive *tropism* that skims the surface of words, as Nathalie Sarraute[4] (1939, 1996) understood, who, while denying any affiliation with psychoanalysis, built her work on the principle of undecidable meaning. In this connection, it is worth recalling Freud's first elaboration of the theory of language (Freud 1915e),[5] presented in terms of thing-presentation and word-presentation, underlining the irreducible disjunction between a thing, which is in itself indefinable at the level of its status (sensation, affect, emotion) or its topology (internal or external, psychical or biological, conscious, unconscious or preconscious) and its verbal representation. French psychoanalysis draws on all this complexity when attesting to the functioning of the psychical apparatus.

In addition to the role of writing as a means of reflecting on psychoanalysis and its practice, the philosophical approach to psychoanalysis remains a distinctive feature of French psychoanalysis (Anzieu-Premmereur, Gibeault, Vanier). Apart from the role played by Lacan's and Green's reading of Hegel, Laplanche and Pontalis were philosophers before they became psychoanalysts. The dialogue between philosophy and psychoanalysis in the 1970s helped to give psychoanalysis its credentials, at a time when psychiatry and psychoanalysis were getting on relatively well together, despite the rich influence of the antipsychiatry and antipsychoanalysis movements that developed under the aegis of Deleuze and Guattari (1972), with a programme that was more political than clinical.

Finally, the specific nature of the training of French analysts, accredited by the International Psychoanalytical Association (IPA) organization (Gibeault), alongside the Eitingon and Uruguayan models, contributes to the creation of freethinking analysts insofar as the training of analysts is essentially based on the significance of the candidate's own pathway to psychoanalysis, on a personal and possibly professional basis. In concrete terms, the French model of psychoanalytic transmission requires the validation of a personal analysis prior to training and outside the targeted training institute. In addition, theoretical and clinical training is the result of a personalized programme, with a large place given to "independent study", which leaves the choice of seminars, courses and group supervision open. In this way, the analyst-in-training becomes the author of their own training, which they can orient and enrich according to their own interests. Nevertheless, validation of the training depends on the approval of highly demanding committees, which examine the psychoanalytic, theoretical and clinical relevance of the candidate's individual way of thinking rather than their didactic achievements. It is arguable that the merit of such a system is that it produces analysts who develop a personal and committed voice thanks to the continual renewal of their reading of the fundamental texts of psychoanalysis.

The theoretical, clinical and stylistic roots of the history of French psychoanalysis documented by Roudinesco (1994) deserve to be mentioned as a prelude to the reading, which I hope will be receptive to the interviews in this book. In this respect, it is worth recalling in broad outline that while British psychoanalysis, following in the footsteps of Melanie Klein, was built around the object and object relations, and American psychoanalysis, in the wake of Viennese psychoanalysts established in the United States, developed around ego functioning (Hartmann) and on the development of the notion of the self (Kohut), paving the way for intersubjectivist and relational currents, French psychoanalysis endeavoured to theorize and explore in greater depth its understanding of the primary processes in the formation of the psychical apparatus. It has thus chosen to preserve what it considers to be the essence of psychoanalysis, namely the unconscious and the role of sexuality and drives in psychic life. The Freudian topographical model[6] and, in particular, the first topography, remain the touchstone of contemporary French psychoanalysis, to which new trends have recently been added, represented in this book by Evzonas, Laufer and Mendelsohn, under the impetus of societal issues that psychoanalysis today cannot ignore if it is to continue to be relevant among the human and clinical sciences (Kapsambelis, Vanier).

French psychoanalysis continues to be inspired by Freud's methodology for analysing psychical phenomena, which he developed in his article "The Unconscious" (Freud 1915e) and which is based on a combination of dynamic, economic and topographical points of view. As a result, the role of the drives (economic) and the places and modes of their representation (topographical and dynamic) remain the pillars of French psychoanalytic thought (Chabert, Denis, Kahn, Scarfone). Following these fundamental principles, rooted in Freudian metapsychology, has led French analysts to constantly question the first forms of symbolization and action under the pressure of drives (Aisenstein, Anzieu-Premmereur, Chabert, Denis, Kapsambelis).

In this respect, it should be noted from the outset that André Green's (1999a/1973) work on affect in *The Fabric of Affect and Psychoanalytic Discourse*, which sought to rehabilitate the role of drives in psychic life in opposition to the linguistic theory of Lacanian psychoanalysis, marked a turning point in the orientation of French psychoanalysis. Close attention was paid thereafter to the link between the life of drives and affects and their visual and pre-verbal representations, thus relegating the role of the signifier and the symbolic to secondary processes of elaboration.

For anglophone psychoanalysts, the notions of representation or symbolization are generally understood as conscious formations that produce meaning; or, in a strictly Kleinian sense, representations result from a collusion between affects and phantasy. For French psychoanalysts, representation is a highly complex unconscious, or even pre-psychic, process that governs the primordial organization of the psyche.

French psychoanalysts thus anchor their approach to psychoanalytic speech in the *thing*-presentation inherent in the word-presentation. According to this model, the thing-presentation is an unconscious visual, acoustic or tactile image, formed from memory traces of sensory experiences whether or not they are conveyed in the analysand's speech. It is this pre-language sensory phase that Green was interested in, in his conception of affect as the first form of representation of the drive, and which determines the *link* to the object, whether internal or external. For Green, this binding between the drives and the object, or its absence (unbinding), was one of the major causes of dissociative pathologies, linked, as he explained in *Life Narcissism, Death Narcissism* (Green 2001/1983) and *On Private Madness* (Green 1986), to the death drive. In his view, the death drive is a negative force that runs counter to the work of representation and psychic thought (Green 1999b/1993).

Within this line of research, it is important to mention the early work of Julia Kristeva (1984/1974) in resonance with her later thoughts on the feminine and its humanistic roots expressed in this book. In alignment with Green's work at the time, Kristeva developed the concept of *semiotics* which designated a proto-communication embodied in the instinctual bodily life prior to, and preparing for, the emergence of language. Similarly, Piera Aulagnier (2001/1975) developed, at the same time, the notion of *pictogram*, as being the first representation driven by bodily sensations. Finally, the work of Pierre Marty (1980), the psychosomatician, stems directly from the observation of a disjunction between affect (thing-presentation) and ideas (word-presentation) in psychosomatic illnesses, giving rise to the famous notion of "operational thinking" (*pensée opératoire*), i.e., a way of thinking that is separate from the drives and thus from the psychic thing.

Those currents of psychoanalytic research focusing on the role of the body and affects in the representation of preverbal states—which clearly stands out from the Lacanian monism of the signifier—had two consequences for the orientation of French psychoanalysis: the reference to sexuality as the permanent background of psychic life and the interest in the condition of the *infans* as distinct from Winnicott's conception of the mother/child duo.

For the vast majority of French psychoanalysts, sexuality is linked to the theory of the drives in their economic and polymorphic aspect. In this sense, sexuality, whether pregenital or genital, is not based on a conception of development in different phases, nor is it recognized as a problem of message, deemed to be enigmatic,[7] rather it concretely concerns the life of the body in terms of its psychic impact, particularly at a conflictual level (Anzieu-Premmereur). French psychoanalysis is interested in the psychic processes involved in sexuality more than in sexual orientations, that is to say in unconscious phantasies, conflicts of identification, destructive desires, fears of castration, fear and desire for pleasure, inhibitions and transgressions, and otherness of self and the other. For most of the authors of this book, the link between the body and the id in its unconscious manifestations, whether symptomatic or not, remains the very foundation of erotic/psychic life. In their view, the gendered approach seems to water down or even sidestep these issues. Rightly or wrongly, as the reader may judge, gendered identity is often implicitly seen, by French psychoanalysts as a denial—or de-sexualization (Green 1995)—not so much of the diktat of the biological realm, but of the naturally conflictual, polymorphous and fluctuating dimension of sexuality.

Finally, the question of the *infans* or the infantile[8] (Guignard 2021), mentioned above, refers not to the child or infant per se, but to the origin of each person's preoedipal phantasy and sensory experiences, the memory traces of which remain diffuse in the psychosexual life of the adult. For many contemporary analysts, this human infantile dimension is the primordial driving force that inhabits adult life, determining its neuroses. Here we find again the fascination of French psychoanalysis with the first stages of psychic life, revealed in the transference—this "regressive" return is often seen as a necessary aspect of analytic treatment. This *infans* in the adult does not correspond to a distinct entity (ego or self), nor to an identity or an object, but is the matrix of a psycho-instinctual drive history developed in the aura of the maternal realm. The very notion of the maternal, developed in particular by Julia Kristeva (1989/1983, 2000/1996, 2014),[9] is to be understood as a lifelong function of the psychic apparatus and not just as an instrument of infantile development, as it is seen in anglophone approaches. In this way, the maternal is a matrix for the transmission and transformation of the primordial feminine dimension in each and every one of us. Just as in French psychoanalysis the *infans* cannot be reduced to the child (Ainsenstein, Anzieu-Premmereur, Brun, Chabert), the feminine is neither sex nor gender, nor the opposite of the masculine (Leguil). These approaches open up innovative ways of thinking about the societal issues of gender and race that cut across psychoanalytic societies, notwithstanding the resistance or reluctance of some of the psychoanalysts in this book to incorporate LGBTQAI+ issues into their thinking and theory.

Nevertheless, it is undeniable that all the authors in this volume remain highly sensitive and attentive in their clinical practice to the psychic and physical suffering of their patients. This suffering, or "cruelty", which Derrida (2000) described as the ethical reason for psychoanalysis, remains at the heart of these debates, which no psychoanalytic approach can claim to ignore dogmatically.

Faithful to the history of psychoanalysis and its power relations, this volume of interviews reveals the currents and tensions that spur French psychoanalysis, linked to its own history, like any other psychoanalytic tradition. Confirming its critical capacity, *The "Here and Now" of French Psychoanalysis* gives us the opportunity to dialogue with the past, the present and the future of psychoanalysis as an ongoing transformative thought process.

Rachel Boué-Widawsky

Notes

1 After their excellent work, *The Language of Psychoanalysis*, originally titled *Vocabulaire de la psychanalyse* (Laplanche and Pontalis 1973/1967), Laplanche and other collaborators undertook to translate Freud's complete works (OFC). This translation was poorly received by the French psychoanalytical community because it was not so much a question of translating Freud's German into French but of translating Freud's thought, Freudism, the translators considering themselves "Freudologists". The result of such a translation, based on interpretation and inspired by the German etymology of words applied to the French language, is a presentation of Freud's work in incomprehensible French. On this subject, read the last chapter of *Histoire de la Psychanalyse en France*, by Elizabeth Roudinesco (1994).

2 In the absence of an official, unified translation, it is significant that writers (André Breton, Romain Rolland, André Gide, etc.) showed a keen interest in psychoanalysis from the 1920s onwards, despite Freud's reservations about this infatuation, particularly regarding André Breton. See Oliner (1988, 22–24).

3 It is the English-speaking method, validated by the International Psychoanalytical Association (IPA), that is criticized here by French psychoanalysts. This critique needs to be placed in the context of each culture, which places value on the sovereignty of its language.

4 See my book on this subject, *Nathalie Sarraute. La sensation en quête de parole.* (Boué-Widawsky 1996).

5 The first conception of language for Freud which dates back to his study on aphasia (1891) and was taken up again in "The Unconscious" (Freud 1915e) is that there is a hiatus—which Laplanche was to develop as a fundamental problem of translation of the unconscious—between unconscious psychical life and language, which manifests itself between two forms of representation, *thing*-presentations and *word*-presentations.

6 French psychoanalysts view the whole psychical apparatus as literally *topographic*—dividing, as Freud did, the functions of the mind into different locations (*Ucs, Pcs, Cs* [1915e]) and entities (ego, id, superego (1923b)). In French, the term *première topique* refers to what in English is called the *topographic model*. The *deuxième topique* is what is called in English the *structural model*, which is Strachey's conception/translation of Freud's new model of the mind presented in *The Ego and the Id* (Freud 1923b).

7 It is important to mention the fact that the influence of Laplanche's writings on these questions has disappeared from current debates in French psychoanalysis—which stands in contrast to the author's popularity on the American continent today. In this sense, Dominique Scarfone's ideas on translation, rooted in Laplanche's theory, are all the more distinctive and seminal in this book.

8 This was the theme of the 2021 IPA Congress in Vancouver.

9 For a full review of the concept of the maternal in Kristeva's work, see my own writings in the reference section (Boué-Widawsky 2014, 2019, 2020).

References

Aulagnier, P. (2001/1975). *The Violence of Interpretation: From Pictogram to Statement*, trans. A. Sheridan. London: Routledge.

Birksted-Breen, D., Sanders, S., & Gibeault, A. (2010). *Reading French Psychoanalysis*, trans. D. Alcorn, S. Leighton, A. Weller. London: Routledge.

Boué-Widawsky, R. (1996). *Nathalie Sarraute, La sensation en quête de Parole*. Paris: L'Harmattan.

Boué-Widawsky, R. (2014). "Julia Kristeva's psychoanalytic work". *Journal of the American Psychoanalytic Association*, 62(1): 69–85.

Boué-Widawsky, R. (2019). "Maternal eroticism and the journey of a concept in Kristeva's work". In: *The Philosophy of Julia Kristeva, The Library of the Living Philosopher*, ed. S. Beardsworth. Chicago, IL: Open Court, pp. 627–638.

Boué-Widawsky, R. (2020). "The maternal and the necessary risk of madness". In: *Eroticism*, ed. S. Akhtar, R. Gulati, London: Routledge, pp. 25–36.

Deleuze, G. & Guatarri, F. (1977/1972). *Anti-Oedipus: Capitalism and Schizophrenia*. London: Viking.

Derrida, J. (2000). *Etats d'âme de la psychanalyse: l'impossible au-delà d'une souveraine cruauté*. Paris: Galilée.

Freud, S. (1953/1891). *On Aphasia*. Madison, CT: International Universities Press.

Freud, S. (1905c). *Jokes and their Relation to the Unconscious. S. E.* 8. London: Hogarth, pp. 9–236.

Freud, S. (1915e). "The unconscious". *S. E.* 14. London: Hogarth, pp. 166–216.

Freud, S. (1923b). *The Ego and the Id. S. E.* 19. London: Hogarth, pp. 3–66.

Green, A. (1977). "Conceptions of affects". *International Journal of Psychoanalysis*, 58: 129–156.

Green, A. (1986). *On Private Madness*. London: Hogarth Press and The Institute of Psychoanalysis.

Green, A. (1995). "Has sexuality anything to do with psychoanalysis?" *International Journal of Psychoanalysis*, 76: 871–883.

Green, A. (1999a/1973). *The Fabric of Affect and Psychoanalytic Discourse*, trans. A. Sheridan. The New Library of Psychoanalysis. London: Routledge, Kegan and Paul.

Green, A. (1999b/1993). *The Work of the Negative*, trans. A. Weller. London: Routledge.

Green, A. (2001/1983). *Life Narcissism, Death Narcissism*, trans. A. Weller. London: Free Association Books.

Guignard, F. (2021/1996), *The Infantile in Psychoanalytic Practice Today*, trans. A. Weller. London: Routledge.

Kristeva, J. (1984/1974). *Revolution in Poetic Language*. New York, NY: Columbia University Press.

Kristeva, J. (1989/1983). "Stabat Mater", *Tales of Love*. New York, NY: Columbia University Press, pp 234–263.

Kristeva, J. (2000/1996). *The Sense and Non-Sense of Revolt*. New York, NY: Columbia University Press.

Kristeva, J. (2014) "Reliance, or Maternal Eroticism". *Journal of American Psychoanalytic Association*, 62(1): 69–85.

Lacan, J. (2006/1953). "The function and field of speech and language in psychoanalysis". In: *Écrits*, trans. B. Fink. New York, NY: Norton, pp. 197–268.

Laplanche, J. & Pontalis, J.-B. (1973/1967). *The Language of Psychoanalysis*. London: Routledge.

Marty, P. (1980). *L'ordre psychosomatique*. Paris: Payot.

Oliner, M. (1988). *Cultivating Freud's Garden in France*. London: Aronson.

Roudinesco, E. (1994). *L'Histoire de la Psychanalyse en France*. Paris: Le Livre de Poche.

Sarraute, N. (1939). *Tropismes*. Paris: Minuit.

Sarraute, N. (1996). *Oeuvres complètes*. Paris: La Pléiade, Galllimard.

Chapter 1

Conversation with Marilia Aisenstein

Abstract

Marilia Aisenstein explains her psychosomatic approach to psychoanalysis, highlighting the role of ego splitting and operational thinking in the repression of affects. This leads her to address the question of primary masochism in the formation of the psychical apparatus.

• Could you describe the intellectual and personal journey that led you to psychoanalysis?

Having been born in an African country and brought up in several languages and different countries, I was led to ask myself questions very early on in life about the nature of thought. This question, one I constantly struggled with, naturally led me to study philosophy. While studying for a doctorate, I underwent an analysis. This first encounter with psychoanalysis was a revelation that changed my life. I began studies in clinical psychology and changed course.

I was accepted for training at the Paris Psychoanalytical Society (SPP) and had the immense good fortune to benefit from a great variety of ways of thinking and styles. In the years between 1980 and 1985, psychoanalysis was flourishing in Paris. I attended seminars by Green, Lebovici, Diatkine, Laplanche, Evelyne Kestemberg, Pasche, Widlöcher, Pierre Marty, de M'Uzan, Joyce McDougall, Benno Rosenberg, among others.

I was soon recruited by Evelyne Kestemberg to work with the team at the Centre for Psychoanalysis and Psychotherapy of the Mental Health Association in the 13th district of Paris (ASM 13)—in France, psychiatry is organized by districts—in other words a psychoanalytic centre located within the psychiatric sector. Shortly afterwards, Pierre Marty asked me to join IPSO, the Paris Institute of Psychosomatics, which had just been founded.

• What is the cornerstone of your theoretical and clinical work?

My interest in psychosis on the one hand and in psychosomatic patients on the other has certainly guided the evolution of my theoretical work, but it is deeply rooted in

DOI: 10.4324/9781003342502-1

clinical practice. I must add that I have also always kept up a classical analytic practice of treatments with neurotic patients three or four times a week on the couch. I think that it is important to continue practising analysis with neurotic patients. I consider that working with psychotics, borderline cases or somatic patients requires technical adjustments to the "standard treatment". However, I believe that it is important both to have integrated and to be very familiar with the Freudian model of analysis before diverging from it in full knowledge of what one is doing and why one has chosen to do it.

I have written a great deal on the theoretical and clinical aspects of working with psychosomatic patients, but the heart of my research concerns the psychosis/somatosis axis. I think that there are common elements between the two, to do with the relationship with the primordial object, but that the modalities of the early splitting of the ego differ. Ego-splitting is an early "tear" in the ego that enables the child to accept reality while denying it; these two attitudes coexist without influencing each other.

I consider myself to be essentially Freudian and while I read Melanie Klein, Bion, Winnicott, Green and so many others with interest, even passion, it is always in reference to Freud's work.

This is why I have a particular admiration for André Green who knew how to innovate while continuing to deepen the Freudian roots of his own theorizations. Pierre Marty also based his theoretical approach on his knowledge of Freud. One of the starting points of the theoretical edifice of the Paris School was inspired by a remark made by Freud in *Beyond the Pleasure Principle* (Freud 1920g) where he explored in greater depth what he had said about somatic illness in "On Narcissism: An Introduction" (Freud 1914c). He wrote: "[P]ainful and feverish illnesses exercise a powerful effect, so long as they last, on the distribution of the libido." A little further on we read, "It is also well known that [...] such severe disorders in the distribution of the libido as melancholia are temporarily brought to an end by intercurrent organic illness, and indeed that even a fully developed condition of dementia praecox is capable of a temporary remission in the same circumstances." (Freud 1920g, 33)

Both Green and Marty's theorizations are deeply rooted in Freudian metapsychology. Although they followed divergent paths, they seem nevertheless to have nourished an inner dialogue concerning their original theorizations, both of which open up psychoanalysis to non-neurotic modes of functioning. They built two new paradigms of mental functioning: for Marty, it was the paradigm of "operational" states of mind (*états opératoires*) and for Green, it was borderline states of mind. Very different from borderline states, where affect, often poorly elaborated, is in excess, "operational states" or "operational modes of thinking" are antitraumatic modes of functioning that involve a drastic repression of affect and fantasy life. It is thus a concrete mode of thinking close to the state of alexithymia described by Sifneos (Apfel & Sifneos 1979). I follow in the footsteps of these two great thinkers with whom I have had the pleasure of working closely.

I have been very close to two other French analysts who have had a great impact on my thinking, namely Michel Fain and Benno Rosenberg, who are less known to the Anglo-Saxon public because they have not published in English. I have written an introduction to Fain's thought (Aisenstein 2018), while Rosenberg left us a fundamental book on masochism (Rosenberg 1991). I have penetrated further into his thinking in my latest book, *Désir, douleur, pensée* (Aisenstein 2020/2023).

• What is your theoretical approach to psychoanalytic practice?

My conceptions of psychoanalytical practice are very classical as far as couch analyses with patients with more or less neurotic functioning are concerned. However, they are not very classical when it comes to psychosomatic or psychotic patients, treatments that require technical adjustments.

In the first case, I would say that I have retained a certain rigour that I learned during my training. I value the classical setting and the structure it provides. I continue to state the fundamental rule, something many young colleagues no longer do. I do not see myself as a particularly silent analyst, but I am much more silent than my Anglo-Saxon colleagues, as I have seen in international conferences or clinical exchanges. This position is based on the idea that if you intervene often, you break the associative flow of patients.

• In your opinion, what are the points of divergence between French psychoanalysis and English-speaking psychoanalysis?

I want to emphasize here a difference between French analysis and Anglo-Saxon analysis, all tendencies taken into account (Kleinian, Bionian, New Contemporary Freudian, etc.). In France, what we call "indication of analysis" takes on great importance and is considered after two or three preliminary meetings.

We have a narrow spectrum of indication for couch analysis according to several criteria: Can the patient tell a life story rather than reciting a biography? Is there associative thinking? Is there guilt, which allows one to assume the existence of a functional superego? Do they have a dream life or the ability to recount a dream, even an old one? Depending on this understanding of mental functioning, we choose classical analysis or face-to-face psychoanalytic psychotherapy, or even the use of the couch—but at a very sustained rhythm (four or five weekly sessions)—for a patient who is in a borderline state and with whom the interpretative modalities are different from the standard treatment.

After many clinical exchanges with my British and American colleagues, I noticed that the "indication" did not carry the same weight as in France and was not given so much attention. This attention is not only clinical but also theoretical because it should make it possible to acquire real knowledge of the mental functioning of each patient.

I have noted great theoretical divergences between the Anglo-American and European schools and particularly between Kleinians and non-Kleinians. I will come back to this later. There are also technical differences. However, I must say here that in the course of my clinical exchanges (in the Centre for Advanced Psychoanalytic Studies (CAPS) in the USA or in our annual Franco-British colloquiums), I have never seen any really serious and profound oppositions in the clinical understanding of cases. For example, in spite of sometimes radically opposed theoretical positions, whenever I have been confronted with an account of a treatment by hardline Kleinian colleagues I have always been in agreement and often admired the clinical work. The understanding of the case was the same but the technical methods of intervention very different.

This is a phenomenon that has intrigued me a great deal, but also reassured me. Melanie Klein was the founder, following Ferenczi, of the current that we now call "object relations". She elaborated a coherent and original theoretical edifice, and I will try to briefly summarize my points of agreement and disagreement here. I believe that we are all convinced of the crucial importance of the relationship to the primordial object, but I regret the absence in Klein's work of the father as a third party and bearer of the law.

I find it very difficult to conceive of the existence of an early superego that is no longer the "heir of the Oedipus complex". While I can agree with the place given to unconscious phantasies, I nevertheless feel that the role of conscious ideation (which supports free association) is underestimated.

I think the categories of the paranoid-schizoid and depressive positions, as well as the concept of projective identification are remarkable and conducive to reflection and research. The concept of projective identification is very close to Pierre Marty's conception of countertransference (Marty 1952). But Klein's use of this concept seems to have led us to overlook the work of countertransference as described by Paula Heimann (1950) and I think this is a pity. Let me add that I feel very much in agreement with Winnicott and wish to draw attention to an article in the *Revue française de psychosomatique*, highlighting the closeness of the ideas of Pierre Marty and Winnicott (Jaeger 2015).

Bion, for his part, was particularly interested in thought processes, which for him had their roots in the emotional experience with the mother. His conceptualization of thought processes was based on his clinical experience with psychotic patients, as well as with small groups. He places considerable emphasis on the analyst's reverie in the session, which transforms the transference movements and is indispensable for interpretation. In my view, this is a rich and complex theoretical construction that is indispensable to me theoretically as well as in my clinical work.

• What is your theoretical approach to psychoanalytic practice (the couch, frequency, the setting, teletherapy, interpretation and silence)?

I must now share my views on remote analysis or analytical psychotherapy, that is, by telephone, Skype, Zoom and so on. I have long been opposed to these practices. If I criticize them, it is because of the absence of the bodies of the two protagonists.

Affect and thought are related to the body. In his article, "Psychical (or Mental) Treatment", Freud (1905, 208) writes:

> The affects in the narrower sense are, it is true, characterized by a quite special connection with somatic processes; but strictly speaking, all mental states, including those which we usually regard as "processes of thought", are to some degree "affective", and not one of them is without its physical manifestations or is incapable of modifying somatic processes. Even when a person is engaged in quietly thinking in a string of "ideas", there are a constant series of excitations, corresponding to the contents of these ideas, which are discharged into the smooth and striated muscles.

For me, the presence of bodies is fundamental to analytical treatment. Like so many others, the pandemic and containment forced me to offer telephone sessions to my patients. I gave all of them the choice between waiting for the health measures to end or resorting to telephone sessions; three of them preferred to wait. I chose the telephone over Skype or Zoom precisely because the telephone makes it possible to focus on the voice, which I believe conveys affect more than images. Only one patient insisted on Skype appointments, but she suffers from a representational deficit and cannot retain the image of the object.

As soon as the lockdown was lifted, all my patients returned in person. I am very concerned to hear that many colleagues have chosen to continue their practice by tele- or videoconferencing; in Europe this is relatively rare, but apparently more common in both North and Latin America. I am familiar with the argument that the analyses went "very well" during the lockdown. My response is that without the presence of the two bodies the resistances are weakened considerably. But in classical analysis resistances are an important part of the work. This option seems to me to be the essence of the current of ego psychology from which French psychoanalysis has largely emerged. In an article (Aisenstein 2010), I described French analysis as stemming from Hartmann's ego psychology revisited by the contributions of the Lacanian current and then by the conceptualizations of the Paris School of Psychosomatics. It should be noted that Hartmann lived in Paris after the war and analysed a whole generation, including Sacha Nacht, Jacques Lacan, Kestemberg and others, before emigrating to the USA.

In a podcast in which our colleague Harvey Schwartz from New York asked me about remote analysis, I said that it was true that on the telephone patients speak without difficulty, but that they speak as one easily talks to a taxi driver. That they usually have difficulty in speaking with their psychoanalyst, precisely because of the transference and physical presence, seems to me to be a healthy situation.

I am aware that my opinion is somewhat harsh and no doubt highly controversial. Nevertheless, I hold to it because I fear a deviation that would, in my opinion, be dangerous, one that would consist in authorizing training analyses and training programmes without the presence of bodies. Yet I have learned that certain American institutes are considering this possibility.

• What is your view of the transmission of psychoanalysis?

I have not yet touched on the fundamental question of the transmission of psychoanalysis. To do so, I will return to my training in Paris in the 1980s.

Before doing so, I must say a few words about the "French model", which was officially recognized by the IPA at the 2007 Berlin Congress. According to this model, the analysis precedes the training of candidates; it is not part of the training and is therefore strictly personal and free. It can be done with any member of the IPA. Consequently, it is the supervisions that are the centre of the training. The function of the of training psychoanalysts is therefore only to teach and supervise analytic treatments.

At the SPP training lasts between five and seven years. Two supervisions are compulsory, but most supervisees do more. One is individual and the other is a collective supervision. Compulsory group supervision is a speciality of the SPP; no other European society seems to practise it in this form. They are weekly and are usually held in the evening as they last three hours and often more. The groups consist of three, four or five supervisees maximum, who present their work (three or four sessions) every week, plus two or three "auditors", who are candidates who have already been admitted and are waiting for a place in supervision. They attend and intervene but do not present material. The advantage of this format is that each presentation is followed by a group discussion, after discussion by the supervisor. Everyone present knows all the ongoing cases and can intervene as they wish. This usually leads to enriching exchanges during which the supervisor highlights theoretical points and recommends reading material in relation to what is being discussed.

I believe that supervision should also be an occasion for spontaneous theoretical teaching. Indeed, gifted candidates often do well intuitively, but they do not know what they have done or why they have done it, so the supervisor has to "translate" for them what has happened with metapsychological concepts.

For me, both as a supervisee and then as a supervisor, these collective supervisions are clinical moments of immense richness and transmission. I would say that they are the "cornerstone" of the Paris Society's training process.

Apart from the supervisions, no seminar is compulsory and the candidates choose those that interest them from among the large number of seminars and lectures on offer. It is obvious that the question of transmission is crucial for the future of psychoanalysis in the world. I am in favour of rigorous standards and consider that the validation of training should never be granted easily or in cases where there is any doubt.

The transmission of analysis is in my opinion complicated by the effects of transference in supervision, especially in individual supervision. The transference of the supervisee corresponds to the countertransference of the supervising analyst. I have very often seen end-of-training discussions in which a supervisor has hinted at the weaknesses of their supervisee but nevertheless defends them in the end. This, at any rate, is a phenomenon that I have seen in the SPP and also in the Hellenic Psychoanalytic Society of which I am a member.

I fear that today Freudian metapsychology and the fundamental texts are no longer studied and transmitted as they were 30 years ago but are replaced by more diverse teaching: a little Freud, a little Klein, a little Bion, a little Kohut, etc. But to really understand and integrate psychoanalysis, the Freudian roots of all these theoretical models should be truly acquired. Otherwise, one is building one's own theory "on quicksand".

I believe that after a few years of experience, each psychoanalyst works with the theories to which they adhere and also with what I have called an "implicit theoretical magma" which is their own.

• What is your psychoanalytic approach to the societal debates on racial, gender identities or/and on the new forms of reproduction and parenting?

As my colleagues will have understood, I am an old-school analyst who is currently faced with considerable societal upheavals that we psychoanalysts will obviously have to take into account.

In the last 20 years, my generation has had to go through the shock of AIDS, the explosion of assisted pregnancies, egg donation, surrogate pregnancy, access to adoption by homosexual couples and others. More recently, the phenomenon of transsexuality has emerged. The latter dates back to ancient times. There have always been men and women who were unhappy in their gender.

For years I have been doing supervisions in a psychiatric ward for adolescents from 15 to 26 years old. They are hospitalized or followed in psychoanalytical psychotherapy by a psychoanalyst from the hospital's (outpatient) centre.

Ten years ago, 2% of the population were transgender. Recently, one in five teenagers has declared themselves transgender and is considering undergoing hormonal bombing and surgery. Teenage unease concerning identity is now "transferred" to "gender dysphoria" which they believe condenses all their problems. For me it is a fad maintained by trans associations and social networks. I also believe that a number of doctors have been carried along by this fad and have agreed to start hormonal bombing at the age of 12, i.e., before the legal age of "sexual maturity" at 15.

I regret that many analytical societies have not taken any position on the subject until now, which seems to me to be something of a denial.

Some Lacanian analysts linked to the Observatoire de la Petite Sirène,[1] to which I and some of my SPP colleagues have signed up, have had the courage to militate against this trend.

The Observatoire, which is frequently attacked on social media, has collected numerous testimonies from families and teenagers who bitterly regret having embarked on a path of no return. Thanks to its action, the Observatoire has obtained a "European Manifesto for the objective treatment in the media of the 'transidentity' of minors" and a declaration from the Ethics Committee, which does not prohibit transidentity but calls on practitioners to reflect seriously before making any decision. I myself have followed adult transsexuals in treatment who were seriously depressed because, although they had changed sex, their sense of ill-being had not disappeared. Moreover, they have often lost their jobs. I am thinking of one of them, a children's judge, who had to start a career as a lawyer at the age of 45 and saw his lifestyle decline. He had lost his friends and family and was severely depressed. That there is a small minority of people with genuine gender dysphoria who need to be helped and supported is undoubtedly true. Nevertheless, I believe that we are going through a crisis that is a societal crisis that we cannot hide from.

Having touched on them all too briefly, let me return now to the debate on gender identity, new forms of reproduction and parenthood. It is obviously a good thing that more and more women are able to become pregnant thanks to the new methods of assisted reproduction. I would like to point out here that, in France, the National Authority for Health does not authorize surrogacy and surrogate mothers. I feel in agreement with this measure, not for the sake of the child's future but for reasons that concern the dignity of women. I am deeply shocked that money can reduce a young woman to renting out her womb, to carrying a pregnancy to term with the emotional climate it implies, and then have the child taken away from her.

As a general rule, and with regard to these scientific advances that are magnificent on the one hand yet frightening on the other, I would like to recall the Greek concept of "*hubris*".

In ancient Greece and tragedy, hubris referred to the insolence of humans who defied the laws of the gods, of nature in fact. Hubris is always punished in the end. I have often wondered if our era is not in a state of hubris. Always in pursuit of improvement, we have ended up destroying nature. We have turned forests into crops, drained marshes and threatened the climate. Global warming is inevitable today; perhaps pandemics are the response of outraged nature.

I think it is a pity that these questions are given little discussion by the French psychoanalytical societies. Those who do talk about them are analysts who are faced with transsexuality, gender changes or sometimes with dramas linked to excesses of assisted reproduction (I am talking about ovarian cancers as a consequence of too many attempts at in vitro fertilization involving hormonal bombing). In France, these recourses are limited, but many women seek them abroad.

I recently learned that Anglo-Saxon psychoanalytical clinical practice has been challenged by various antiracist, feminist, LGTBQIA+ social movements. It seems to me that this is not the case in France, or at least, I have not heard about it. This is probably linked to the discretion of the analytic societies, which are not in the habit of expressing themselves on these societal issues. I remember some concerns at a congress held in Paris a few years ago on "Psychic Bisexuality". We feared the presence of militant transsexuals, but the congress was closed to non-psychoanalysts, so there was no turmoil, although the question of the failures of psychic bisexuality in transgender people was debated.

The last point I wish to address here concerns the idea of the "engaged psychoanalyst" as André Green wrote. Like him, I believe that analysts can no longer, and should no longer, remain private analysts working only in the city. This was the case in the 19th and early 20th centuries, until the 1980s, but it no longer holds up today. In my opinion, if psychoanalysis wants to continue to live, it must become involved in psychiatric hospitals, general hospitals, prisons, schools, universities and finally the life of the "city" in the Greek sense of the term.

Note

1 Translator's note: A multidisciplinary Franco-Belgian collective of practitioners and re-searchers, founded in 2021, interested in transidentity and particularly transgender minors.

References

Aisenstein, M. (2020/2023). *Desire, Pain and Thought.* Routledge.

Aisenstein, M. (2018). "An introduction to Michel Fain's thought". *International Journal of Psychoanalysis*, 99(2): 495–509.

Aisenstein, M. (2010). "Letter from Paris". *International Journal of Psychoanalysis*, 91(3), 463–468.

Apfel, R. J. & Sifneos, P. E. (1979). "Alexithymia: concept and measurement in psychotherapy and psychosomatics". *Psychotherapy and Psychosomatics*, 32(1–4): 180–190.

Freud, S. (1914c). "On narcissism: An introduction". *S. E.* 14. London: Hogarth, pp. 69–102.

Freud, S. (1920g). *Beyond the Pleasure Principle. S. E.* 18. London: Hogarth, pp. 1–64.

Heimann, P. (1950). "On countertransference". *International Journal of Psychoanalysis*, 31: 81–84.

Jaeger, P. (2015). "Winnicott et l'École psychosomatique de Paris, convergences". *Revue française de psychosomatique*, 47: 13–36.

Marty, P. (1952). "Les difficultés narcissiques de l'observateur devant le problème psycho-somatique". *Revue française de psychanalyse*, 16(3): 339–362.

Rosenberg, B. (1991). *Masochisme mortifère et masochisme gardien de la vie.* Paris: Presses Universitaires de France.

Chapter 2

Conversation with
Christine Anzieu-Premmereur

Abstract

Christine Anzieu-Premmereur reflects, as a child psychoanalyst, on archaic processes, emphasizing the Freudian economic model in the sensory and psychic
life of children and adults. She discusses transitional psychoanalysis as shoring
a mental space between narcissism and object.

- ## Could you describe the intellectual and personal
  ## journey that led you to psychoanalysis?

As a student in France in the 1970s, I was immersed in the intellectual and critical richness of the period following the youth uprising of May 1968. I was able
to take advantage of the way higher education was organized at the time, going
from Khâgne[1] classes to several bachelor's degrees in classics, philosophy and
20th century literature at the Sorbonne. Dissatisfied with this abstract view of the
world, I went to the new Paris Dauphine University to try to better understand
the mechanisms of the economic world. The teaching method, based on small
groups, led me to take an interest in psychological and sociological dynamics,
and I found myself, albeit neurotically unconscious with regard to the choices I
was making, in the Paris Nanterre University psychology department, of which
my father, Didier Anzieu, was the head. Having started school at a younger age
than most, I had time to devote myself happily to studies, but I also suffered
from depression during adolescence. I underwent psychoanalysis with Janine
Chasseguet-Smirgel, who had the patience to cope with my resistant depressive
silence. She was able to make me associate and remember, despite my obstinacy.
Not feeling recognized or understood was a tenacious defence in the face of two
famous psychoanalysts. I had found a way of remaining opaque to others.

This analysis shed light on my intellectual and scientific curiosity. During
my Master's degree in psychology and a student placement at the Sainte-Anne
Hospital, one of the great centres of enlightened psychiatry at the time, I had
access to Lacan's presentations of patients. Lacan's writings (Lacan 2006/1966)

DOI: 10.4324/9781003342502-2

were read in the on-call rooms, and Foucault's (2009/1961) *History of Madness* was an essential work.

My grandmother, whom I loved very much, suffered from paranoia, but was superbly intelligent as well as a writer. This put me in touch with psychotic pain and the need for containment and limits at a very early age.

I was born into a family of peasant origin but rose to middle-class status through educational success, and this has left me with a rigorous work ethic.

Psychoanalysis had enabled my parents to live with their private madness better, and their passion for analysis had created an intellectual atmosphere: my father would read to us in the evenings from his writings on Freud's dreams or his creation of the skin ego. Meetings and dinners with J.-B. Pontalis, Jean Laplanche, René Kaës[2] and Gisella Pankow, not to mention invitations to meet Lacan and his court, or Francis Bacon and the intelligentsia of the time, were a source of constant stimulation for my interests in literature and art as much as in analytical thinking.

I attended Lacan's seminar, where I witnessed the mingling of colleagues with socialites and, despite Lacan's talent, the obscurity of original thought distorted by narcissistic triumph.

My essentially critical view of Lacan was not helped by the story of my grandmother, the case of Aimée in Lacan's thesis, and the comments she made about her psychiatrist's lack of ethics, her smile when she saw him appear on television—she compared him to the extravagances of Salvador Dali, who was doing commercials for chocolate at the time— and learning years later about my father's experience on Lacan's couch and the compromises Lacan made and the lies he told in connection with the psychoanalytic institutions. This flood of unpleasant information made me distance myself from fashionable phenomena in psychoanalysis.

What I particularly recall of Lacan was his phenomenal energy in understanding the unconscious, the interplay of illusions and ideals; and I observed, like everyone else at the time, the seductive and absurd clinical deviation that has wreaked havoc on our contemporaries.

At one and the same time, I was dining with my parents, who were talking about the skin-ego, femininity and borderline or autistic patients and soaking up this passion for psychic care.

I heard my father discussing psychoanalysis's tendencies towards radicalization with his colleagues. "Idolatry", he would say, "consists in using mentors as sacred leaders." As a result, the spontaneity of the Freudian experience is stifled, which is always marked by the surprise of the unexpected. He warned against both the risk of a biblical reading of Freud and its opposite, discrimination against Freud in the name of novelty.

Years later, I wrote a text on the humour of the analyst, based on a phrase used by a child patient: "An analyst is someone who understands jokes." It's a legacy of my father's great sense of humour.

• **Could you comment on any opportune encounters in your journey and in your training?**

Clinical training

It was Professor of Clinical Psychology, Roger Dorey, who gave me rigorous training, enabling me to carry out thorough assessments of new patients. He taught me to observe psychic processes, resistances and defences. I gained access to a mental geography of internal dynamics.

I was fortunate to be a psychologist at Sainte-Anne because I found myself exposed to a formidable psychiatric role model in the person of Professor Georges Daumezon, a reformer of asylum psychiatry and a pioneer of "institutional psychotherapy". This period was a formative experience in terms of knowledge of the history and transformations of psychiatry. It was there that I began the task, which is still relevant today, of seeking to understand and treat severe depression and psychotic disorders. With the support of my parents, who were happy to see me achieve what they had not been able to achieve on account of their family environment, I set about studying medicine with a view to becoming a psychiatrist.

As soon as the first year of working relentlessly on maths and physics to take the entrance exam to medical school was over, I quickly realized I was in danger of losing my knowledge about psychic functioning. So, in parallel with my first years in medicine, I did a doctorate in psychology under the supervision of J.-B. Pontalis, then R. Dorey, on ambivalence towards motherhood. This was the period when contraception and then abortion became legal in France, in 1967 and 1973 respectively.

Medicine introduced me to the body and the vicissitudes of biology, the complexity not only of pathologies but also of therapeutic approaches. I was fortunate enough to meet Professor Philippe Jeammet, famous for his work on adolescence, as soon as I turned to psychiatry, and I taught medical psychology with him, using Balint and the effectiveness of his model of groups of doctors discussing their practice, discovering the unconscious in their patients' reactions. Serge Leclaire and François Perrier, then Jean Laplanche, led discussions on the unconscious, repression and foreclosure, while the first neuroleptics made it possible to work with psychotic patients.

As an intern in psychiatry, again at Sainte-Anne, I worked in the emergency department, the CPOA (Centre psychiatrique d'orientation et d'accueil); thanks to the remarkable nurses, I learned to cope with the dangers of acting out and destructiveness. I then trained in child psychiatry with the psychoanalyst Pierre Bourdieu, again at Sainte-Anne. Michel Soulé's teaching complemented my knowledge of the world of sick infants, always centred on observing the body as well as feelings and behaviour.

Psychoanalytic training

As a young-child and adult psychiatrist, I took the path of psychoanalysis, the royal road, at the beginning of the '80s.

Interested in the links between the biological body and psychic life, I became a trainee at the Institute of Psychosomatics (IPSO). My encounter with Pierre Marty (Marty 1968) and Michel Fain and their rigorous way of thinking, as well as early childhood specialists Rosine Debray (Debray 1987) and Léon Kreisler (Kreisler, Fain and Soulé 1978), confirmed my interest in psychosomatics from the very beginning of life, and so I turned towards clinical work with infants.

Training at the Paris Psychoanalytical Society (SPP) was an experience of freedom and discovery, as you could choose your seminars without constraint. These work meetings on a theme, decided for the year—and often for several years— involved presenting a paper in front of analysts who were full members, a difficult but formative exercise because of the quality of the discussion that followed.

Pontalis published Winnicott, Masud Khan and Bion in French translation in the *Nouvelle revue de psychanalyse*, anthropologists discussed with analysts, Beckett's theatre was performed in Montparnasse, cultural life was flamboyant and I expended a lot of energy on that which paid off in terms of the pleasure I took in thinking and discovering.

Paul Racamier and his work on the incestual, Guy Rosolato and Piera Aulagnier, centred on the primal and the body and also the discovery of Ferenczi's work were to have a lasting impact on me. Karl Abraham's work on depression and its influence on Melanie Klein and the Hungarian school broadened the teaching on depression and psychosis.

The work of Nicolas Abraham and Mária Török (1978) on intergenerational transmission was an enriching follow-up.

André Green's seminar was an experience of rigorous theoretical and clinical work, opening up possibilities for research into a metapsychology that was constantly being revised and supplemented. What struck me when I arrived in the USA was the lack of understanding of metapsychology, which was ridiculed as a false science, and the ignorance of Freud's thought process, which was taught academically, removing all the power of a mind that persisted in making hypotheses rather than asserting dogmas.

During my training at the SPP, I was supervised by J.-L. Donnet; I am grateful to him for making me aware of the power of transference dynamics in the process of managing the analytical setting (see Donnet 2018).

Listening to the Botellas (Botella & Botella 2005) exploring in detail their thinking on the capacity for representation and the analyst's work as a double was to have a profound resonance and provide me with a source of rich work years later when I gave conferences in New York to show how alive French psychoanalysis was.

Moving towards child psychoanalysis

At the SPP, I became a child psychoanalyst thanks to the supervision and seminars of René Diatkine and Serge Lebovici, as I had always been interested in early childhood. Despite the regrettable lack of training in child analysis in French institutes, I did my own training by attending numerous seminars, working groups and supervisions, with the immense advantage of being able to go off the beaten track. I visited the Anna Freud Centre in London and attended the annual colloquia where the analytic rigour restructured me in relation to psychotherapy. Anne-Marie Sandler was a grand lady of clinical finesse. The vitality of the Tavistock Clinic, where infants and early psychic life were tackled in the tradition of Esther Bick, Bion and Meltzer; the lectures and writings of Martha Harris, then Margaret Rustin and Anne Alvarez were the basis of my attachment to the diversity of thought in psychoanalysis.

At Nanterre, Didier Anzieu continued to teach Bowlby and attachment theory along with analytic thought from different horizons; furthermore, psychodrama, which is still practised today, and group techniques developed under his impetus.

The annual meetings of psychoanalysis for infants in Geneva with Bertrand Cramer, then with Palacio Espasa (Manzano & Espasa 1999), enriched my practice of working with babies and parents and gave me the opportunity of meeting the paediatrician T. B. Brazelton. Observing the mental, cognitive, motor and sensory development of the infant along with parental projective tendencies is an area of ongoing discovery. Listening to Geneviève Haag in Paris was also a space of freedom for me in a French analytical world that has tended to remain either dogmatically Lacanian, and ignorant of the bodily and affective dimension of the human being, or fixed on an interpretation limited to the Freud of the ego and its relations to the external world, excluding the universe of the sensory, fantasy and the work of the preconscious. A meeting at the Société Européenne pour la Psychanalyse de l'Enfant et de l'Adolescent (SEPEA) with Antonino Ferro and hours of supervision happily opened up the field of countertransference activity to me. Reading Winnicott's pupil, Lore Schacht, and her cases of child analysis that are so detailed on primitive functioning in the transference, oriented me more and more towards Marion Milner and Winnicott, transforming my listening to patients, moving away from overly rational, psychological or medical thinking, and becoming more sensitive to emotional and sensory movements in my self-analysis.

My reflections on the feminine and bisexuality, which really came into their own in the 2000s when I met Virginia Ungar, had their seeds in my reading of Juliet Mitchell and Julia Kristeva (Kristeva 2014).

My mother, Anne Anzieu (Anzieu 1989), together with Florence Guignard, founded the SEPEA and worked with autistic children at the Pitié Salpêtrière hospital. She used Kleinian thinking and, like my father, was always close to the body of sensoriality and the universe of drive impulses in all its expressions or pathological exclusions.

The happy experience of motherhood and my passion in applying my knowledge to the way I brought up my children enriched my ability to listen to and associate with patients, particularly those who were very regressed.

At the Alfred Binet Centre,[3] where I managed a child psychiatry department for 15 years, the notion of therapeutic consultation—from the outset an analytical encounter with patients of all ages—gave me a great deal of freedom to intervene dynamically in consultations, getting the patient to associate rather than questioning them about their history. The enthusiastic creation of a parent–infant consultation department was the starting point for my work with infants and their parents.

Encounter with American psychoanalysis

In 2000, I moved to the USA. The experience of emigrating to an international environment, even under the best of conditions, and the trauma of September 11, affected me personally and taught me about the mechanisms of resilience and their limits. Traumatic separations without transitional issues, the brutality of losses and their influence on early childhood, were the source of the learning that would later enrich my work in the parent–infant programme at Columbia's psychoanalytic centre, which I became part of as soon as I arrived thanks to Fred Pine, a child analyst close to Margaret Mahler. I became director of the programme in 2003 and went on to develop training in parent–baby psychotherapy, which led me to reflect on the issues involved in any analytical training.

As a long-term psychological disaster, the 2020 pandemic revealed the extent to which denial and addiction are now taking centre stage in society. My work on autoeroticism and the lack of capacity for representation and play in the individual and relational spheres is therefore taking on its full importance. Therapy with very young children, which involves a work of symbolization centred on the countertransference, is the best way to think about the transitional space and its pathologies, which are sources of symptoms such as addictive phenomena, somatic disorders and a craving for concrete solutions that short-circuit the world of representational play.

I work in parallel with my husband, a doctor in immunology research, who makes me aware of the rigorous nature of research and the links between biological movements and the forces of the unconscious. His work on Spinoza and the continuity between living systems and external reality, as well as between soma and mind, is always in dialogue with mine; the notion of epigenetics seems to me to be an excellent example of this link. It always forces me to stay close to the living body.

The support of welcoming colleagues such as Francis Baudry, Gail Reed and Graciela Abelin-Sas Rose opened the doors of psychoanalytic centres in New York to me. My multicultural and international work led me to take the helm of the IPA Committee on Child and Adolescent Psychoanalysis (COCAP), thanks to Florence Guignard and Virginia Ungar, who was president of the IPA, developing training projects in child analysis around the world, with a remarkable team of colleagues on every continent. Thinking of child analysis as an essential part of all analytic training seems to me to be an important goal. Many adult analysts no longer have any contact with the origins of psychic life or with the child within them. This sometimes limits their ability to listen to adult patients. This leads to resistance to making use of post-Kleinian thought, such as Winnicott's, in many institutes, whether in France, where post-Lacanian notions of the quest for symbolic meaning take precedence over attention to the early failings of narcissism, or in the USA, where focusing on the ego and its adaptive faculties has turned it into a rehabilitative and explanatory therapy far removed from any consideration of unconscious processes and their early origins.

Meeting Vaia Tsolas, a colleague who had sought a way to open up her thinking in her American training via psychosomatics, gave me the impetus to develop my own personal thoughts. In 2022, we founded the Pulsion Psychoanalytic Institute, oriented towards a knowledge of Freud as a whole, while keeping as close as possible to metapsychology and its dynamics and remaining open to post-Lacanian and Kleinian points of view as well as to more recent schools of thought.

Didier Anzieu's notion of transitional psychoanalysis, explored in greater depth by René Roussillon, is at the heart of this institute: this way of being an analyst is essential nowadays with young people who are detached in a blank depression associated with addictions; the psychoanalytical situation potentially offers the possibility of feeling alone in the presence of the other. But this potential can only be realized if the patient has the necessary internal psychic space. This is the precondition for the "transitional" and organizing character of a seduction fantasy to be evoked, without which the situation oscillates between a risk of impingement by the presence of the other and an experience of radical solitude. As in childhood, transitional objects can be chosen as "representatives" of a maternal imago. Through their materiality and existence, they guarantee the persistence of a private space, a psychic space, in other words a space of representations. Quick, pragmatic responses reduce the possibility of being in a living relationship with one's own self. Goldberg's (1995) work on dissociation is at the heart of the clinical experience of detachment, from depressive withdrawal and the false self to autism and psychotic dissociation.

• What is the cornerstone of your theoretical and clinical work?

It seems to me of the utmost importance not to refer to a single school of thought and to work on understanding and using different points of view in clinical practice, without becoming dogmatic, while keeping to the essence of analytical thinking. In other words, to analyse one's irrational emotional reactions, blind spots and history, to integrate different conceptions of mental life, to see their technical consequences, to think of psychoanalysis as an attitude of receptivity in the countertransference, in issues of identification, and finally to maintain the necessary energy to invest in critical knowledge.

I work to maintain a capacity to play, to be associative and alive, even when caught up in the networks of the patient's death drive or masochism, to preserve an active memory that is quick to make connections and never to forget infantile sexuality in its interactions with part objects and parts of one's own body or that of the other, in investments that are essential to maintaining the eroticism that is essential to vitality.

This implies constantly rereading Freud's work in its entirety and in a critically revised translation, staying close to André Green and his theory of affects and the work of the negative (Green 1999/1993), Didier Anzieu's theory of the skin-ego (Anzieu 2016/1985) and psychic envelopes (Anzieu 1990/1987), and the work of

René Roussillon (2011) in his wake. For me, Winnicott and his subtleness in talking to us about ourselves at the deepest level is essential.

- **What is your theoretical approach to psychoanalytic practice (the couch, frequency, the setting, teletherapy, interpretation and silence)?**

I put emphasis on the place of the body in the session. Although working remotely on screen facilitates meetings and training abroad, it leaves us with the illusion of being nothing more than an image, with no depth, no physical feelings, no experience of the transition between presence and absence.

The key factors are the analytic frame and its paradoxes, the role of silence and waiting for the patient to be ready before interpreting and attention to the analytical process. Active interventions from the very first meeting reveal the analyst's particular way of thinking. I am in favour of intervening quickly, encouraging associations, showing empathic presence and distance in observing unconscious processes, when patients are not using narcissistic defences in the negative register.

Following Winnicott (1971), I believe that play is the very model of psychic work that the psychoanalytic situation seeks to establish. It is when play has disappeared that pathology sets in, when the compulsion to repeat "identically" tends to exert its domination over psychic functioning, and when interpretation is immobilized. When an event is traumatic, memory fixes it like a pure photographic perception. It loses its vital potential, an expression of the life drives, and in repetition tends towards the death drive. Conversely, elaborating the trauma revives interpretative mobility, re-establishes the capacity for linking, the free circulation of psychic representation and the generativity of associative chains.

On the other hand, psychoanalytic work with children and adolescents, along with all forms of psychoanalytic practice based on psychodramatic expression, involves perception and motor skills in which the dynamics of presence and encounter also play a decisive role.

The unconscious issues that are operative in play and that contribute to the symbolization of subjective experience need to be identified. In other words, the latent aspects of its manifest expression conceal potentials to be discovered and explored. It is the slow revelation and shaping of these unconscious issues that constitutes the essence of "symbolizing" play. It is in this sense that play can provide a model for psychoanalytical work.

To propose play as a model for psychoanalytic work is not to fetishize play, but rather to envisage it as a "royal road", an alternative to that of dreaming.

- **What is your view of the transmission of psychoanalysis?**

The transmission of psychoanalysis begins with a personal analysis that is sufficiently integrated to be thought of as psychic work that can continue without the presence of the analyst and by reading and commenting on major texts and clinical cases. It also involves our personal way of being in society, of being attentive to others and, if possible, in harmony with ourselves, thereby transmitting an art of living. The richness of clinical experience and of oneself as an analyst facing up to doubt enables us to avoid dogmatism and to show curiosity about the unknown and surprise when faced with novelty.

The training of colleagues has to be based on the rigour of Freudian technique and thought. It is important to have exposure to clinical work with infants and children, archaic processes, interplays of regression, transformation and progression, pregenital and Oedipal conflicts and the quality of the solidity of narcissism to confront the depressive position and gain access to thinking. This is also the case with adolescents, where there is risk of psychosis, and during the different stages of adulthood.

In the Pulsion Institute created in New York, the project is to read Freud's work in chronological order, with commentaries from different horizons—Lacanian, Kleinian, Bionian and Winnicottian—in relation to Freud's biography and his unique way of using his personal experiences to maintain constant curiosity and self-analysis.

It is important to learn to establish an analytic frame and, in silence, a transitional space where the play of representations can get under way, from the most concrete to the most symbolic, in the playful "as if" realm of creative illusion and metaphors.

Although I understand that candidates in the USA are much younger than in France, where you can only start your training after you've been through personal analysis, I have reservations about the passivity of an educational system that leads to an academic vision of psychoanalysis and neglects the dynamics of the unconscious by reifying the psychic world. The analytical function is seen as reparative, or too intellectual, and not as an experience of oneself with one's own unconscious impulses.

• In your opinion, what are the points of divergence between French psychoanalysis and English-speaking psychoanalysis?

I would not want to lump together psychoanalytic practice in the USA with the history of psychoanalysis in England, the British Society and its controversies; the work of Winnicott and Bion are enrichments for psychoanalysis, not just for native English speakers.

On the American East Coast, where ego psychology reigned, the gap between it and French psychoanalysis is immense; and the West Coast, under the influence of Bion, has sailed just as far away from Freud. The drives, the body and sexuality in the Freudian sense, Eros, have disappeared.

The notion of frame is no longer mentioned in terms of something that can foster free association.

In many institutes, the medical model is essential: The patient must be assessed during several consultations according to Diagnostic and Statistical Manual of

Mental Disorders (DSM) or International Classification of Diseases (ICD) diagnostic criteria. This puts the analyst in the position of a consultant who is not involved in transference processes.

It is the interpersonal relationship that becomes the therapist's domain. It is not a matter of drive impulses but of "motivation". Anxiety is thought to be created by the inadequacy of the environment. Such a picture induces reparative and empathic desires in the therapist.

Another notion that has disappeared is temporality, a key point in Franco-American debates. An analysis centred on the here and now of the relationship eliminates any notion of the operation of après-coup.

Another debate revolves around the aim of analysis: Is it to help the patient adapt to reality and achieve emotional maturity? French psychoanalysis tends to think that the main aim is to prepare the patient for self-analysis through the experience of being alone in the presence of the other in an associative process where objects of the preconscious and unconscious phantasies can come into play, with the patient "using" the object/analyst in the sense that Winnicott speaks of using the object.

• What is your psychoanalytic approach to the societal debates on racial, gender identities or/and on the new forms of reproduction and parenting?

Motherhood is now being re-examined in the light of new cultural values and medical sophistication. Medical fertilization has changed the framework of family models, the question of origins and the evolution of maternal and paternal functions.

Some mothers are faced with their own unconscious dilemmas about femininity and reproduction. Conflicts surrounding the life debt towards her own mother will play a role in an adoptive mother's capacity to feel legitimate after an egg donation or surrogacy. Young adults who become parents, both men and women, are faced with their bisexual and social identities in an interplay of identification with and receptivity to the movements of infantile sexuality and the distress of the infant. Here too, the life and death drive impulses create a psychosomatic dynamic specific to each family.

The hypersexualization of school-age children can be observed. It is not so much a matter of pleasurable sexual activities as of compulsive behaviour. A lack of libidinal capacity is combined with a need for self-soothing activities.

It is a world of excess and insufficiency. An excess of stimulation and novelty, and a lack of relationships and attention. Psychoanalytic theory applies perfectly with its economic view of the psyche as regulating the quantities of affects.

The feminine has undergone a problematic erasure in analytical contributions, with the erasure of psychic bisexuality. The identity and erotic value of the self within a gendered identity has been replaced by a lack of differentiation that increases the narcissistic crisis associated with assertions of identity which are always painful. Psychoanalysis is familiar with the misfortunes of narcissism weakened by the lack of constructive identifications and the compulsive search for reflections of oneself in the mirror of the other who is, unfortunately, indifferent. Dogmatism on all sides makes it difficult to speak analytically, since it threatens wounded identity and seeks to remind us that our energy comes from our drive impulses towards another person, who is different from us. Thus, femininity and infantile sexuality are denied and forgotten. I note the disappearance of the role of the breast and the fantasies it generates throughout life.

Working with United Nations psychologists based in Africa has helped me a great deal to think about the racism within each of us, questions of identity and difference that are often dealt with in radical ways, and the movements of transformation that are possible in sessions with oppressed patients.

• Any other topic you would like to discuss?

The place of child and adolescent psychoanalysis, knowledge of infants and parenting issues, is an area of knowledge and experience that I think is essential to analytical practice and that I would like to see developed in all institutes.

In my work and teaching, I try to maintain the central role of infantile sexuality, the links between the life drive and the death drive, and consequently the role of primary masochism in the capacity to wait. Finally, I would add the importance of the pathology of ideality and the central role of the maternal foundations of psychic life. Maintaining a playful, but not manic, spirit, with the use of body metaphors, helps me to stay alive and creative.

Notes

1 The second year of a two-year preparatory course for entering the competitive school École normale supérieure (ENS).
2 Editor's note: See this psychoanalyst's chapter in the book.
3 A renowned paediatric psychological clinic in the 13th district of Paris.

References

Abraham, N. & Török, M. (1978). *L'Écorce et le noyau*. Paris: Flammarion.
Anzieu, A. (1989). *La Femme sans qualité. Esquisse psychanalytique de la féminité*. Paris: Dunod.
Anzieu, D. (2016/1985). *The Skin-Ego*, trans. N. Segal. London: Karnac Books.
Anzieu, D. (1990/1987). *Psychic Envelopes*. London: Karnac Books.
Botella, C. & Botella, S. (2005). *The Work of Psychic Figurability: Mental States without Representation*, trans. A. Weller. London: Routledge.
Debray, R. (1987). *Bébés/mères en révolte. Traitements psychanalytiques conjoints des déséquilibres psychosomatiques précoces*. Paris: Le Centurion.
Donnet, J.-L. (2018). *The analyzing situation*, trans. A. Weller. London: Routledge.
Foucault, M. (2009/1961). *History of Madness*. London: Routledge.
Goldberg, P. (1995). "'Successful'; dissociation, pseudovitality, and inauthentic use of the Senses." *Psychoanalytic Dialogues*, 5: 493–510.
Green, A. (1999/1993). *The Work of the Negative*, trans. A. Weller. London: Free Association Books.

Kreisler, L., Fain, M. & Soulé, M. (1978). *L'enfant et son corps. Études sur la clinique psychosomatique du premier âge*. Paris: Presses Universitaires de France.

Kristeva, J. (2014). "Reliance, or maternal eroticism". *Journal of the American Psychoanalytic Association*, 62: 69–85.

Lacan, J. (2006/1966). *Écrits*, trans. B. Fink. New York, NY: Norton.

Marty, P. (1968). "A major process of somatization: The progressive disorganization". *International Journal of Psychoanalysis*, 49(2): 46–49.

Manzano, J., Espasa, F. P. & Zilkha, N. (1999). "The narcissistic scenarios of parenthood". *International Journal of Psychoanalysis*, 80(3): 465–476.

Roussillon, R. (2011). *Primitive Agony and Symbolization*, trans. D. Alcock. London: Karnac.

Winnicott, D. W. (1971). *Playing and Reality*. London: Routledge.

Chapter 3

Conversation with Danièle Brun[1]

Abstract

Danièle Brun takes an original and sensitive approach to the theory of the father in psychoanalysis, in Freud and Lacan, and enquires about the father before father-hood. At the same time, with the aim of establishing a dialogue between psychoanalysis and medicine, she reflects on the possible responses of psychoanalysis to physical illness and the way it is handled by the medical establishment.

• What is the intellectual and personal journey that led you to psychoanalysis?

I was led to psychoanalysis by chance, need and desire, like a triad that does not need to be given any precise order in order to grasp how these three elements are intertwined. Chance took its time to manifest itself as a need, since I had children before looking for the child within myself when I took up my studies again. [After having children,] I felt a need to take up studies again that I had abandoned ten years earlier due to changes in my life. As chance would have it, in the autumn of 1968, a new university opened in Vincennes, built during the summer after the events of May. Psychoanalysis was taught in the philosophy department there under Michel Foucault. This course gave me the desire to undertake an analysis and to become a psychoanalyst. It was the first time that a psychoanalyst at the university had addressed neophytes. His lectures throughout the academic year covered key concepts, including transference, loss and castration, repression and the drive and its objects. He evoked the theme of separation from the "mother" object and the moment when this separation became operative—a moment that was never really reached. According to Serge Leclaire, this irreducible gap between the satisfaction expected and the satisfaction obtained illustrated the work of an analysis, reflecting the specificity of temporality in psychoanalysis and its difference from ordinary temporality. I had the impression not of having understood everything but of having recognized, once it had been put into words and because I carried it within me, knowledge that was in fact, as Freud says in *The Three Essays*, a rediscovery, the gap being in the "re" of rediscovery. I had the impression that I had nothing more or

DOI: 10.4324/9781003342502-3

different to learn than what I had always carried within me. Such was the familiarity with which I approached psychoanalysis on both a practical and theoretical level, which of course did not prevent me from being surprised and bewildered. This intellectual, academic desire for psychoanalysis was also, and above all, sensory. In fact, I now realize that it had been there since childhood, reaching deep down inside me.

Once I had got beyond this feeling of having an immediate connection with psychoanalysis, I was surprised to discover the diversity of positions between Freudians, Kleinians and Lacanians. Reading the most significant works in each of these fields was very fruitful, particularly the work of Winnicott, Melanie Klein, Hanna Segal and, of course, Jacques Lacan. They were all opportunities to perceive the multiplicity of approaches to the unconscious and to infantile sexuality and, thereby, to *rediscover* my own. I was thus better equipped with arguments to explore Freud's theory of infantile sexuality more deeply.

• Could you comment on any opportune encounters in your journey and in your training?

Very early on in my student life and in my professional life, I met women who encouraged me from the outset, both clinically and as a writer. One of these was Nina Rausch de Traubenberg, a Rorschach practitioner who invited me to join her clinical work group, though in the end I did not join it. But I taught Rorschach at university for over 20 years. Then there was the founder of children's oncology, Dr Odile Schweisguth, who, despite her avowed ignorance of psychoanalysis, trusted me immediately and got me involved in doing research into curing cancer in children. I then met Juliette Favez-Boutonier, who, in 1968, had set up the Clinical Human Sciences Department at the Denis Diderot University (now Paris City University), and as it happened, I was her last doctoral thesis student. She was interested in the theme of death and thanatology. She introduced me to Didier Anzieu who chaired my thesis jury and published my first book, *L'Enfant donné pour mort* (Brun 1989), in his collection. Jean Laplanche chaired the jury for my state thesis, entitled "Psychopathologie de la guérison. La maternité et le féminin". Pierre Fédida was my supervisor.

I also met Joyce McDougall, who wrote a preface for my book on child psychoanalysis *Mikael, un enfant en analyse* (Brun 1997). The work of Michel de M'Uzan also had a major impact on me. I've had several psychoanalysts, both men and women, including Conrad Stein. His book *L'Enfant imaginaire* (Stein 1987) and Serge Leclaire's *On tue un enfant* (Leclaire 1981) had, and still have, a very important place in my view of psychoanalysis and in my practice. And last but not least, Julia Kristeva and all her studies on the feminine. I'm always very receptive to her proposals for meetings and discussions about her texts.

• What is the cornerstone of your theoretical and clinical work?

Questions relating to motherhood, the feminine, the status of the child in a girl's life and the process of her becoming a woman have mobilized my attention and my writing since the beginning of my work. They organize and concretize the question of loss, death anxieties and so-called castration in women.

I've been guided by Freud's notion of the infantile, as developed in *The Interpretation of Dreams* (Freud 1900a). The role of the infantile in psychic life illustrates the timelessness of the unconscious and the instinctual drive issues at stake. It is in their name, and with the images they produce, that every dream, says Freud, makes room for the "lost paradise of prehistoric childhood", where the child is still alive.

I also believe it is essential to know about man's life before he becomes a father in order to appreciate how he integrates his paternity. If it is ignored, this life of the man who becomes a father can create what I have called "an insidious maleficence" (Brun 2013). Freud's renunciation of the theory of seduction by the father left me perplexed because it exonerates the father's role in infantile identifications.

With Freud, psychoanalysis had its origins in everyday life and its psychopathology. The reason for entering analysis is a starting point that discovers its deeper meaning over the course of the sessions. Giving an account of dreams, even fragmentary ones, and of parapraxes provides a new way of looking at life and its traumas. I also attach importance to the intimate links between body and psyche, where psychoanalysis reveals itself beyond psychologizing explanations.

- **What is your theoretical approach to psychoanalytic practice (the couch, frequency, setting, teletherapy, interpretation, silence)?**

It is difficult to think of psychoanalytic practice today in the same way as in the 1980s. The anatomical difference between the sexes as conceived by Freud can no longer be regarded as a pivotal element. Women have spoken out. Children make themselves heard at a very early age. Although somewhat marginalized in comparison with other therapies that are reputed to be quicker and more effective, psychoanalysis remains the only real means of gaining access to the unconscious. For me, the couch and regular sessions, even twice a week, are essential. Silence is less essential. Today's patients expect reciprocity and words, which does not prevent them from gradually entering into the dynamics of an analysis. With the pandemic, the use of the telephone and videoconferencing has become widespread, ushering in another way of talking about oneself, sometimes seemingly free, but much more difficult to explore in depth. In the end, there's no substitute for attending sessions.

- **What is your view of the transmission of psychoanalysis?**

If transmission through personal analysis remains the first necessary condition, I no longer believe in transmission through personal analysis alone because it fades with time to a greater or lesser degree depending on the person.

To this must be added the reading of the written works of authors who left their mark on their time. The works of Freud, Melanie Klein and Lacan raised fundamental questions for psychoanalysts, both in their own practices and in the seminars they regularly held in their respective institutions. From this point of view, the work that emerged in France for over 20 years from the 1960s onwards ensured the transmission of psychoanalysis. We must continue to read and quote them. Without returning to those authors I have already mentioned, the contributions of Piera Aulagnier and François Perrier still bear fruit and have lost none of their relevance. The same may be said of the contributions of the English-speaking world, including, of course, Melanie Klein and Winnicott, who were translated at the time and whose clinical illustrations counted for a great deal. The works of Harold Searles, Louis Wolfson and Marion Milner follow in their footsteps.

The influence of psychoanalysis on the contemporary world of culture is particularly important, notably in the work of Julia Kristeva. The contribution of literature to psychoanalysis is also noteworthy. Examples include Jacques Lacan's work on Joyce and Duras, and Didier Anzieu's on Beckett.

- **In your opinion, what are the points of divergence between French psychoanalysis and English-speaking psychoanalysis?**

Theoretical references in English-speaking psychoanalysis are more Kleinian than Freudian. The interventions of the Anglo-Saxon psychoanalysts I listened to, particularly in London, focused more on the daily lives of patients than those of French analysts, as a means of gaining access to their psychic lives. Perhaps it depends on the training and habits they have acquired.

- **What is your psychoanalytic approach to the societal debates on racial, gender identities or/and on the new forms of reproduction and parenting?**

Numerous seminars and colloquia are being held on social issues and their impact. What are the potential changes for psychoanalysis and its invariants: transference and repression? Speaking about the new challenges for psychoanalysis is also a way of questioning its social ties. Think of the role played by the ebullient atmosphere of fin-de-siècle Vienna (Schorske 1980) in Freud's discovery.

I do not have any preconceptions, and I do not mix my personal opinions with my practice. I listen to what patients tell me and pay attention to how the current situation has developed over time since childhood. How did we get here? On the basis of what identifications?

- **Is there any other topic you would like to discuss?**

There is one question that is essential today but barely discussed or examined in institutional settings: that of the place of psychoanalysis in medicine. Why? Because life expectancy is getting longer, and because medicine is making enormous progress and becoming more protocolized. The patient is the object of inevitable passivity with regard to treatment. We need to work on the weight of medical rhetoric and on accompanying patients through their illness, particularly in oncology. My current work is devoted to contemporary medicine and its dehumanization. How can one continue to inhabit one's body when it is requisitioned by the side effects of treatment and by the external authority represented by medicine and its practitioners? The speaking body is an essential element of access to the unconscious, and today, the way in which treatments are coded and automated tends to turn the patient into a little automaton eager for medication. The words of the body are encrypted like a dream. We often ignore them, taking into account only their manifestation in practical life. This does not mean wallowing in the masochism of malaise. We need to train doctors, nurses and psychologists to listen to the malaise of the speaking bodies of patients. Pierre Fédida used to say, encouraging me, that medicine and psychoanalysis were truly hyperdisciplinary fields, and Conrad Stein, recalling Ferenczi, used to say: "an infant's body in an adult's carcass". This is a subject that has preoccupied me since the beginning and one that I have explored extensively.

Note

1 Editor's note: Danièle Brun passed away during the production of this book while she was finishing her last essay (Brun 2023). Not only does this interview reflect her last thoughts about psychoanalysis, it also conveys a lifetime of psychoanalytic experience with its rigor and subtlety.

References

Brun, D. (1989). *L'Enfant donné pour mort*. Paris: Dunod.
Brun, D. (1997). *Mikael, un enfant en analyse*. Paris: Calmann-Lévy.
Brun, D. (2013). *L'Insidieuse malfaisance du père*. Paris: Odile Jacob.
Brun, D. (2023). *Madame Vertigo et son cancer, Rencontre avec une médecine déshuamnisée*. Paris: Odile Jacob.
Freud, S. (1900a). *The Interpretation of Dreams. S. E.* 4–5. London: Hogarth.
Leclaire, S. (1981). *On tue un enfant*. Paris: Seuil.
Schorske, C. (1980). *Fin-de-siècle Vienna, Politics and Culture*. New York, NY: Alfred A. Knopf.
Stein, C. (1987). *L'Enfant imaginaire*. Paris: Denoël.

Chapter 4

Conversation with Catherine Chabert

Abstract

Catherine Chabert emphasizes the dangers of avoiding the role of the drives in transference. She sees this avoidance as an escapism from the inevitable pain associated with separation and loss. She also proposes an inverted conception of seduction, based on her clinical work with anorexic patients.

- **Could you describe the intellectual and personal journey that led you to psychoanalysis?**

Unlike many psychoanalysts of my generation, I did not encounter psychoanalysis during my secondary education: I now think that my teachers were not really interested in Freud, their struggles were elsewhere. I must say, however, that my philosophy teacher, in preparatory classes for the *grandes écoles*, essentially taught me how to read, that is, a method for listening to what others write, which was a real contribution to my training as an analyst. After obtaining a degree in philosophy, I enrolled in psychology without committing myself at all to psychoanalysis. It was when I arrived at Paris Nanterre University that, almost by chance, I met Didier Anzieu and found myself studying psychopathology, which was the starting point for my entire career, since it was there that I discovered psychoanalysis.

- **Could you comment on any opportune encounters you had in your journey and training?**

Other encounters had a truly decisive effect at this time: Daniel Widlöcher who supervised my first thesis, Roger Dorey who convinced me of the richness of psychopathology and, of course, Didier Anzieu who supervised my PhD. These encounters at university "naturally" led me to the French Psychoanalytical Association (APF) for my analyses and training. It was there that I met Jean Laplanche, François Gantheret, Guy Rosolato, Pierre Fédida and, above all, J.-B. Pontalis.

My long university career enabled me in turn to pass on clinical psychopathology and psychoanalysis. I really enjoyed teaching, sharing both my knowledge and clinical experience with my students, growing with them over time and over the

DOI: 10.4324/9781003342502-4

years: it is wonderful to be able to develop your own thinking by passing on that of others and speaking to others!

While working as a psychoanalyst in Paris, I was heavily involved in the Adolescent and Young Adult Psychiatry Department run by Philippe Jeammet at the Institut Mutualiste Montsouris (IMM)[1] for almost 30 years. It was a wonderful experience working with young psychotic and borderline patients: psychodrama, therapies in institutions, group dynamics, working with healthcare teams and other therapists who were all involved in caring for very ill adolescents and young adults and were supported by a spirit of theoretical and practical research that was entirely committed to psychoanalysis. It was a truly fertile period when psychiatry was opening up to psychoanalysis, when madness was no longer restricted to asylums: Freud's insistence on the dialectic between the normal and the pathological was a fundamental principle for everyone at that time. My analytical training and teaching activities gave me the chance to combine experience, methods and theories from both a clinical and a metapsychological perspective. Theory completely divorced from clinical practice makes no sense to me, and clinical practice without theory is no better. I think that while clinical practice regularly offers singular configurations that enable us to discover astonishing psychic forms, metapsychology is indispensable because it opens up another way of thinking that ensures listening maintains a certain height and distance. It is in this sense that psychoanalysis is a science, a "young science" as Freud used to say, and not the old lady of the last century as is too often said today.

I tend to return regularly to texts I have already read and to reread them regularly (Freud, first and foremost!) with the renewed conviction of discovering something different each time. It is true that I also return regularly to certain old treatments. What transference effects does this repetition obey? I would like to make it clear that, in these returns, I am looking for modifications, transformations and essential novelties. In the end, it is more the hope of escaping the violence of unchangeable repetition that mobilizes my approach. Is it an attempt to tame something within myself? It could be that, in this case, repetition is stripped of its alienating dimension and finds a way forward: a way of returning to, of returning towards, sustained by the desire to go further and to change rather than remain permanently fixed in the same point of view. It is also a way of considering that analytical work is never completely satisfactory, of course, never definitive, that is clear.

• What is the cornerstone of your theoretical and clinical work?

Freud and the analytical method

For me, Freud's work is the essential reference in terms of the foundations of psychoanalysis. It accompanies my clinical and metapsychological work, guides my writing and is at the heart of my transmission to universities and to analysts in training. If I attach great importance to the links between clinical practice and theory it is also because it allows me to get involved in new fields while keeping the foundations alive. There are strong currents in Freud's work, sometimes contradictory, sometimes complementary, which reveal extremely fertile sources for thinking about today's clinical work: masochism, or failure when faced with success, the negative therapeutic reaction, melancholia and mania, not to mention the two topographies and the two drive theories. For me, the Freudian epistemological approach retains its heuristic value: the regular to-and-fro between observation and theory and their interactions are still important to me; they are part of a dynamic of research in psychoanalysis that allows us to move forward again and again. For Freud, observation already contains preconcepts that influence perception and, therefore, the description of clinical facts. This movement, present from the outset, is repeated and renewed. Such clinical work is inhabited, alive, animated by the experience of transference/countertransference and a metapsychology that is constantly being put to the test but which nevertheless continues to be essential as it is revised. Freud never really gives up; there is not just a chronological sequence in his work but stages, affirmations and doubts, constructions and defeats, scaffolding and edifices. And I share his conceptions with my colleagues in the APF, in defence of a psychoanalysis that remains Freudian in spite of, or thanks to, change: Is not change the driving force and the major challenge of all psychic treatment?

However, I do not feel confined in the association to which I belong and I have always enjoyed looking elsewhere. Very early on, I had the opportunity to follow the seminars of other "great" analysts like Piera Aulagnier, Evelyne Kestemberg and André Green. It is very important for me not to confine myself to a single circle, and it is also a pleasure to compare different points of view because I have always had a strong taste for debate. Consensus bores me, and moreover, I think it is dangerous due to the risk of a dogmatic drift that it implies. If there is one lesson to be learned from Freudian epistemology, it is that progress in research depends on ideas being tested and challenged! Moreover, if I chose the APF, it was also because, despite basic agreements, the "great" psychoanalysts of the time were capable of thinking differently: Some memorable debates[2] between the founders were at the heart of my training. What's more, from the outset our training institute had the particularity of welcoming analysands from a variety of couches, and not just from the APF.

There is nothing original about my career path; it is characteristic of a generation of analysts trained in the 70s and 80s, at a time when a wind of freedom was blowing through France, thanks in particular to the work of Winnicott, and precisely at a time when the indications for analytic treatment were expanding well beyond neurosis, giving rise to debates and conflicts within the various analytic currents. That there was a desire or need to go elsewhere in order to grasp these "new" clinical situations seems to me to be entirely justified, provided that Freudian metapsychology is not abandoned: It clearly provides a powerful analysis of these modalities of psychic functioning! One only has to read and reread "On Narcissism: An Introduction" (1914c), "Mourning and Melancholia" (1917e) or *The Ego and the Id* (1923b) to appreciate their value and meaning!

Let me give an example: At the time of my first readings, I was working as an analyst mainly with adolescents suffering from serious psychological disorders. The fragility of these adolescents' sense of identity, whether borderline or psychotic, revealed major narcissistic problems in a context of analytic thought where many authors were devoting their work to them.[3] In the analytical treatments of these young patients, it seemed necessary to support or ensure the maintenance of a minimal narcissistic cathexis, and the conquest of the self clearly constituted a purposive idea in the conscious sense, since, at the same time, the development of a specific method for treating these flaws was gradually being put in place. Why not? But an approach that involves going through stages of analysis successively seems questionable to me because how can one separate narcissistic cathexes from object cathexes? How can the ego be thought of without the other? How can we abandon sexuality, particularly at the time of adolescence, a period of life that disrupts previous reference points precisely because drive functioning is exacerbated? This is where, for me, Freud's brilliant discovery (along with that of the unconscious and infantile sexuality) gives its essence to the method: I am speaking of the transference, where the intertwining of the self, the object and drive functioning are played out again. The more time passes, the more I am interested in it, for it is a constant source of new experiences and lines of questioning. Nothing is more disconcerting than to see it confined in categories that immobilize it (Chabert 2020)!

The influence of D. W. Winnicott

Very early on, I had access to the work of Winnicott[4] (whom I discovered almost at the same time as Freud, albeit in very different ways), who accompanied me in my first experiences in child psychiatry. This obviously made me very aware of the concepts of the ego and the self and therefore of the existence of different perspectives between French psychoanalysis and Anglo-Saxon psychoanalysis.

Here is a theoretical example: The construction of the ego through the sedimentation of identifications with lost and abandoned objects, as defined by Freud (1923b) in *The Ego and the Id*, constitutes, in my opinion, a decisive pivot in the conception of psychic functioning based on the second topography. It is a divided ego, torn between the demands of the id and the superego, grappling with its unconscious roots and conscious expectations, an agency that bears witness to the highest degree of the fundamental mental conflicts defended by psychoanalysis. This ego is quite different from the one conceived by the proponents of ego psychology, who insist much more on its capacity for synthesis, regulation and adaptation in relation to external reality.

As for the self, it might appear to be a relevant notion with regard to narcissism, reserving the field of conflicts with objects for the ego within the psychic apparatus itself. It seems to me that its success is due to a rather hasty amalgam between the self and narcissism, of which it is alleged to be the representative; except that the self too often expels drive activity, whereas narcissism depends on it! However, J.-B. Pontalis's (1977) definition of the self is still very meaningful to me. According to him, the self is the representative of the living, perhaps a fulfilment of the sense of a continuity of being promoted by Winnicott, with the added element that the living implies movement and therefore the drive.

What I also retain from Winnicott is the importance of giving a transitional function to the analytical situation, particularly when the boundaries are lost between inside and outside, between self and object—a space which, at the outset, belongs to no one but which can be created/found thanks to the transference. I have also put forward another reading of "Fear of breakdown" (Winnicott 1974), while fully respecting Winnicott's point of view concerning the failure of the environment and the way in which its repetition can be handled in analysis. I also understand it from the angle of the sexual, with regard to the nonrecognition, the psychic nonregistration of the primal scene as the primordial scene, as the scene of origins. I support the idea that the child's loneliness and distress, triggered by environmental failure, are not exclusively the result of maternal failings, and that they can also be understood in relation to the primal scene and the exclusion it imposes. This is a way of understanding both what is *in-between* and what is *in-between-the-two-of-them* (Chabert 2003).

The teaching of Pontalis

J.-B. Pontalis's genius was not to confine himself to a few notions that are relatively easy to grasp in Winnicott's work but to tackle what is more difficult, more complicated, in spite of appearances. The self is a fine example of this, but the use of the object even more so. It is a real driving force in analytic treatment, indispensable for constructing legends or versions of a patient's history, and above all for its essential action in the transference. In what ways is the patient capable of using the analyst-object? In what ways is the analyst likely to use the object represented by the patient? These questions were subtly developed in Winnicott's (1969) article "The use of an object", which Pontalis (1983) took up and explored further.

I have focused on object loss and its links with pain, once again with reference to Pontalis (1977). Drawing on the addenda to *Inhibitions, Symptoms and Anxiety* (Freud 1926) as a starting point, I wanted to explore the difference between pain and suffering. At the moment it occurs, in the immediacy of its emergence, pain could be a pure experience, a naked experience, devoid of any representational connection. It could be seen as an unimaginable narcissistic violation, in the literal sense of the term: There is no possible link with even a minimal representation, no doubt due to the effect of splitting. We may wonder about the psychic operations that deal with the instances of pain, which may or may not allow them to be registered psychically. The inner scene and its private theatre, the cathexis of psychic reality, that is, of representation, dreams and fantasies, guarantee the permanence of internal objects. We separate, of course, but we do not lose ourselves for all that because the traces are there, making it possible to summon the absent object, making it exist in representation, assuring ourselves of its continuity.

Any situation of loss can engender both immense despair and insurmountable anger, nagging self-blame and a persecutory threat. The projection of hatred can affect the other person and transform them into a bad object, while at the same time hounding the ego in the form of permanent separation anxiety to do with never being loved again, being left or abandoned forever. I have developed these reflections over the course of my career but more particularly in my book, *Maintenant, il faut se quitter* (Chabert 2017).

I want to return now for a moment to Freud, to mourning and melancholia and to the drive trajectories that characterize and differentiate them: openness to new objects when the mourning process is over, and the narcissistic turning back that is more characteristic of the melancholic movement. By not falling into the trap of self-destruction, Freud clearly showed how, by attacking itself, the ego seeks to reach the object: not differentiating between the ego and the object precludes experiencing hatred for the object that it encompasses; it avoids the separation between the two since the object and the ego are indistinguishable. There is no separation and therefore no loss—manic triumph is not far off, even if the shadow of the object and the risk of being carried away by death lurk constantly.

In varying configurations, it is nonetheless against the yardstick of the capacity to separate that primary identifications are established. Whether fusional, narcissistic, manic or melancholic, they are formed in the soil of drive life and in the possibility of accepting ambivalence towards the object, whether differentiated or in the process of being differentiated.

- **What is your psychoanalytic approach to the societal debates on racial, gender identities or/and on the new forms of reproduction and parenting?**

Infantile sexuality: the Oedipus complex and its multiple configurations

It is too often forgotten that psychosexuality begins at the very beginning of life and that sexuality, in the Freudian sense of the term, is not the same as genital sexuality. Winnicott's (1966) notion of *pure femininity* may be partly responsible for this, but not entirely!

For me, the difference between the sexes is not only the basis of sexuality (in the analytical sense of the term), but it is also the paradigm of difference. This means that, whether recognized or not, denied, disowned, flouted or destroyed, the difference between the sexes is there as a fundamental reference point, just like the Oedipus complex. Whatever the modalities of psychic functioning, the density of the problems of object choices and identifications means that its vicissitudes vary. They can acquire a structuring value when the difference between the sexes and generations is recognized, but they can also exist in the most confusing configurations when incest and murder are involved. The Oedipus complex is not only understood according to its most classic or conformist configurations; referring to the difference between the sexes and generations does not mean that these are psychically accepted without hesitation, or even without confusion. Nor does it mean that we are systematically confronted with fusional and dependent infantile fixations, like a distressed infant, always in search of a helping other, with no expectations other than self-preservative satisfactions. The infantile is sexual, and remains so: In adult treatments, it never confines itself to the most troubled zones of nondifferentiation. It is inevitably confronted with the difference between the sexes and generations and comes to terms with it to a greater or lesser extent, which in no way prejudges the choice of objects in the reality of love life.[5] Bisexuality is still very much alive, and only shifts in orientation in terms of "a little more" of one or the other. It does not mean confusion between the sexes, still less "indifferent gender", but rather the existence of both, masculine and feminine, and their representations, both singular and plural. In my opinion, whatever the modalities, it is still this reference to the Oedipus complex that traces the path of identifications, which I think are essential in the transference and countertransference with regard to object choices.

Seduction fantasies

In the hysterical construction of seduction fantasies, and in the genesis of the theory that underlies it—it is the gap, the asymmetry, that creates the trauma in the earliest Freudian theory. The difference between the sexes and generations, flouted by the act of a "perverse" father, underpins the transition to the fantasy and its translation into fiction. In the construction of the "nuclear" Oedipus complex and its repression, it found a path of resolution through the setting-up of the prohibitions of incest and murder. Mixing gives way to separation.

My experience with adolescent girls and young women with severe compulsive symptoms (eating disorders, repeated suicide attempts, scarification, etc.) has brought me face-to-face with another version of the seduction fantasy: In this version, fuelled by the daughter's conviction that she has actively seduced the father and not been seduced by him, the seducing agent is no longer the adult pervert, but the subject herself. The hysterical version, beyond its manifest content, leaves open the question of "who is seducing whom", of the respective responsibility of each of them. (This was a "solution" Freud found to the problem of trauma, through the affirmation of joint forces that come from without *and* within.) In the "melancholic" version of seduction, there is a crudely formulated belief in the guilt of the young girl charged with the crime of incest, the idea of which is not repressed. This guilt is massively fuelled by masochistic compulsions reflected in the recourse to implacable sacrificial mortification. The seduction fantasy then undergoes a shift in orientation sustained by self-accusation, repeatedly demanding humiliating and mortifying retaliatory measures. The girl is no longer the innocent victim; she is both criminal and executioner. The punishment she inflicts on herself involves attacks on the body, the gendered and sexual body, considered to be the root of all evil, since it is the source of violent excitation for the ego and for the other.

- **What is your theoretical approach to psychoanalytical practice (the couch, frequency, setting, teletherapy, interpretation, silence)?**

Transferences

As psychoanalytic thinking has evolved, certain currents of thought have considered the Freudian point of view to be obsolete, arguing that cultural changes as well as clinical and psychopathological modifications require new concepts to be found—very often neologisms, moreover—and further that Freudian metapsychology has become, in their opinion, inadequate to account for the new indications of psychoanalysis, not to mention the changes in method recommended to adapt to new psychic disorders. This results in undoing the essential principles of Freudian psychoanalysis. Changes of method do not do away with the transference, but they do make its dynamics difficult to deal with; if we hinder free association and above all the frustration that is necessary for its deployment, for ideas and affects to emerge, for the action of fantasy and the drives, if we abandon all these components and many more besides, what is left of analysis? Adopting an overly reparative approach for fear of repeating frustration in the transference seems to me to be highly questionable. Reparation is no consolation for the unconscious, and there is a great risk, particularly in avoiding hatred or destructiveness in the transference, of encouraging or aggravating dependence on the environment, that is on parental imagos and the original objects they attempt to represent.

What is essential lies elsewhere, in the analytic situation itself: Only the real presence of the analyst and the response that it elicits in the initial and massive forms of the transference allow this movement to inaugurate the process. Just as Freud's presence enabled the child of the *Fort-Da!* to throw his wooden reel far away and to rejoice at its disappearance at least as much as at its return (Freud 1920) so the analyst's presence, close to the patient, makes it possible to ensure the return, the survival of the representation of the object. In such instances, it is the perception of the analyst's presence and his or her constancy that offers the opportunity to "say everything" without excessive risk. This is why remote analysis (of which I had some experience during the lockdowns of 2020 and 2021) seems to me to betray the essence of analysis and transference.

I would like to return to another criticism of the method, namely the *supposed neutrality of the analyst*: In my opinion, this apparent neutrality does not imply actual indifference, that is, the absence of feelings. Their quality remains even if practising the method attempts to reduce their quantity. In so-called classical treatments, the analyst's reserved position is accepted, even recommended. On the other hand, in so-called borderline cases, the analyst's neutrality is still clearly called into question, and there is a strong temptation to engage in a process in which "benevolence" distorts its original conception. It is confused with a reparative attitude that seeks to make up for the failings of the original objects. The analyst could be tempted to identify with the "good object" that compensates for the misfortunes caused by the "bad" ones! What is most surprising is that this position is in complete contradiction with Winnicott when he considers that analysis repeats the failings of the environment, thereby making it possible for these experiences to be registered psychically.

The pain of transference

In my opinion, the presence of the analyst, his or her physical and psychic presence, constitutes a foundation, a guarantor, to which is linked the possibility of repeating what did not occur, as a result in particular of the failures of the object, along with the disappointment they cause and the dejection they provoke. If transference always has to do with the past, the repetition that is inevitably at its source is also a matter of fidelity to that past, of a relentless clinging to the early parental figures, and this repetition, precisely, is in the service of this mad attachment. This is what I call the pain of transference, as it reveals itself and unfolds in the analytic process, attaching its lineaments to the analytic experience when the most naïve bonds of seduction, or the more tragic ones of idealization, have come undone. In such situations, analysis offers the opportunity to repeat a nonencounter, to repeat it over and over again, provided that both partners, the analysand and the analyst, are willing to put up with it, that both accept that they do not always occupy their place, that they accept this rout, this defeat, this infinite dispossession of oneself which will enable them to accept the opposite of what is regularly sought in analysis: the sharing of meaning first and foremost, and the sharing, equally expected, of affects. Such intimacy is constitutive of the ego, of the certainty (however occasional and ephemeral it may be, as long as it is regularly experienced) of existing now, in pain, creating what Winnicott calls the sense of a continuity of being.

In analysis, the fact that the analyst accepts their passivity (i.e., the fact that they too can be afflicted, affected by pain or pleasure as a result of the transference) may be seen as a psychic event ensuring a new conquest, thanks to the now possible reversal of opposing drive movements. There is a change of point of view, a mobilization on both sides, that of the analysand and that of the analyst.

• What is your view on the transmission of psychoanalysis?

I have already mentioned the transmission of psychoanalysis at university, which involves transmission via teaching, not training. Let me explain: The university has been a significant place for raising awareness of psychoanalysis, its discoveries, its concepts, the foundations of metapsychology and the method. The reference to psychoanalysis underpins the study of clinical psychopathology, analysing the sometimes excessive forms of psychic operations that deal with general and singular problems. Training in clinical interviewing provides a solid foundation that can be deployed in the experience of analysis. These components can be developed in great depth and form the basis of knowledge and training in analysis. However, they are not sufficient. It is not possible, in a university curriculum, to require actual experience of analysis, which presupposes private personal involvement, the first condition for training as an analyst. On the basis of this fundamental experience, it is up to the psychoanalytic societies to provide candidates with training in the method through supervised treatments, and in the theory through seminars and the scientific life of the associations at national and international levels.

• What, in your view, are the points of divergence between French psychoanalysis and English speaking psychoanalysis?

This is a complex question, and I'm not sure that I can give an exhaustive and relevant answer. I can only speak for myself! As I have already said, I am interested in debates, very curious, and I pick up ideas here and there that interest me. My training was heavily influenced by Melanie Klein and D. W. Winnicott: my critical stance towards the former has developed over time and concerns, above all the ways in which references to phantasy are interpreted too quickly, sometimes in a clichéd way, without making the necessary detour to grasp their singular forms. But I absolutely adhere to Melanie Klein's construction of the depressive position and her work on projection. For Winnicott, about whom I have already spoken at length, the situation is different and relates to the effects of his work on contemporary psychoanalysis: the triumph and omnipresence of the mother and the abandonment of psychosexuality. There is undoubtedly a gap between the way Anglo-Saxon psychoanalysis is understood and interpreted in France and the way it is actually practised. What I have mentioned in terms of changes in the method, which supposedly aims to repair psychic damage by relying heavily on the mother–child relationship, is perhaps a question of French translation and interpretation! I can have much more relaxed and direct discussions with my English and American colleagues, no doubt because there is mutual respect for the other person's analytical language.

Notes

1 Translator's note: A private healthcare establishment in Paris.
2 The debates concerning the second drive theory and especially the death drive continue to be topical, starting from the different initial positions of Jean Laplanche and J.-B. Pontalis. Others are based on the varying importance of Lacan's influence concerning the place and function of language—of signifiers—in the work of Daniel Widlöcher, Jean-Claude Lavie or Pierre Fédida. Yet other debates are, to a greater or lesser extent, oriented towards the question of beginnings (Didier Anzieu).
3 Among French psychoanalysts, André Green and Guy Rosolato; among Anglo-Saxon psychoanalysts, Heinz Kohut and Otto Kernberg.
4 It was J.-B. Pontalis who introduced Winnicott's work to France.
5 It might be supposed today that this does not prejudice identity choices, but I cannot really take a position on this question, especially when one thinks of early gender changes and of the questions they raise.

References

Chabert, C. (2003). *Féminin mélancolique*. Paris: Presses Universitaires de France.

Chabert, C. (2017). *Maintenant, il faut se quitter*. Paris: Presses Universitaires de France.

Chabert, C. (2020). *Les Belles espérances. Le transfert et l'attente*. Paris: Presses Universitaires de France.

Freud, S. (1914c). "On narcissism: An introduction". *S. E.* 14. London: Hogarth, pp. 69–102.

Freud, S. (1917e). "Mourning and melancholia". *S. E.* 14. London: Hogarth, pp. 237–260.

Freud, S. (1920g). *Beyond the Pleasure Principle. S. E.* 18. London: Hogarth, pp. 1–64.

Freud, S. (1923b). *The Ego and the Id. S. E.* 19. London: Hogarth, pp. 3–66.

Freud, S. (1926d). *Inhibitions, Symptoms and Anxiety. S. E.* 20. London: Hogarth, pp. 77–174.

Pontalis, J.-B. (1977). *Entre le rêve et la douleur*. Paris: Gallimard.

Pontalis, J.-B. (1983). "Naissance et reconnaissance du soi". In: *Entre le rêve et la douleur*. Paris: Gallimard, pp. 159–191.

Winnicott, D. W. (1966). "The split-off male and female elements to be found in men and women". In: *Psycho-Analytic Explorations*, ed. C. Winnicott, R. Shepherd, M. Davis. Cambridge, MA: Harvard University Press, pp. 169–192.

Winnicott, D. W. (1969). "The use of an object". *The International Journal of Psychoanalysis*, 50(4): 711–716.

Winnicott, D. W. (1974). "Fear of breakdown". *The International Review of Psychoanalysis*, 1: 103–107.

Chapter 5

Conversation with Bernard Chervet

Abstract

Bernard Chervet develops the concept of après-coup beyond repressed memories and extends it to the totality of the human psychic life in its resonance with sexuality, memory and trauma.

- **Could you describe the intellectual and personal journey that led you to psychoanalysis?**

Overdetermination and cryptomnesia

Any reflection on our inheritance combines Goethe's (1808) famous words, repeated on various occasions by Freud (1940a [1938]) right up to the last lines of *An Outline of Psychoanalysis*—"*Was Du ererbt von deinen Vätern hast,/Erwirb es, um es zu besitzen*" ["What thou has inherited from thy fathers, acquire it to make it thine"] (from Goethe 1808, Part I, Scene 1)—and the fact that what is passed on is also the result of cryptomnesias and reminiscences that contribute to the specific overdetermination of psychic functioning, a passive overdetermination that includes the attraction of the goal to be achieved.

It is a question of acquiring freedom in relation to our inheritance, opening up new psychic pathways and using the historical and singular lines of identification to gain access to the impersonal principle of identification and to the pathways that have been neglected, avoided or even discarded by previous generations.

After studies during my childhood and adolescence that were deemed "brilliant", my future lay in mathematics, with an appetite for abstraction and for the very specific mechanism for solving maths problems, the leap between the statement and the solution, a leap often linked to intuition, which I later found in psychoanalysis with interpretation. When I was a teenager, I experienced this transition between moments of tension and perplexity when faced with a statement and moments of sometimes dazzling resolution in a state of jubilation and exaltation, a mixture of inspiration and idealization.

However, a reminiscence came into conflict with this destiny mapped out by my school results, and finally imposed itself: the wish I expressed as a child to become

DOI: 10.4324/9781003342502-5

a doctor or even a surgeon. I later realized that it was to do with the question of the body, reactualized by puberty and the instinctual drive upheavals of adolescence that animated my student years.

It was obviously no coincidence that I discovered psychoanalysis at the end of my secondary education, thanks to works by Freud that I found in my elder sister's library. I devoured them, was fascinated by them, and transferred immense aspirations onto Freud's texts. I now began to envisage a different future, that of undergoing psychoanalysis and improving my psychic functioning in order to make psychoanalysis my profession and to contribute to the development of psychoanalysis through original theoretical contributions.

To achieve this goal, doing medicine made sense, as did specializing in psychiatry. This project enabled me to overcome my disappointment with medical studies. I took advantage of them to continue my reading, both in psychoanalysis and in many other areas of culture, and at the same time I enrolled at the faculty of psychology, where psychoanalysis was at the forefront of the teaching programme at the time.

It was only logical that my youthful passion should find a field to blossom in studying psychiatry. As soon as I took on professional responsibilities, I began my own psychoanalysis and, to this end, organized my family and professional life between two French cities, Lyon and Paris.

The overdetermination that can be seen in these lines ran through my childhood and adolescence. It can be followed, through my sister and my childhood "loves", through all the twists and turns of the vicissitudes of my instinctual life, along the path of the maturation of adult desire. And also through my parents and the adults invested with a transference of authority insofar as they helped establish the psychic processes needed for processing my instinctual life and the correlations established between it and the realities of the external world; hence the easily identifiable influence of certain desexualized activities of my ascendants, entering into an analogy with my interest in psychic functioning.

• Could you comment on opportune encounters in your career and training?

Transference of authority

A propensity for a transference authority, which consists in attributing another person with abilities that confer authority on them, has led me to elect a wide variety of characters with the aim, recognized after the event, of acquiring their presumed abilities and thereby gaining access to psychic maturity. This type of transference is the common thread running through all the transferences that have helped me to grow and evolve. A latent imperative to establish a superego and an internal world governed by it, coupled on its obverse side with idealizations conducive to the unfolding of family romances, is at the origin of such a transference of authority.

Freud and psychoanalysis were major sources of inspiration, as were many analysts I considered to be the "thinkers" of psychoanalysis; hence my critical reading, in the sense of a reflective reading, of the works of Freud's successors. Along the way, I learned the value of the interplay between the verticality of the mentors and the horizontality of peers.

This approach resulted in my choice of a highly respected analyst who was very committed to psychoanalytic work and writing, and considered by his peers to be one of the leading thinkers of psychoanalysis in France. Another consequence was that I only had one analyst and that I had a very long analysis with him (almost 18 years). I was an analysand occupied by my internal world and my psychic productions, by my idealizations and my ego ideal. I did not question the analytical situation or the fundamental rule by acting out. I gave psychoanalysis the power to enable me to fulfil wishes in an atmosphere of idealization. Analysis itself was a wish-fulfilment, which could be translated into the infantile wish to be a great thinker of psychoanalysis.

The process of après-coup and the beyond

Gradually, through the publication of a large number of articles and collective works (around 280 articles and 13 books), it is the process of après-coup that has become the cornerstone of my thinking, my clinical listening and my reading of psychoanalytical contributions. I have published a book in English called *Après-coup in Psychoanalysis: The Fulfilment of Desire and Thought* (Chervet 2023), in which the process of après-coup is at the foundation of human thought and desire.

The history of the theorization of metapsychology, and in particular the reading of Freud's work, can be approached linearly and chronologically, but also according to the method of the après-coup process, whereby each stage illuminates the previous one through retroactive reverberation. This reading includes discontinuity, leaps, interpretation and overdetermination, hence revisions that consist in considering that what has been elaborated previously is not to be rejected but is to be thought of as a "symptom" containing an element of "illusion" and an attempt to fulfil some unconscious wish.

This is why the function of dreams, infantile sexuality and then of narcissism, can only be understood after the writing of *Beyond the Pleasure Principle* (Freud 1920). The stumbling blocks of each of them are linked to disturbances in psychic work required by the extinctive tendency of the drives, that is to say the tendency of every drive to return to an earlier state of things, and even back to the inorganic and inanimate state. In 1920, in *Beyond the Pleasure Principle*, Freud proposed this new definition for both the life drive and the death drive.

All psychic work plays a role in this mission of restraint, of libidinal regeneration, of the intrapsychic registration of cathexes and their orientation towards objectality.

This way of reading shows the extent to which Freud's work is a system of thought and not an accumulation of successive bodies of knowledge. Confronted with our daily work, this work is far from being exhausted or outdated.

In my work, a new aspect of clinical work is raised by this constantly renewed approach. It concerns the possibilities for each patient to be able to use the thinking of another person, to deploy a transference of authority and to use it for their own growth. Again, what we find here is the question of transmission within an analysis, of how a patient makes use of their analyst's mind. This is another aspect of reminiscence, revealed within the analytic situation, that of the identificatory legacy of the parents and the identificatory call they supported.

- **What is your theoretical approach to psychoanalytic practice (the couch, frequency, the frame, teletherapy, interpretation, silence)?**

Psychoanalytic work and its contextualization

The theory of psychoanalytic practice is a very important field in my work. As such, I edited and wrote a large part of a book published in French titled *Pourquoi la règle? Méthode analytique et règle fondamentale* (Chervet & Donnet 2014), and in addition to my individual and group supervisions (a specific feature of the French model), I run two seminars on analytic practice as well as my seminars on psychoanalytic theory and reading Freud's work.

Thinking about our practice requires us to think about the situation of analysis itself, how the two protagonists think and the type of associativity of the patients, whether we see them in our practices or in specialized institutions, individually or in groups (in psychodrama, for example).

We therefore need to think about the organization of the sessions and everything that comes up in the session and also pay attention to what does not come up in the discourse of this or that patient. These various semiologies are generally lumped together under the all-encompassing term *setting*, a term that refers both to the concrete protocol, to the thought processes of the analyst and analysand, and to the organization of the patient's discourse, a "setting" that each patient repeats in the service of their defensive needs.

The protocol includes the analyst's environment, their consulting room or the private place in which they see their patients, providing the latter with information about their tastes, choices and identifications. The role of the protocol is essential. It serves as the materiality onto which the patient's mental mechanisms can be transposed when they are attracted by the traumatic regressive tendencies. This requires a detour via external tangible material realities. Created by the analyst, this environment serves as a second skin, a second nature that expresses their internal world but also their own defensive needs. The protocol is designed to be used in the transference by the patient, and it offers an image of the analyst's countertransference needs.

The second meaning of the term setting is the notion of an *internal setting*, that is, the analyst's thought processes stimulated by the patient's discourse and by the analytic conceptions that inform their listening. There can be no psychoanalytic listening without evenly suspended attention combined with a latent theoretical conception of psychic functioning. This attention cathects all the material of the session as evenly as possible, even if this evenness does not eliminate qualitative differences. Indeed, the analyst does not listen to a dream, acting out and defective impulses in the same way as they listen to free associative discourse.

The protocol and thought processes of the two protagonists are mutually dependent. The notion of *respecting the setting*, so often used in training, refers to the use of the protocol, by both the analyst and the patient, when their thought processes are in difficulty. An analogy has often been made between the analytic situation and sleep, which is the precondition for dreaming at the same time as dreaming ensures its maintenance; similarly with children's play, the toing-and-froing in the session evokes the toing-and-froing of the wooden reel game necessary for the construction of thought processes.

The third register implied by the term *setting* refers to the fact that, during childhood and with their family group, the patient organized ways of relating that met the defensive needs of each person. In this way, the child becomes part of their parents' defensive needs and maintains their Oedipal ties without renunciation. The setting then refers to a stable organization with symbiotic and incestuous value, which the patient seeks to impose on the analysis; hence the conflict between this historical and family setting and the analytic setting, which seeks to replace the former with freer and more efficient psychic processes. This conflict is sometimes resolved by swapping the alienating identifications of childhood with those of analysis that are equally alienating.

In all cases, the result of such alienating solutions and dependence on a material environment organized with the aim of denying the feelings of lack recognized in certain external realities is that the relationship to lack and the superego will not be mentalized.

The link between the protocol and the fundamental rule, that is to say the thought processes the latter elicits, is to make it possible for psychic contents to unfold and for the patient to come into contact with the extinctive tendencies that are at the origin of the feelings of lack. These correlate with the perception of non-tangible external realities, such as absences, losses, disappearances and all manner of differences. The psyche responds to these correlations by using psychic materials derived from tangible realities. The anti-traumatic use of the environment is only recognizable when it is lacking.

All the concrete elements of the analytical situation can be used in this way. The couch is both a tangible material reality and a metaphor for the correlations that exist between regression in the session and the sleep-dream system, between the repetition of the sessions and children's play, between the recumbent position and regressive tendencies towards extinction.

Compared with face-to-face sessions, using the armchair-couch setting makes it possible to link two aspects: the facilitation of regression, that is, the priority given to psychic productions, and the possibility of identifying as session material the patient's anti-traumatic appeal to the perception of tangible elements in the consulting room.

In the face-to-face situation, providing direct perceptions of the analyst makes it more difficult to observe these appeals to tangible perceptions. On the couch, the patient is more alone with themselves in the presence of another who is supposed to be in a position of evenly-suspended attention turned towards the unconscious mental functioning revealed by regression and elaborated by interpretation.

All analysts have noticed the existence of moments when their patients open up to perception and take an interest in the ceiling, the walls, the decoration, the time of day, the objects present in the consulting room, objects that may have been there for years and that they discover in the strongest sense of the word, at the moment when they need them.

In childhood, the difference between the sexes is discovered in the same way. Although the child has been aware of it for a long time, it remains without effect until the mind is the locus of traumatic experiences that force it to give up the previous denial, to clear its perception and to use the anatomical difference between the sexes to process the traumatic extinctive tendency.

The number of sessions, fixed session times, whether or not missed sessions are replaced and payment issues are also part of the protocol. There is no ideal number of sessions, but a sustained frequency is useful for both the patient and the analyst, to obtain an internal tension that requires the intervention of psychic processes, to ensure the presence of material in the preconscious memory and to observe the psychic work carried out between sessions.

The fixed duration of the sessions is a consequence of the fundamental rule which imposes, on both protagonists, their specific modes of psychic functioning. The traumatic issue at stake at the end of the sessions is thus delegated to the conventions of the protocol to which both patient and analyst are subject. The persecutory dimension of the interruption is attenuated and there is recourse to passivity.

The COVID period highlighted the importance of bodily proximity in analytical work and the work of abstinence during the sessions. The lockdowns stimulated comparisons between working in the presence of bodies and working in the presence of voices alone.

Thinking is influenced by the presence of bodies. The main reminiscence is the quality of parents, in the mental sense of the term, with regard to their children during care and education involving their bodies. These bodily exchanges are governed by the principle of abstinence, even if they carry messages disturbed by sexuality. In the session, this interplay between the awakening of unconscious desires, that is to say seduction, and the imperative of abstinence is repeated, hence the mentalization of instinctual drive impulses. Seduction and abstinence are the two levers of analytical work. Their common function is to oppose the extinctive tendencies that occupy mental life and to register the instinctual drive impulses in the mind and in object relations with the world.

Our experience of telesessions existed long before the COVID period since the practice of shuttle analysis had already given rise to reflection and encouraged the addition of remote sessions during periods of separation due to relocations and other temporary impediments. A psychoanalytic treatment cannot be based on remote sessions alone. The resolution of the Oedipus complex and the mourning of Oedipal objects is achieved through oscillations of presence and absence, but in the presence of the bodies and minds of living parents. Teletherapy is a form of analytical work, but not psychoanalysis.

• What is your view of the transmission of psychoanalysis?

Becoming a psychoanalyst, becoming a psychoanalyst again

Psychoanalysis is transmitted by means of a tripod which combines personal analysis, supervision and the teaching of psychoanalytical concepts with an openness to culture.

Personal psychoanalysis is one of the requirements for becoming an analyst; it must begin prior to any application for training in the French model but at the same time in the Eitingon model.

In France, the training analysis has gradually been abandoned in favour of personal analysis. This aspect differentiates the mindset transmitted by the two models. The French model considers that the candidate has to experience an improvement in their psychic suffering through analysis before applying for training. Analysts in training have been or still are patients.

Certainly, after their training, analysts trained within one model or another have in common the experience of personal analysis. Nevertheless, the initial steps towards analysis and the profession of analyst are not the same.

The second element of the training tripod is supervision; generally, two supervisions of an analysis by a training analyst. There is a difference here linked to the history of psychoanalysis in France in that, in the French model, there are group supervisions. In France, analysts in training undergo individual supervision and group supervision, which encourages fraternal transfers and horizontal sharing of their experiences.

Some of the parameters of the French model arose for pragmatic reasons. They should be distinguished from the principle of the model. Just after the Second World War, there was a craze in France for psychoanalysis; hence the large number of requests to undergo analysis and become an analyst. The few training psychoanalysts working in France informed the IPA of this fact. By mutual agreement, it was decided to allow three forty-five-minute sessions per week for training analyses, and to practice collective supervisions. This made it possible to train many more analysts in the same amount of time.

The specific nature of the French model lies in one principle: the strict separation between personal analysis and training. This principle arose from the major reflection on training provoked by the upheavals introduced by Lacan (short sessions and scansion). There was clear opposition to "reporting" and a refocusing on personal analysis. This was the principle on which the French model was based until it was recognized by the IPA, more than 50 years after the adjustments made in response to the circumstances of the postwar baby boom.

The third point of the tripod concerns teaching proper, with seminars, conferences, participation in working groups, the reading of Freud's work and the teaching of the contributions of his successors. This teaching concerns metapsychology and psychoanalytic practice, knowledge and know-how.

To this teaching should be added the acculturation of the analyst-in-training and the support given by the institutes to an openness to culture. This point is essential to the development of psychoanalytic theory. Culture is certainly necessary to feed our preconscious and satisfy our curiosity and our need to approach psychic functioning by means of analogies. But it is also part of the epistemological approach to psychoanalytic research. Indeed, the elaboration of metapsychology includes making a detour through external cultural fields; during this intermediary phase the elements being elaborated are transposed and underpinned by theories and human productions belonging to other disciplines. All speculation is underpinned by analogies and metaphors with other cultural fields. This first phase is followed by a second phase of differentiation and refocusing on metapsychology itself. The epistemology of psychoanalysis includes this detour and is carried out according to the two-stage process of après-coup.

What the training tripod transmits are thought processes themselves, those acquired through identifications. Each pole participates in and is used by an identification with analytic thought and its method, that is, with a way of thinking that remains in contact with the unconscious and has the duty to bring about an elaboration through interpretation. This brings us back to the duality inherent in thought itself, the tendency to return to an earlier state of things, even to extinction, linked with an imperative of registration and elaboration. This is the duality that determines the form in two stages of the process of thought and desire, the process of après-coup.

It is this duality that is transmitted by means of identifications: identification with the analyst in order to gain access for oneself to this way of thinking that can be described as analytic; identification with the supervisor, in order to enable another person to benefit from this analytic tool; identification with the training analyst in order to enrich our theoretical corpus and our analytic thinking. Each of these three vertexes enriches us and brings us into contact with lack, at the level of healing, knowing and being ideal.

Transmission has an essential role in giving us the means, through contents, methods, theories, affects and sensations, to respond to what we discover and continually try to deny, the existence within us of extinctive tendencies.

Transmission enables us to become analysts. It also teaches us that we are not analysts all the time, that our internal analytical disposition is never acquired definitively, that it is subject to dangers of reduction and that it is one thing to become an analyst and another to have to become one again.

• In your opinion, what are the points of divergence between French psychoanalysis and English-speaking psychoanalysis?

The moments of the process of après-coup

Schematic opinions have set French psychoanalysis and Anglo-Saxon psychoanalysis in opposition to one another. We need to look at the differences between them.

It is common to say that Anglo-Saxon psychoanalysis refers to the here and now, whereas French psychoanalysis is concerned with determination by history. In fact, we are all attentive to the recomposed past of infantile amnesia and to the construction of thought processes in the here and now.

Infantile sexuality and instinctual drive activity are more manifestly present in French psychoanalysis, whereas Anglo-Saxon psychoanalysis favours the emotional approach. Similarly, there is a difference between the place given to empathy and to an elaborative approach involving language; the same goes for the importance given to hysterical identification and projective identification. The influence of the philosophical traditions of each culture can be seen here.

Having taken part in numerous conferences and congresses throughout the world, but above all having worked with colleagues in New York in the Centre for Advanced Psychoanalytic Studies (CAPS) in order to share and compare our clinical experiences, it is not possible for me to assert such clear-cut positions. During our discussions, local consensuses were certainly visible, but they were easily abandoned, and ultimately, the various approaches could be taken into account and become a source of mutual enrichment.

Other differences sometimes caused controversy, such as the number of sessions per week. We all agree that frequency is important, but we also agree that the number of sessions is no guarantee of the analytical value of the work done.

Rather than stir up controversy between these different points of view, it seems to me important to refer them to mental functioning and psychoanalytic theory, in other words, to consider these differences as a clinical application of psychoanalytic theorizing. It is interesting to identify which clinical practices, moments of mental functioning and processes each model and each author is referring to.

My interest in the organization of thought according to the process of après-coup leads me to make the following remark. French psychoanalysis focuses on deferred effects as the result of the process. The logics of determination are therefore in the foreground. But a simple linear temporal logic is often used, neglecting the economic function of this process, which requires temporal regression.

Anglo-Saxon psychoanalysis makes little overt reference to this process, except to consider it as a missing concept.

Anglo-Saxon colleagues have focused on the initial "traumatic moment" (coup) itself, on the fate of the traumatic moment, given that the process is only very partially realized and repetition, or even compulsions of repetition and reduction, dominate the clinical situation.

Beyond the concept, psychoanalysts, whether of French or Anglo-Saxon obedience, work with their highly organized psyches in which the process of après-coup is operative. They transmit this through their interventions, their interpretations and their way of being in the session.

- ## What is your psychoanalytic approach to the societal debates on racial, gender identities or/and on the new forms of reproduction and parenting?

The question of emergences and contextualization

As psychoanalysts who are concerned with the fundamental rule and the specific listening that follows from it, it is possible for us to listen to the world in a similar way. This approach is partial in terms of the intelligibility it offers. As human beings, we are concerned with registers and intensities that go far beyond those we encounter in our consulting rooms, although their respective content is not entirely different.

The notion of gender emerged in sociology at the beginning of the 20th century. It became widespread at the end of the 20th century and is now manifesting itself at the beginning of the 21st century by exerting pressure on bodies and the transformations they undergo. Initially, it concerned masculine and feminine features from a social point of view. The aim was to restore freedom from the constraints of group psychologies, which imposed contingent criteria as a universal definition of the masculine and the feminine. The notion of gender gradually became the banner of a freedom to be acquired over anatomy, biology and genetics.

From the point of view of civilization, the desire of human beings to free themselves from constraints emanating from matter, whether external or psychic, has always been a major driving force. Numerous devices have been created to develop and even exacerbate certain qualities in human beings, but also to give them powers that they do not spontaneously possess, and of course to compensate for the reductive tendencies that inhabit them.

From the psychoanalyst's point of view, gender is a way of dealing with the difference between the sexes and freeing us from this passive imposition. Bisexual fantasy is not enough. It is an attempt to attenuate the traumatic impact of the extinction of the drives as transposed onto the double difference between the sexes (masculine–feminine, endowed–unendowed) and onto all differences, using the body and bodily transformations. The question of lack is central. Every difference gives rise to a comparison between the tangible realities that constitute it, and between what is lacking in each of the parties in question (the trauma of small differences). The traumatic factor is linked to the major difference between what exists in a tangible way and what exists as a lack, which are two different orders of reality.

Of course, the question of racism is affected by this approach to differences. It runs through all civilizations and comes to the fore whenever civilization is dominated by a sense of disquiet.

The hope of freeing ourselves from group constraints and conventions also concerns new ways of procreating, as well as new ways of organizing parenthood. This wish even extends to freeing ourselves from the laws of nature. Certain artistic movements (Carnal Art) make use of this wish and modify or shape bodies themselves during performances, with the aim of turning them into a work of art.

The debates around gender concern dizzying problems that psychoanalysts face as human beings in their daily lives and in their professional activities. Once again, they are facts of civilization that call into question the passivity and powerlessness of each and every one of us, but also our denial.

All institutions are places where psychic modes of functioning known as collective, group or mass psychology are revealed, from hysterical identification, which enables several people to support some sort of generic hallucinatory Oedipal wish-fulfilment, to group psychologies centred on the pooling of narcissisms in order to avoid the vexations of incompleteness and the threats of resexualization and, finally, mass psychologies, which are much more difficult to understand on an individual level but which are deployed in large groups.

It seems to me that these questions that are a feature of our societies today, particularly the question of gender, are characterized by the desire to be free of the question of lack, and to free ourselves from the psychic work that lack mobilizes in us, and by the use of unlimited means to achieve this goal.

References

Chervet, B. (2023). *Après-coup in Psychoanalysis. The Fulfilment of Desire and Thought*, trans. A. Weller. London: Routledge.

Chervet, B. & Donnet, J.-L. (eds.) (2014). *Pourquoi la règle? Méthode analytique et règle fondamentale*. Paris: Presses Universitaires de France.

Freud, S. (1920g). *Beyond the Pleasure Principle. S. E.* 18. London: Hogarth, pp. 1–64.

Freud, S. (1940a [1938]). *An Outline of Psychoanalysis. S. E.* 23. London: Hogarth, pp. 144–207.

Goethe, W. (1808). *Faust*. Oxford: World Classics.

Chapter 6

Conversation with Paul Denis

Abstract

Paul Denis explains the metapsychological role of the libidinal cathexes of the drives as a quest for mastery and satisfaction but also, paradoxically, as a quest for pain. He also develops a critical reflection on the technical aspects of analysis, such as the limits of the analyst's silence, interpretation *in* the transference vs. interpretation *of* the transference and the difference between treatment on the couch and face-to-face.

• Could you describe the intellectual and personal journey that led you to psychoanalysis?

I was brought up in a cultured Catholic family, and one of my grandfathers was a well-known painter and art critic, while the other was a doctor who had written a thesis on hysteria, far from the Freudian perspective. Between them they had raised 21 offspring. I was a child and adolescent who enjoyed reading, and I learned to read with Victor Hugo's 1862 novel, *Les Misérables*. I came to psychoanalysis following medical, paediatric, neurological and psychiatric training. But I would not have become a psychoanalyst if I had not had the personal need to undertake an analysis on my own behalf. At the very beginning of my studies, I read Freud's *Introductory Lectures on Psycho-Analysis* and *Moses and Monotheism*, and I was interested in my own dreams. I was encouraged to undergo this analysis by a half-brother of my father, a psychiatrist who had started training as a psychoanalyst but never completed it.

• Could you comment on any opportune encounters you had in your journey and training?

My medical internship allowed me to meet great clinicians from various disciplines, in neurology in particular, who had an admirable way of thinking about clinical problems. As far as child psychiatry and psychoanalysis are concerned, I am particularly grateful to Serge Lebovici, a psychoanalyst and child psychiatrist who was president of the IPA from 1973 to 1977. He had confidence in me when

DOI: 10.4324/9781003342502-6

I was his intern and entrusted me with a study on the latency period, which was my first publication in *La psychiatrie de l'enfant*, a French-language journal listed in *Current Contents*. I would also like to mention Anne-Marie Sandler, through whom I came into contact with the work of the British Psychoanalytical Society, and above all René Diatkine, who helped me to see the nature of psychoanalytical theory as a model and not as a revealed truth.

• What is cornerstone of your theoretical and clinical work?

The cornerstone of my theoretical approach is the notion of the drive, which is central because, for Freud, the drive is what causes psychic life to emerge from bodily life. It is essentially a theoretical psychosomatic model. It is the notion of the drive that allows Freud to say that the ego is "bodily", and it is the drive that articulates psychic formations, such as fantasy, with bodily experiences such as affect and desire, allowing us to form a picture of the unity of psychosomatic functioning.

Drawing on Freud's formulations describing, on the one hand, the erogenous zones that are capable of giving orgasmic-type pleasure and, on the other, "an apparatus of mastery" capable of acting on the external world (and of registering the actions of the external world) but not providing specific pleasure, I have put forward a model of the organization of the drive itself as the result of the cathexis of the libido (Denis 2002). This first pleasure-producing path for the libido creates a usable path for a subsequent increase in libido. When libidinal excitation increases in the mind, the available libido will cathect, through the apparatus of mastery, elements of the external world—the mother's breast for example—and an erogenous zone, the mouth, the stimulation of which will lead to an experience of satisfaction. This experience renders cathexes in the form of mastery useless; the libido that was devoted to them is freed and will cathect the experience of satisfaction itself. The drive thus results from the combination of two libidinal currents, one in the form of mastery, the other erogenous, "in the form of satisfaction". The experience of satisfaction is thus crucial for the constitution of mental life. It is as if cathexis in the form of mastery—through sight, touch, motricity—created a sort of mnemic network to which the colour of the satisfaction was fixed. A representation results that is enriched by repeated experiences of satisfaction. The evocation of such a representation is partly accompanied by the satisfaction that gave rise to it. What Freud called hallucinatory satisfaction is thus more a kind of *mnemic* satisfaction sustained by the evocation of the representation.

According to the "pleasure/unpleasure principle", "pleasure" is the consequence of a reduction of excitation in the ego, even if this is not on a scale that can give it the quality of "satisfaction". It follows that every cathexis has a hedonic value, because of the reduction in floating libidinal excitation that it implies. The cathexis of motor, coenesthetic, sensory and painful sensations can therefore be a recourse in states of disorganization and depersonalization linked to an overload of formless excitation. Thus, an important path of cathexis offered to the libido is that of pain, a "pseudo-drive" Freud said. The libidinal cathexis of pain does not produce an experience of satisfaction, but it mobilizes part of the libido in an unproductive way. Bodily masochism is thus a recourse in certain states of disorganizing anxiety. Alongside erogenous cathexes and cathexes in the mastery mode, a third path involves the different ways of cathecting pain.

The destiny of the libido is thus to cathect any object, person, object of love or erotic exchanges, but also neutral objects, not directly sexual or sensual, thereby opening up the field of sublimations and the minor satisfactions they bring. But there are also forms of cathexis that do not develop sufficiently to have a hedonic value and instead seem to be limited to an unproductive dissipation of libidinal energy.

This model makes it possible to account for destructiveness without introducing the "death drive". The subject in search of an experience of satisfaction increases their cathexes in the mastery mode as long as an experience of satisfaction does not stop them. The subject then becomes the victim of "mastery mania" that aims to destroy the very object from which they hoped to obtain satisfaction.

• What is your theoretical approach to psychoanalytic practice (the couch, frequency, the frame, teletherapy, interpretation, silence)?

As a therapy, psychoanalysis, with four sessions per week—plus or minus one—the patient lying on the couch, with sessions of fixed duration, remains the best form of psychotherapy, and it should be used more often. As far as the length of the sessions is concerned, I give my appointments every three quarters of an hour. Fifty-five minutes would be better, but would increase the cost of the sessions too much. Shorter sessions would not be favourable, as the temporality of affect is long; time is needed for tears, but also moments of psychic rest. There is no music without moments of silence.

This classical framework does not have to be reserved for what is deemed to be "neurotic". The experience of psychoanalytic centres, which allow patients to do an analysis free of charge, shows that patients with significant pathologies, serious neuroses, characteropathies or borderline disorders have benefited greatly from an analysis undertaken within the classic framework (with the exception of fees). The obstacle is precisely the cost linked to the frequency of sessions over a long period of time.

The problem for such pathologies is that a wait-and-see, silent attitude takes the patient back to infantile situations of rejection and nonrecognition from which they have suffered terribly. The analyst's silence duplicates these experiences of rejection. The analyst must therefore intervene frequently to interpret, of course, but above all to support the expression of affects and the patient's psychic functioning by means of constructions, "relay representations", and not leave them alone in unspeakable pain or nameless anxiety, waiting for them to "associate" by themselves.

The analyst's silence is tactical; they must only speak from what their patient has formulated and not speak for themselves. They must be silent about themselves so as to let the patient imagine what they want from their analyst. What the patient imagines reveals their transference experience. Any sharing of a secret by the analyst deprives the patient of what they might have expressed in their transference.

Strachey's "mutative" interpretation remains the implicit model for any "interpretation" of the transference: "Here and now you dread my absence just as you were once afraid when your mother was about to leave the house ..." is a type of interpretation that is particularly necessary to allow the patient to elaborate the negative aspects of the transference. But constructions and relay representations play an important role in the progressive construction of an interpretative chain. From this point of view, it is necessary to distinguish the simple reference to the transference, which is useless and often hurtful, from its *interpretation* in relation to the patient's past experiences.

When psychoanalysis itself is impracticable, it is necessary, according to Winnicott's expression, to do something else, which opens up the field of psychoanalytic psychotherapy. This will mostly be face to face: The patient's perception of the analyst's facial expressions and gestures can limit their projections and facilitate the verbalization of certain conflicts. In any psychoanalytic undertaking, two sides can be recognized: one relational, constituted by the cathexis of the person of the analyst in terms of what the patient perceives of his or her reality, and the other, transference proper, which is constituted by the projections onto the analyst of the patient's imagos and unconscious fantasies. The classical analytical situation favours the transference dimension, the face-to-face encounter favours the relational register. The analysis of the transference occurs in a way through the difference between the two registers: the patient knows that their analyst is a woman *but* fears her just as they feared their father.

The frame must be respected, particularly concerning the rule concerning payment for missed sessions; failure to enforce this invariably leads to conflict between patient and analyst and jeopardizes the depth and continuation of the analytic process.

From my point of view, psychoanalysis proper can only be experienced in the presence of the two protagonists of the treatment in the same room, that is, with all the parameters that this presence implies: physical closeness, perception of the voice, smells, the possibility of the occurrence of sexual excitement, the frustration of this dimension of excitement requiring an inhibition of the aim of the drive impulses aroused and their transposition, by means of words, on to the seductive characters of the patient's past. In the event of a major long-term hindrance (hospitalization, professional stay abroad), the treatment must be suspended for as long as necessary. Maintaining telephone or visual contact at a distance is only justified if the patient is in crisis at the time when the hindrance occurs. In this case, except in exceptional circumstances, it is more of a relay psychotherapy intended to allow for the resumption of the analytical process once the hindrance has disappeared.

• What is your view of the transmission of psychoanalysis?

This is a crucial point for the future of psychoanalysis, and the different models each have their qualities and their defects. The IPA recognizes three models today: The Eitingon model: preselection of candidates, personal analysis with four sessions per week and two supervisions of analytic cases; the French model: no preselection, selection takes place after a preliminary analysis of the candidate with a minimum of three sessions per week and two analytic case supervisions; and the Uruguayan model, which, if I have understood it correctly, is comparable to the French model, but analysis continues during the early stages of the supervisions and candidates are involved in the life of the society early on. But, in fact, each society that uses one of these models applies it in its own way. The Paris Psychoanalytical Society (SPP), which long ago abandoned any involvement of the candidate's analyst in his or her selection and accreditation—the reporting analyst—has also abandoned the obligation to use a training analyst authorized to conduct analyses of future analysts; it examines applications from people who have undertaken a personal analysis with a member of the IPA. One of the two individual supervisions must take place in a group of other candidates presenting their cases and candidates who will present their cases later; this is an individual supervision in front of the small group of other candidates. The situation does not lend itself well to an in-depth analysis of the candidate's countertransference, but it does have the merit of offering the participants in the group the experience of other analytical treatments in addition to the one they present to the group.

The French Psychoanalytical Association (APF) examines applications from "any couch". The supervision of the two analytical cases must be successive. The Belgian Society of Psychoanalysis, which is based on the French model, conducts the training of its candidates in a very different way from ours. What counts most, in fact, is the conception of analysis underpinned by each model. The place of infantile sexuality, the place of the Oedipus complex and so on. I feel that anything that has an influence that is similar to the role of the reporting analyst is detrimental to the candidate's analysis, as is the candidate's swift involvement in the practice of supervised analyses, which, as Phyllis Greenacre (1966) has pointed out, can lead to a kind of split in the candidate's transference, between the analyst and supervisor, limiting the depth of his or her personal analysis.

I feel that my experience of individual supervision in a group setting helped to broaden my field of perception of analysis in the course of my training, and becoming a supervisor myself has broadened my experience of analytic practice.

• What, in your view, are the points of divergence between French psychoanalysis and English-speaking psychoanalysis?

The question could be put differently: What are the divergences between French and English *psychoanalyses*? Neither of them are globally individualizable. I feel quite close to some English colleagues, such as Rosine Perelberg, or North Americans, such as Glen Gabbard, but very distant from others and also very distant from some French psychoanalysts, in particular from various Lacanians whose theoretical references justify practising sessions of variable duration, often very short, which is a break with the Freudian tradition. I feel very far removed from most of the Kleinians and, in particular, today's Bionians, for whom emotion takes the place of sexuality. Whatever the interest of the perspectives opened up by Melanie Klein, we can see, for example, two essential points of divergence in the way the Kleinians approach clinical practice and theory. On the one hand, there is the simplistic use of the notion of death drive: Love is the life drive and hate, its opposite, comes from the death drive. Hate, however, is not the opposite of love but a product of its degradation, one could even say that hate is a form of love. The opposition between good objects and bad objects introduces a kind of Manicheanism that does not account well for the nuances and ambivalences of object relations. The other point is the disappearance of references to sexuality. During clinical meetings between analysts from the SPP and the British Society, I was struck by the fact that all the content of the sessions reported by Kleinian colleagues was interpreted in terms of good and bad objects, without taking into consideration all the erotic and sexual nuances of the transference. Among today's Bionians, the disappearance of the reference to the drive is striking, and as a result, the notion of sublimation loses its Freudian meaning and becomes a thrust towards the sublime. Finally, among many North American analysts, there is a tendency to abandon the notion of drive, which is considered too "biological". Kohut, for example, reverses the Freudian schema and considers the drives as products of the disintegration of the self. For me, instinct is a biological notion, and the drive is what the mind does with instinct. The drive is a fundamental metapsychological concept; it is the linchpin of mental life.

- **What is your psychoanalytic approach to the societal debates on racial, gender identities or/and on the new forms of reproduction and parenting?**

What intrigues me most is the shift in emphasis from sex to gender. This shift should be reconsidered. The notion of gender is cultural, so why today should it replace the entirely biological notion of sex? Sex and gender, it should be remembered, are two different registers: one is in the order of anatomical reality, genetically fixed and absolute, while the other is relative, the product of different constitutive movements of the mind, contrasting movements, leaving room for contradictions and variations in mental life.

We can see this today, since the number of requests for sex changes is steadily increasing in our consulting rooms. We should ask ourselves about the possible meanings of these requests, the number of which is growing exponentially. However, these requests correspond to very diverse psychic situations, and they cannot be reduced to a single formula, which would imply a standardized behaviour, a protocol, logically leading to a transition. Each request, behind the same manifest formulation, is in fact underpinned by a particular psychological configuration that is more or less problematic, raising questions of varying seriousness. From this point of view, bringing all these situations under one term, transidentity, gender dysphoria or other, has the disadvantage of blurring the differences, of merging diverse psychopathological situations into one.

It is astonishing that the psychic suffering of the gender dysphoric child is immediately attributed to the fact that he or she was born in the wrong anatomical body, in contradiction with his or her gender, which supposedly corresponds to the opposite sex. The question could be raised as to whether there is not prior emotional and mental suffering, which the child then seeks to resolve by requesting a sex change.

To endorse this request of the child or adolescent, and to treat it as if it were a fact, when it essentially implies an uncertain relationship to the aspect of reality that is the difference of the sexes, is questionable. In my opinion, providing support in the direction of transition supports a form of denial of reality. Taking the request for a sex change at face value, listening only to this request, is a way of refusing to listen to the malaise that is expressed through this request, of leaving the child or adolescent alone with their psychic suffering bound up with the affirmation of their gender, and of sharing with the child the illusion that the medical/surgical transition will fix everything.

It is important to remember that the psychic disorganization linked to the transformations of adolescence, which is sometimes unbearable, can be contained by the hypercathexis of various behaviours, which then form a makeshift point of reorganization. This is the case with anorexia nervosa, sectarian commitments, self-mutilation, suicidal actions and others. The fixation on the idea that one is not of the sex corresponding to the gender one affirms is perhaps another. Asserting that one belongs to a sex other than one's own, asserting a gender in opposition to one's anatomy is a symptom. Saying that one is transgender is not a state; it does not describe a fact: What is a fact is the psychological suffering that this assertion expresses.

The question I ask myself is the following: If gender is independent of anatomy, why do we want to modify it? Why not leave these children with their genetically programmed erogenous capacities—and their potential for procreation—and let them later develop the sexual life and social gender life that they want, male, female, homosexual, heterosexual, queer or nonbinary?

Femininity or masculinity is not reduced to the possession of a penis or its absence, which is an infantile conception of the difference between the sexes.

It goes without saying that removing a boy's testicles and penis will not change his genetic basis, he will remain genetically and biologically male; equally a girl who has been given male hormones and had her uterus and breasts removed will remain biologically female. We are forced to admit that the difference between the sexes is inescapable. This difference is not symbolic; it is a reality. Sex is not the result of an *assignment* by a doctor, but the *observation* of a reality over which we have no power.

On the psychic level, in a child's evolution, the difference between the sexes will be the subject of a gradual recognition—perceptive, cognitive, erotic, emotional—and will give rise to a considerable and fundamental fantasy-related and intellectual development. The construction of identity is based on this recognition and its developments. The direction of these developments invariably leads to psychic bisexuality, whose destiny depends on multiple choices and experiences and is expressed in the choice of a more or less heterosexual or more or less homosexual life, and to gender, which is a quality of identity and is not expressed in a univocal way. There are effeminate men and masculine women. Sex is self-affirming, a fact of nature, while gender is a fact of culture. As for the orientation of sexual preferences, it is the result of the evolution of the psyche, of various cultural facts and of a largely unconscious "choice".

In France, we are also faced with original clinical, but above all, societal, situations. The clinical and psychopathological pictures are not fundamentally different, but the conditions for monitoring and treating them are subject to the weight of ideological and regulatory pressures and also to the fact that clinical practice in France is called into question by a sort of negation of the specificity of psychiatry. Psychic suffering tends to be approached according to the medical model that applies to organic pathology. The relational dimension of the treatment of these disorders, the psychotherapies that derive from them, and psychoanalysis are decried. To say that a condition or behaviour is pathological is considered an insult. For example, autism is no longer considered a pathology but a disability.

This tendency extends to the question of gender, where invoking the possible presence of psychopathology is ideologically prohibited. Psychoanalysts thus find themselves in a paradoxical situation; taking a child who is considered to be gender dysphoric into psychotherapy can lead to accusations of practising conversion therapy, a term used to designate treatments applied to homosexuals to force them into heterosexuality—treatments that are explicitly, and wisely, prohibited by French law.

Indeed, it is striking to see that the reflections and recommendations on this question of transidentity are infiltrated by a number of contradictions. The American Psychiatric Association (APA) considers that gender dysphoria—the suffering of a person who believes that their identity (female or male) does not correspond to their anatomical sex, and who therefore considers that they belong to a gender that is different from that of their anatomical sex—is not a psychic disorder but a form of "clinical suffering" that must be treated by "medical, not psychiatric" care. So what then is "clinical suffering"? Why should it not be psychic suffering? And why not use a psychiatric, psychotherapeutic or psychoanalytic approach if necessary?

On the other hand, if one considers the *Yogyakarta Principles*, presented to the UN Human Rights Council,[1] prescribing the application of human rights to LGBT and intersex persons, one reads the following, which aims at "protection from medical abuses":

> No person may be forced to undergo any form of medical or psychological treatment, procedure, testing, or be confined to a medical facility, based on sexual orientation or gender identity. Notwithstanding any classifications to the contrary, a person's sexual orientation and gender identity are not, in and of themselves, medical conditions and are not to be treated, cured or suppressed.
>
> (International Commission of Jurists, Principle 18, p. 23)

This is an entirely appropriate prohibition against imposing a therapeutic injunction or medical treatment on anyone on the basis of their sexual orientation *but also their gender identity.* According to these prescriptions, no medical treatment or protocol should be applied to anyone on the basis of their gender identity. The transition protocol with its prescription of hormones and the series of surgeries involved is clearly in contradiction with the Human Rights Council's prescription and would therefore constitute "medical abuse".

Trying to understand what may have led a child to experience themselves as belonging to another sex is almost illegal. As a psychoanalyst, I can only be perplexed ...

Note

1   26 March 2007.

References

Denis, P. (2002). *Emprise et Satisfaction.* Paris: Presses Universitaires de France.
Greenacre, P. (1966). "Problems of training analysis". *Psychoanalytic Quarterly*, 35(5): 540–567.
International Commission of Jurists (2007). *Yogyakarta Principles: Principles on the Application of International Human Rights Law in Relation to Sexual Orientation and Gender Identity.*

Chapter 7

Conversation with
Nicolas Evzonas[1]

Abstract

Nicolas Evzonas demonstrates how psychoanalysis can address the diversity of sexual modalities through the lens of intersubjective processes. He also draws his attention to the role of the emergence of "techno-subjectivities" in treatments.

• Could you describe the intellectual and personal journey that led you to psychoanalysis?

During my childhood in Cyprus, a small island in the Mediterranean Sea situated at the crossroads of the rational West and the colorful East, I was fascinated by tales and myths, which made me delve into novels, theatrical plays, films and anything that put these extraordinary narratives into creative action. I was particularly keen on family dramas and representations of erotic and aggressive drives in ancient Greek tragedies. This made me go to study classics at the University of Athens and sparked my initial interest in psychoanalysis.

My growing passion for metapsychology led me to the truly Freudian city of Paris, where I completed a PhD at the Sorbonne on erotic desire in the work of Alexandros Papadiamantis, known as the "Saint of Modern Greek Literature" because of his profound religious faith. I remember that one member of my PhD jury criticized me for conducting research on psychoanalysis instead of literature, whereas the other members vigorously protested that he was being biased and unfair. However, in reality, this overly rigid professor was the only one to clearly see that the emperor had no clothes, namely that my genuine passion lay in a different field. To cut a long story short, after pursuing a rather ungratifying career as academic scholar in Greek studies, I decided to train as a clinical psychologist in the Department of Psychoanalytic Studies at Paris Diderot University (also known as Paris 7, now Paris City University). This department was founded in 1970 by Jean Laplanche, who took the initiative to introduce psychoanalysis into academia by creating a complete cursus of psychodynamically oriented training in psychopathology and clinical psychology for undergraduate, postgraduate and PhD students. I feel extremely grateful to be currently working as an associate

DOI: 10.4324/9781003342502-7

professor in this department and to be able to share my psychoanalytical experience with students of all ages and all backgrounds who come from all over the world to deepen their understating of the unconscious.

I realize that I have mainly spoken about my attraction to psychoanalysis as a cognitive object. However, I find Nietzsche's (2001/1887) comments, from the preface of *The Gay Science*, that all philosophy and intellectual expression are the autobiography of a body, insightful and relevant. Indeed, my academic and clinical interest in psychoanalysis had deep personal roots, being related to some unsettling issues that had troubled me from my teenage years onwards. Thanks to three extremely different analytic treatments, I radically transformed my life. Psychoanalysis was like the most unexpected miracle for me, so I could not help saying to myself: "If you manage to make your analysands benefit from just 10% of this wonder that you have experienced, you should feel fulfilled." And I can honestly say that I am much more than fulfilled. As I mentioned at the beginning, I have always been fascinated by extraordinary tales. My patients have shared the most amazing stories with me, and I consider some of them to be more powerful and moving than any piece of artistic creation. I feel incredibly rewarded when, through the magic of transference, we rewrite these life narratives and make them more meaningful and less repressive, less symptomatic and even less traumatic.

• Could you comment on any opportune encounters you had in your journey and training?

When I was training in clinical psychology, I was privileged to be tutored by psychoanalyst Patrick Chemla, head of Antonin Artaud Psychiatric Centre in Reims. The latter is an innovative mental health care institution, which uses polyphonic transference, that is, a constellation of transferential agents such as psychiatrists, psychologists, nurses and ergotherapists, in response to the split-off elements of psychotic patients. The experience at this particular psychiatric framework made me understand the fruitfulness of the psychoanalytic method beyond the "pure gold" of analysis in the classical setting. Is this extended psychoanalysis not what Freud (1926e) dreamed of in "The Question of Lay Analysis"?

During my training at Paris Diderot University, I became close with two academic professors and analysts whom I like to call "free spirits" as they do not belong to any psychoanalytical society: Sylvie Le Poulichet and Philippe Givre. The former conceptualized the "terrors of formlessness", that is, the primitive anxiety of losing one's sense of body continuity that is frequently revived in the transference with patients who suffer from addictions, depersonalizations and identity issues. The latter, who specializes in male anorexia, delves into primary interactions between the baby and the (m)other. In my view, the work of these two analysts provides the most amazing samples of clinical writing in French literature, hence their influence on my style as psychoanalytic author.

Professor Laurie Laufer[2] was another decisive encounter in my career. This Lacanian and Foucauldian thinker initiated me to queer studies, gender theory and feminist epistemology, with a special emphasis on the social situatedness of sub-jective enunciation and historicization of knowledge. She subsequently became the supervisor of my PhD dissertation on trans and countertransference. I will be for-ever indebted to her for encouraging me to think in my own way and also for help-ing me develop a rich academic network of international psychoanalytic thinkers.

On a personal level, my transference love with my third analyst, Marina Pa-pageorgiou, made me attentive to the polysemy of signifiers, the wordplay of the unconscious, the power of timely interpretation, the flexibility of the setting and analytic creativity in general. Moreover, my experience with this admirably erudite clinician allowed me to discover the theories of the Paris Psychosomatic School on somatic regression—to be distinguished from libidinal psychic regression and the symbolically laden hysterical bodily symptoms, André Green's dialectical ap-proach to the drives and the object and Howard Levine's work with patients tradi-tionally considered to be unanalysable.

• What is the cornerstone of your theoretical and clinical work?

As can be easily surmised from my personal trajectory, diversity is the cornerstone of my work: diversity of concepts, epistemologies and spaces of thinking. I am privileged to work in three different languages—French, English and Greek—and with patients from diverse countries and cultures, which further enhances my perspective of multiplicity.

My approach to psychoanalysis is consubstantial with the bracketing of any adap-tational end and has absolutely no predefined aim. Therefore, I do not adhere to the popular Lacanian argument in France that the goal of analytic treatment is to accept one's castration, which I deem normative and ultimately anti-Freudian. Psychoa-nalysis is about singularity and processuality. In this respect, I am sceptical about the structural model of "neurosis, psychosis and perversion", as established in French psychoanalysis by Lacan. Does the term "structure" not suggest a fixed and immu-table psychic organization? Accordingly, does it not contradict the very notion of transference, which involves multiple movements, becomings and transformations?

If neurotic, psychotic and perverse mechanisms can be identified, they should not confine our patients to psychopathological categories, which are not only reductive but can also generate suffering through the performative power of language, not to mention the countertransference anxiety involved in the use of these catego-ries. Accordingly, instead of speaking of "psychotic," "perverse," "borderline" or "unanalysable" patients, I prefer to think in terms of complex treatments and unrep-resented or weakly represented mental states, which require technical adaptations. This reminds me of Howard Levine (2010) who argues that we can *create* analytic patients if we are theoretically fluid, technically flexible and convinced about the usefulness of analysis for a given analytic dyad.

Theoretical fluidity and technical elasticity necessarily entail multiple psychoana-lytic references as well as interdisciplinary thinking. In my view, this multireferentiality, which de-essentializes theory and denormativizes clinical practice, can help us avoid blind spots. Freud encouraged analysts to leave behind the insularity of their offices and gain insights from literature, theatre, anthropology and the arts, as he did. Interdisciplinary extraterritoriality can indeed contribute to the broadening of our theoretical countertransference, that is, the attachment to concepts, methods, representations and discursive practices that shape the analyst's listening. In this respect, I very much agree with Michel Neyraut (1974) who argues that countertransference *precedes* transference.

• **What is your theoretical approach to psychoanalytic practice (the couch, frequency, the setting, teletherapy, interpretation and silence)?**

Rather than fetishizing the French IPA model of the psychoanalytic couch and its three weekly sessions, I prefer to create an original framework depending on the singularity of each treatment and each patient. For me, the couch is only a tool and not a prerequisite for psychoanalytic listening. My practice thus varies from two to four weekly sessions on the couch and from one to three weekly sessions of face-to-face psychotherapy. In most cases, I propose the setting to patients, but in some situations, I cocreate it with them. Didier Anzieu (2000) suggests that the setting and its modifications reveal the quality of the patient's psychic envelopes. I think that this can also be applicable to the analyst. I remember one woman who called me several years ago asking for monthly therapy over the phone. I sensed that behind her manifest request that dealt with a family matter, her real issue was the fear of proximity with the libidinal object, hence her need to keep a distance between both our bodies (physical distance) and sessions (psychic distance). I thus negotiated the possibility of bimonthly phone sessions with her. This unusual framework for me gradually evolved to four weekly sessions with transformative results for both the analyst and the analysand.

I have always admired Ferenczi's (1980/1928) emphasis on the elasticity of the psychoanalytic technique. I did not have to wait until the COVID pandemic to allow myself to "play"—in the Winnicottian sense of the term—with the framework. Since I work with artists, politicians and other professionals who travel a lot, I occasionally agree to videoconference consultations instead of having these analysands pay for their missed sessions, which I do not deem to be a viable solution. Generally, I propose video calls to my patients who are already in face-to-face psychotherapy and phone sessions to those accustomed to the couch with the perceptual absence of the object. Nonetheless, I have a clear preference for sessions "in the flesh", because psychoanalysis is not only about language but also about prelinguistic and paralinguistic signifiers or, in other words, a wide range of affects, gestures and sensorial experiences. For instance, an analysand who always comes to the sessions with an overwhelmingly bad smell: Does he or she not convey a nonverbal message to the analyst? Or an aggressive patient who enters the room with a knife visibly attached to his belt?

Nevertheless, each framework has its pros and cons, its benefits and drawbacks. I can recall some analysands who had never dreamed but started dreaming during the online sessions, while others who seemed stuck in their analysis felt emancipated and were more inclined to free associate by telephone during the pandemic. On the contrary, for certain patients with a special need to be close to the libidinal body of the analyst, the imposed virtual sessions during the lockdowns generated anxiety, depression and even collapse.

Interpretation and silence constitute the two major bedrocks of French psychoanalysis. Personally, I have ceased to believe in the omnipotence of interpretation, and I certainly do not recommend silence with all analysands. Let us not forget that Freud could barely keep his mouth shut and that the tradition of silence in French psychoanalysis actually started with Lacan and his encouragement to "play dead", because he hosted on his couch some highly insightful and self-reflective analysands who did not need any assistance to free associate. By contrast, I can recall some severely traumatized patients who were prone to death anxiety when confronted with extended analytic quietness and who seemed unconcerned by interpretations related to the infantile. These cases corroborate what Jean-Luc Donnet realized with a depressed patient who was deported during the Holocaust and had asked him for therapy free of charge as a sort of symbolic repair. As he notes, it would be more constructive for some analysands who had suffered massive trauma

> if we welcomed their request to acknowledge prejudice as it were, without fully elaborating their individual responsibility in the construction of their own internal objects and destiny. In such cases, the recognition of prejudice and the authentication of an experience are more essential therapeutic goals than interpretation.
>
> (Donnet 1995, 67 (my translation))

I also find extremely enlightening the distinction established by Howard Levine (2010) between a Freudian-inspired "archeological" metapsychological model centred on the unveiling of the unconscious conflict and a Bionian-like "transformational" model focused on the co-construction of meaning in the treatment of patients with weakly organized representations. The first model requires opacity, silence and neutrality, whereas the second places countertransference at the heart of the cure with the analyst taking an active role. It is my view that in France, probably out of loyalty to our theoretical father Freud, we remain deeply attached to the archeological model by favoring certain types of candidates for analysis, while neglecting the transformational two-person model based on primary intersubjective relations that applies to a range of analysands traditionally regarded as unanalysable.

• What is your view of the transmission of psychoanalysis?

For more than ten years, I hesitated before finally applying to an institute for psychoanalytic training. Why? Because I was not sure whether my freedom of thinking and my desire for diversity would be compatible with the insularity of French psychoanalytic societies. I am strongly attached to the subversiveness of Freudian metapsychology and disenchanted by the subsequent loss of this subversiveness, which was perhaps the inescapable consequence of the worldwide institutionalization of psychoanalysis.

I have to confess that one of the strongest aspects of the French IPA model of training is the abolition of didactic analysis and what the French Psychoanalytical Association (APF) labels the "extraterritoriality" of personal analysis with regard to any form of institutional interference. I also admire the rigor and depth of the French model, which requires significant clinical and psychic maturity, since candidates are only accepted to psychoanalytic institutes after a lengthy analytic treatment and occasionally a thriving career in another field. Nonetheless, the exigency of this model can sometimes turn into a pitfall, because we end up having analysts-in-training in their fifties or even their sixties who are called "*élèves*" (pupils) and infantilized in several ways.

Having said this, I appreciate the freedom accorded to candidates to choose their seminars in my institute, an approach that distances itself from the school-based system of compulsory courses and a minimum number of educational hours. I also prefer the APF protocol with two extended individual supervised treatments that succeed one another compared with the Paris Psychoanalytical Society (SPP) model involving one collective supervision and an individual supervision, which can sometimes be simultaneously conducted and validated after only four years.

Notwithstanding their differences, I think that training programmes overemphasize the neurotic analytic model and neglect the kind of analytic work presented by Christopher Bollas (2012) or the expanding range of disorders (including perversions, addictions, psychosomatic, autistic and panic conditions) analytically treated by Levine (2021). Of course, French analysts such as André Green, René Roussillon and Alain Gibeault have conducted brilliant research on psychotic, narcissistic and borderline states, but their work is often excluded from the official training programme of psychoanalytical societies.

I would now like to discuss a rather delicate subject. Traditionally, in the IPA institutes, LGBTQ candidates were refused on the ground of pathologizing arguments (i.e., negation of sexual difference, desire for sameness, part-object relatedness), which tended to conflate nonhegemonic sexual practices and psychic dysfunctions. Nowadays, the situation has rather evolved for gay and lesbian candidates but not for transgender people, who would not dare to even conceive the idea of applying to an institute, because they know very well that they will not be accepted. The North American examples of Griffin Hanbury or Jack Pula are perhaps too progressive for Europe. Moreover, in spite of all the advances, homophobia is still alive but in other disguised forms: even though homosexual candidates are allowed to start training, they may not be able to validate their supervised treatments due to the resistance of predominantly male training analysts. In the APF, it is thanks to the tenacious struggle of female analysts that gay and lesbian candidates have been admitted to the institute and can now validate their supervised treatments. In addition, these candidates are still discouraged to be open about their sexuality, while their straight colleagues can flaunt their heterosexuality without being considered indiscreet or ideologically laden. This double standard suggests that we have still a long way to go in France…

• What, in your view, are the points of divergence between French psychoanalysis and English-speaking psychoanalysis?

I think that French psychoanalysis, despite its heterogeneity, remains essentially Freudian and thus embedded in the theory of endogenous drives and their biologizing tendencies. Accordingly, the other is often relegated to the status of a mere intrapsychic object and the external world is interpreted in terms of a solipsistic psychic reality. By contrast, Anglo-Saxon metapsychology focuses on object relations, especially Winnicott and Bion's work, and prioritizes otherness and addressivity with substantial repercussions on the analytic stance and technique (e.g., co-construction versus one-way construction, question versus assertive interpretation, empathy versus apathy). It is not surprising that Laplanche's emphasis on the primacy of the other's enigmatic messages has had a much greater impact overseas than in France.

In my view, it would be better to distinguish between European and North American rather than French and Anglo-Saxon psychoanalysis. I generally consider colleagues from Europe to be more conservative than their peers on the other side of the Atlantic in the sense that they are inclined to *conserve* the traditional psychoanalytic patterns and to resist novelty. This "spirit of resistance" ["*L'Esprit de résistance*"] was a recent conference theme at the APF, which stressed the proud refusal of French psychoanalysis to go with the flow and thus compromise its authenticity. On the contrary, our American colleagues argue that psychoanalysis should keep up with the times and adjust to contemporary trends, which I deem to be a much more interesting approach.

As I regularly receive newsletters from several North American psychoanalytical institutes, I notice the extreme diversity of lectures, seminars and conferences as well as their impressive topicality. By contrast, European psychoanalysis and perhaps French psychoanalysis in particular tend to venerate bygone authors, repeat the same themes and remain entrenched in the past, including their obsessional interpretation of the infantile in the sessions. To play with the title of this book, what is cruelly missing in France is the relevance and freshness of the "here and now", which includes both contemporary readings and the consideration of topical issues in the transference. I also find that European psychoanalytical institutes cling to hierarchy and verticality, while training analysts and candidates are less segregated in American institutes. In France, for instance, as a candidate, I can hardly imagine receiving an invitation to participate in a project like this book or sharing a panel with a training analyst, which is what I regularly do in the IPA. If I have a voice in the Parisian psychoanalytic scene, it is because of my academic accomplishments and certainly not because of my status as an analyst-in-training.

- ## What is your psychoanalytic approach to the societal debates on racial, gender identities or/and on the new forms of reproduction and parenting?

Freud (1926e) argued that psychoanalysis is open to revision. Indeed, the evolution of our societies and recent anthropological mutations suggest that the traditional Oedipal triangle of "father, mother and the child" on which most of our theories are based needs to be revised. I very much like Laplanche's dynamic conception of subjectivity as the outcome of plural enigmatic signifiers transmitted by a constellation of cathected adults and endlessly translated by the child under the sway of afterwardsness, idiosyncratic urges and anatomical as well as social and cultural codes. According to this model, (1) the "fundamental anthropological situation" refers to the asymmetrical relationship between adults (senders of messages) and the child (receiver of messages) and not necessarily between parents and the child, allowing us to go beyond the familial perspective of traditional psychoanalysis; (2) gender and sexuality are not binary but rather, diverse since the senders of messages, the messages themselves and the translations are all plural; (3) gender and sexuality are not fixed but constantly reshaped—detranslated and retranslated; (4) they do not constitute mere intrapsychic choices but rather intersubjective processes further influenced by social and cultural norms. In this sense, atypical genders such as trans and queer identities can be regarded as possible becomings in this complex interweaving between internal experiences and continual relations with the other (including society and culture).

Even though I advocate for plurality, I do adhere to the structuring effects of triangulation but without using gendered terminology. Following Glocer Fiorini's (2017) arguments, I use the expression "third-party function" instead of the traditional psychoanalytic term "paternal function" (or what Lacan called the "name-of-the-father") to describe the child's separation from the primary caregiver. The assumption that the primary object is invariably the mother and that the separation agency refers solely to the father overlooks contemporary family configurations that do not abide by the mother–child–father triangle. Let us not forget that fathers may nowadays have a caregiving role and mothers a third-party function.

Likewise, in our postmodern context, Oedipality (a universal psychic formation to be distinguished from socially and culturally contingent Oedipal complexes)[3] can be understood in terms of aggressive and erotic drives towards caregivers or other invested adults regardless of their gender. As for new reproductive technologies such as surrogate pregnancy and sperm, egg or embryo donation, instead of conceiving them as a threat to the psychoanalytic bedrocks of the "primal scene", "infantile theories" or "family romance", it would be more constructive to view them as challenges that inspire to novel birth myths and alternative narratives. Does curiosity about the analysand's irreducibly singular material, which bears no resemblance to any previously heard discourse, not constitute the core of psychoanalytic listening?

A nonbinary analysand once told me: "You have excellent referrals, but it scares me that your discipline [i.e., psychoanalysis] is so normative and hostile to the

LGBTQ community." Beyond any resistance to the transferential encounter, it is crucial to acknowledge that psychoanalysis has indeed long pathologized atypical genders and sexualities, hence the public apology of the American Psychoanalytic Association (APsA) in 2019 followed by the similar *mea culpa* of the Finnish Psychoanalytical Society (SPY) in 2022. Regarding French psychoanalysis in particular, I would say that the fetishization of sexual difference and massive resistance to the concept of gender, which was deemed antianalytic, have created dazzling blind spots—oxymoron intended—leading to the clinical and theoretical mistreatment of nonheterosexual and noncisgender patients. Given the connivance between psychoanalysis and conversion treatments, is it really surprising that gay, lesbian and queer studies have relegated the Freudian discipline to antiquated and obsolete paternal dogmas? Without being affected by these criticisms, psychoanalytical institutes in France still do not include any substantial training on sexual and gender diversity despite the efforts of the IPA in this direction.

Notwithstanding the famous Lacanian aphorism "the unconscious is politics", mainstream psychoanalysis remains utterly deaf to systemic violence and depoliticized, brandishing the argument of neutrality. I value Adrienne Harris's sane and realistic approach: "We want to keep clinical work as a free space. But we cure with contaminated tools. We are embedded in structures of money, hierarchy, and power and we must keep a double vision" (2005, 62). In my view, the emphasis placed on the solipsistic model of endogenous drives does not leave space for the environment, which should be conceived not only in the Winnicottian sense of the primordial other but also in the sense of power relations in the social field, as analyzed by feminist and gender studies. This unthought environment also explains why intersectional experiences of sexuality, gender, class, religion and race are conspicuously absent from the French psychoanalytic literature. The imperialism of intrapsychic reality engulfs the external reality even when the latter is shaken by a worldwide pandemic, a war in Europe and an impeding ecological disaster.

• Any other topics you'd like to discuss?

As an academic and practising psychoanalyst working with young people, I have been wondering in recent years about the impact of our massive exposure to images on subjectivizing processes. I can give countless examples of patients whose smartphone, computer or iPad is almost an extension of their body, and interestingly, these patients do not desire the psychoanalytic experience of the couch, which suspends the perception of the analyst.

Let me share this clinical snippet: A feisty teenager who was always writing down the topics that he wanted to discuss with me—because, as he repeated, "out of sight, out of mind"—asked for an online session during his COVID infection, and I naturally accepted. Unexpectedly, his internet connection failed, but he immediately called me on the telephone, describing his panic following the loss of my image. He calmed down as soon as he found a picture of me on an academic website and was therefore able to carry on with the session.

The question that I would like to address here is the following: When we are constantly stimulated by images and have been permanently connected to technological gadgets from a very young age, are we able to constitute what André Green (1999) understands as "negative hallucination", that is, the representation of the absence of representation? In other words, the internalization of the missing object? Accordingly, does the boom of technosubjectivities foreshadow the obsolescence of the psychoanalytic couch? This is perhaps another challenge that psychoanalysis will have to face in the future. Nonetheless, the driveness of the unconscious is everlasting, and in my view, psychoanalysis is all about the unconscious.

Notes

1 While other interviews have been translated from French to English, the responses in this chapter were written in English by their author.
2 Editor's note: See this psychoanalyst's chapter in the book.
3 The distinction between Oedipality and Oedipal complexes draws on the work of Barnaby B. Barratt (2019), but the conception of Oedipality here is my own.

References

Anzieu, D. (2000). "Les signifiants formels et le moi-peau". In: *Les Enveloppes psychiques*. Paris: Dunod, pp. 19–41.
Barnaby, B. B. (2019). "Oedipality and oedipal complexes reconsidered: On the incest taboo as key to the universality of the human condition". *International Journal of Psychoanalysis*, 100(1): 7–31.
Bollas, C. (2012). *Catch Them Before They Fall: The Psychoanalysis of Breakdown*. London: Routledge.
Donnet, J.-L. (1995). *Le divan bien tempéré*. Paris: Presses Universitaires de France.
Ferenczi, S. (1980/1928). "The elasticity of psychoanalytic technique". In: *Final Contributions to the Problems and Methods of Psychoanalysis*. London: Karnac Books, pp. 87–101.
Freud, S. (1926e). "The question of lay analysis". *S. E.* 19. London: Hogarth, pp. 177–258.
Glocer-Fiorini, L. (2017). *Sexual Difference in Debate: Bodies, Desires, and Fictions*. London: Karnac Books.
Green, A. (1999). *The Work of the Negative*. London: Free Association Books.
Harris, A. (2005). *Gender as Soft Assembly*. Hillsdale, NJ: The Analytic Press.
Levine, H. (2010). "Creating analysts, creating analytic patients". *International Journal of Psychoanalysis*, 91(6): 1385–1404.
Levine, H. (2021). *Affect, Representation and Language*. London: Routledge.
Neyraut, M. (1974). *Le Transfert*. Paris: PUF.
Nietzsche, F. (2001/1887) *The Gay Science*. Cambridge, UK: Cambridge University Press.

Chapter 8

Conversation with Alain Gibeault

Abstract

Alain Gibeault explains the foundations of the concept of psychodrama, which he sees as a necessary modification of the psychoanalytic technique and setting for psychotic patients. He also discusses his work on the processes of symbolization, understood as the ability to represent absence (of the object) and not to mistake the symbol for the object, as in psychosis.

• Could you describe the intellectual and personal journey that led you to psychoanalysis?

During my secondary studies, I was in charge of a student newspaper at a college in Quebec, and one day, I asked one of the seniors, "What's the difference between Kant and Freud?" This fellow student undoubtedly gave me an informative answer that I no longer remember, but this question was the starting point of a quest and research process that aimed to understand its meaning intellectually and emotionally. I began by studying philosophy at the Faculty of Philosophy in Montreal, where I had the exceptional opportunity of following Paul Ricoeur's teaching on phenomenology and the problems of language. Hence my subsequent departure for Paris to undertake a doctoral thesis in philosophy with Paul Ricoeur, who had just left the Sorbonne for the newly created Paris Nanterre University with the intention of bringing to it the more open spirit of North American universities, in particular those of Montreal and Chicago, where he used to come to teach every autumn before French universities began their new year. Having been deeply influenced by Maurice Merleau-Ponty's philosophical approach of an indirect ontology oriented towards the sciences, I chose as my thesis subject an area of research in philosophical anthropology on the theme of "phenomenology and psychoanalysis", which was a way of pursuing my initial line of questioning!

This was the 1960s in France, which were a golden age for psychoanalysis, with the publication in 1965 of *De l'interprétation. Essai sur Freud* (Ricoeur 1965) and in 1967 of *The Language of Psychoanalysis* (original title: *Vocabulaire de la psychanalyse*) (Laplanche & Pontalis 1973/1967): two books that would clarify the

DOI: 10.4324/9781003342502-8

translation of psychoanalytical concepts into French and their equivalents in other languages through an exegesis of the meaning of these concepts in Freud's work. In this context, I began a personal psychoanalysis with a training analyst from the Paris Psychoanalytical Society (SPP) and, at the same time, had the opportunity of working with Jean Laplanche in his seminar on translating Freud's texts into French.

• Could you comment on any opportune encounters you had in your journey and training?

This passion for research in philosophy and psychoanalysis left me unsatisfied, however, regarding my plans to acquire clinical experience and one day become a psychoanalyst. I had a decisive encounter with Serge Lebovici, director of the Alfred Binet Centre, a psychoanalytic treatment centre for children and adolescents, and one of the co-founders of the Mental Health Association in the 13th district of Paris (ASM 13), a semipublic psychiatric institution that seeks to achieve a complementarity between psychiatry and psychoanalysis. This was an exceptional opportunity to meet René Diatkine and Colette Chiland in my training as a child and adolescent psychotherapist. René Diatkine, one of the creators of individual psychoanalytic psychodrama, invited me to take part as a psychodramatist in one of his newly created teams in the early 1970s. I continued with this for nearly 25 years, learning an exceptional psychoanalytical psychotherapy technique for treating patients with non-neurotic organizations.

When Jean Kestemberg set up a Centre for Psychoanalysis and Psychotherapy at the ASM 13 in 1974, it marked another stage in my research, involving analytic work with adult psychotic and borderline patients. This gave me the opportunity to attend the weekly preliminary interviews conducted by Evelyne Kestemberg and the fortnightly seminars devoted to theoretical and clinical research into psychotic functioning. From 1980 onwards, the creation of a biannual journal, *Les cahiers du centre de psychanalyse et de psychothérapie*, and the first themes that it developed, in particular ego-splitting, negation, the third person, moral masochism and erotogenic masochism, had a definitive impact on the French approach to the theory and psychoanalytic treatment of psychosis. The journal was published from 1980 to 1996 but was then discontinued until 2001 (at this time, I was Director of the Centre), when a new series "Psychose et Psychanalyse" published in *Les cahiers du centre de psychanalyse et de psychothérapie*, was launched, this time on an annual basis, with the same aim of exploring the modes of being of psychosis and the theoretical and clinical issues involved.

• What is the cornerstone of your theoretical and clinical work?

It was at that point [in 1974] that it became possible to fulfil my wish to explore my initial line of questioning in greater depth. In 1981, in an issue of the *Cahiers* on negation, I wrote an article called "Jugement et négation. De la théorie du jugement chez Kant et Freud". My remarks reflected my search for a possible link between a philosophical theory of knowledge and a psychoanalytical approach to thought.

It was a way of delving deeper into the issues of symbolization in psychoanalysis, which was to become one of the major lines of my thinking. Analytical work with psychotic patients raised the question of disorders in symbolization. My philosophical interest in this theme was deepened psychoanalytically by my theoretical and clinical experience of psychosis. Symbolization can be broadly defined as the operation by which something *represents* something else for someone. While it may appear in this way as the substitution of one object for another, it is first and foremost the result of a process that presupposes both the *ability* to represent an absent object and a subject who is capable of knowing that the symbol is not the symbolized object. This research has led me to take part in numerous symposia and conferences on the theme of symbolization and psychosis and to publish a book, *Chemins de la symbolisation* (Gibeault 2010).

• What is your theoretical approach to psychoanalytic practice (the couch, frequency, the frame, teletherapy, interpretation, silence)?

The above-stated understanding of mental functioning in psychosis determines psychoanalytic research into the treatment of psychotic patients. Without going into a discussion of the different conceptions of transference in psychosis, the status of the object and the role of projection in psychotic states determine a specific approach to transference in psychosis. Following Evelyne Kestemberg (2001/1981), it is probably more appropriate to refer to psychosis as a transference cathexis relating to the nondifferentiation of the imagos, rather than a *transference as such*, which presupposes a differentiation of the imagos.

All these remarks on the appreciation of the economic weight of narcissistic and object cathexes are at the root of the different technical variants in the treatment of psychotic patients. As the psychotic ego is incapable of forming a neurotic-style object transference due to serious difficulties of introjection and identification, it is necessary to make technical adjustments. First of all, in the analytical setting, since the inability to displace differentiated imagos onto the analyst determines recourse to variations in technique—face-to-face psychotherapy, individual analytical psychodrama, recourse to a psychiatric third party—compared with the standard treatment on the couch. Visual and motor support is not only a means of encouraging a process of symbolization but also a material third element that intervenes to limit the danger of nondifferentiation and intrusion.

From this point of view, psychoanalytic treatment is not immediately offered to psychotic patients in acute crisis; they are initially offered psychiatric follow-up, which may or may not be accompanied by a prescription for medication. The third-party function of the Centre for Psychoanalysis and Psychotherapy (ASM 13) and the psychiatric institution plays an essential role here, enabling the patient to contain his or her anxiety sufficiently to undertake psychoanalytic treatment.

The technical adjustments also concern the interpretative approach, where initially it is less a matter of interpreting unconscious phantasy contents and the transference than the modalities of mental functioning; it is only at a later stage, once the ego has acquired the ability to bind drive excitation into representations, that it will be possible to interpret unconscious fantasies and transference without the risk of occasioning a breach of the stimulus barrier.

The aim of the analyst's work, both through the *setting proposed* and through his or her *interpretative technique*, is to create a *space for play* that will enable the schizophrenic patient to take an interest in their own productions and to stop experiencing them as sensations without representations or as representations coming from a persecutory external world. For the analyst, it is a matter of offering the patient thoughts and hypotheses for psychic work that the patient can grasp and use as they wish. As René Diatkine (Gibeault 2015) pointed out, schizophrenic patients are "anti-analysands" and "don't know how to play with language". They do not have the ability to let themselves say what comes to mind and be surprised by it. The symbolizing setting of psychodrama makes it possible to find out

> whether the surprise created in them by the therapists' role playing provides them with a way of negotiating between their desires and their needs for immediate fulfilment, thereby creating the possibility of containing delusional transferences. In individual psychotherapy, whatever form it takes, this is often impossible.
>
> (Gibeault 2015, 106)

The paradox of *analytic psychodrama* consists in systematically prescribing in the form of play what is otherwise considered to be an obstacle to the development of the analytic process, in particular the *lateralization of the transference* and *acting out*, whether motor or verbal. It is true that taking up these defences in a playful way avoids the resistance inherent in them, which would otherwise be in the order of acting out as such, and instead makes them a preferred mode of elaboration for patients who are unable to tolerate a transference relationship organized around a single analyst. While the driving force of the process, the transference, and its purpose are the same as in a standard treatment, in psychodrama the differences are in fact to do with the setting.

Psychodrama is a *symbolizing* setting insofar as it relies on a materialized third party who determines differentiated spaces: the space of the role-play leader and the space of the psychodramatists, with the patient in one or the other space depending on whether they are in dialogue with the role-play leader or playing a scene with one or more psychodramatists. It is just as much a question of a dual temporality: the *time with the role-play leader,* closer to the secondary process opening onto the subject's history, and the *time of the psychodramatic play*, closer to the primary process characteristic of the atemporal unconscious (*Zeilos*).

The invention of individual psychoanalytic psychodrama takes us back to the role of the *third character* as theorized by Evelyne Kestemberg (2001/1981). It can also be seen as a therapeutic modality of thirdness, as defined by André Green (2005/2002), that is, as "the generalized theory of triangulation with a substitutable third party", without having to reduce this triangulation to the Oedipal structure (267).

The concept of *thirdness* gives importance to the triangular relationship in general, which is very important in the approach to the *first interview* and in the possible differences between the preliminary interview where the consultant considers whether to take the patient into treatment or to refer him to another colleague, while remaining a possible reference, as in the institutional situation. This materialization of the third party thus provides the necessary conditions for internalizing the third party in psychic functioning, particularly for patients who have difficulty relying on a differentiated psychic topography.

In my professional career, I became Director of the Centre for Psychoanalysis and Psychotherapy in 1997, which gave me the opportunity to conduct all the initial interviews with patients referred to the Centre and to explore in greater depth the theoretical and clinical issues involved as well as the conditions of an encounter that would enable the patient to do analytical work later on. The *virtuality* of the third party is generally sufficient in neurotic organizations. In non-neurotic organizations, it is often necessary for this third party to be *objectified* in the context of an institution, through an initial interview with a consultant who will not be treating the patient himself, or might eventually do so with an assistant. This is typical of consultations in psychoanalytic centres.

From the 2000s onwards, research into the first interview continued, in particular through a collaboration lasting almost ten years with Michel de M'Uzan. Together we reflected on the issues at stake in the analytic process during these first interviews with patients presenting a psychotic mode of functioning and/or a psychosomatic mode of functioning. This process enabled us to work, as he put it, "on the boundaries".

Michel de M'Uzan (2019/2015) insisted on the importance, during the first interview, of the *translation of identity*, that is, the projection of characters as in the theatre on to the person of the analyst, where "the shadow of the imagos covers that of real people" (54). This is why, like Evelyne Kestemberg, he has always wanted to limit the number of preliminary interviews to one, or two at most, so as not to initiate this process of projection. Other analysts, such as Jean-Luc Donnet (de M'Uzan & Donnet 1998), have preferred to multiply the number of interviews, proposing the equivalent of a "trial treatment", so as not to make a mistake in the indication. Michel de M'Uzan (de M'Uzan & Donnet 1998) thought that "depriving a patient of an analysis is more serious than giving the wrong indication" (199).

Finally, this research on the first interview has had an international extension within the framework of the European Psychoanalytical Federation (EPF). From 2002 to 2012, a working group brought together some 15 colleagues from different European psychoanalytical societies; I was a member of this working group, representing the French approach to the first interview.

Different hypotheses were considered to describe the process of these first interviews: first a *topographical* hypothesis, insofar as it was a question of initiating a *"change of level"* during these interviews and giving a place to an unconscious dimension; then the presentation of interviews with patients who increasingly presented non-neurotic organizations led to a more *economic* hypothesis where it was more a question of *"coping with an unconscious storm"* and containing the excitation aroused by the encounter with the analyst. Subsequently, the very wide range of initial interviews and underlying theories led the working group to propose instead the idea of "opening up a psychic space" (Reith et al. 2012; 2018).

• In your opinion, what are the points of divergence between French psychoanalysis and English-speaking psychoanalysis?

These considerations on the setting and the psychoanalytical process led to some fascinating exchanges with Otto Kernberg, which showed that the difference between psychotherapy and psychoanalysis did not always have the same meaning in France as in the English-speaking world (Gibeault 2000; 2001). Moreover, this is a theoretical and technical perspective which differs from the Kleinian approach. Evelyne Kestemberg (2001/1957, 45) noted:

> It seems to me that it is necessary to avoid as far as possible the setting-in of a transference psychosis and to proceed in a way that neuroticizes the psychotic transference manifestations. Only this gradual neuroticization will enable us to rediscover with psychotic patients the margin between fantasy and reality which, as Nacht said, is what we can work on.

And she adds:

> In fact, if we replace the psychotic state with a psychotic transference, the latter is a delusional construction whose defensive character can no longer be effectively demonstrated, since the analyst is an integral part of this construction and constitutes the reality, devoured and devouring, against which the patient struggles and which impedes him from engaging in any autonomous activity other than this type of defence, the extreme point of which is autism or suicide.
>
> (Kestemberg 2001/1957, 45)

These differences between the French and British approaches do not mean that they are locked in irreconcilable opposition. They both aim to bring about lasting psychic change in psychotic states, but their technical approaches to the setting and interpretation differ.

This approach contrasts with the work of the British Kleinian psychoanalysts, Wilfred R. Bion, Hanna Segal and Herbert Rosenfeld, who did not hesitate to offer private psychoanalysis with five sessions a week on the couch to patients with acute schizophrenia, thereby encouraging the development of a transference psychosis. In France, the preference has always been for face-to-face psychotherapy with one or two sessions a week, after psychiatric treatment in an institution if necessary.

- **What is your psychoanalytic approach to the societal debates on racial, gender identities or/and on the new forms of reproduction and parenting?**

Colette Chiland (2003) was a forerunner in research into gender identity problems, since in the 1980s, following on from Stoller's work, she initiated research into the question raised by very early identity disorders in children. Her hypothesis was that these early gender identity disorders resulted from the unconscious, repressed expectations of both parents to have a child of a different sex from that of their child. She suggested that both parents and the child should undergo psychoanalytic treatment. I took two fathers into treatment, one into psychotherapy and the other into analysis, whose sons, from the age of two or three, claimed to be girls. In both cases, it appeared that for their psychic survival, these children had to respond to their father's unconscious desire to belong to the other sex. These questions have become highly topical today, as societal and political pressure is exerted to authorize medical treatment for sex reassignment from adolescence onwards.

- **What are your views on the transmission of psychoanalysis?**

It is here that the issues of research and the transmission of psychoanalysis come together in my commitment both nationally within the SPP and internationally in the EPF and the International Psychoanalytical Association (IPA). I owe this international commitment firstly to Anne-Marie Sandler, who in 1982 asked me to become Secretary of the EPF, and then to Daniel Widlöcher, who in 1999 invited me to take up the post of Secretary General of the IPA, just as I was finishing my term as President of the EPF. From then on, this was an important institutional adventure, which more than once made me appreciate the third-party function of our institutions where individual narcissistic issues can lead to impasses to the detriment of the development of psychoanalysis. It was in this institutional context that the opening up of psychoanalysis in Eastern Europe after the fall of the Berlin Wall in 1989 enabled me to play an active part in the transmission of psychoanalysis in this part of the world, in particular through the creation of an Institute for Eastern Europeans by the IPA in collaboration with the EPF. This was also how I became involved in the teaching of psychoanalysis in Russia after the organization, when I was president of the EPF, of the first international psychoanalytical conference in Moscow in 1998, which marked the revival of psychoanalysis in that country.

It was also under Daniel Widlöcher's presidency that a process of reflection on the different training models within the IPA began, leading to the adoption in 2007 of three models: the Eitingon model, the French model and the Uruguayan model. When it was founded in 1926, the SPP had adopted the training principles recommended by the IPA, but the evolution of training led to major changes in practice: In 1953, Sacha Nacht, who founded the Paris Institute of Psychoanalysis, no longer active, accepted, for purely political reasons, the principle of a training analysis of three sessions per week in order to allow for the analysis of two candidates

per week with three sessions instead of just one with six sessions, with the require-
ment, however, of having done at least three years of personal analysis before applying for the training. In 1979, the position of the reporter analyst was abolished
and the principle of a strict separation between the candidate's personal analysis
and his or her training at the Institute was adopted. In 1993, didactic analysis was
abolished, and it was henceforth possible for any member of the society and of the
IPA to analyse a future candidate for training. Finally, candidates were given a free
choice of seminars to follow during their training. This is how the SPP evolved
from the Eitingon model to what is now known as the French training model!

For six years, from 2016 to 2022, I was Chairman of the Teaching Committee
of the SPP, with the aim of opening up our society to other training methods by
inviting colleagues from other societies. Furthermore, one of the current challenges
concerns the isolation of analysts-in-training, which is the negative counterpart of
often having too much freedom during training. With this in mind, I have recommended an experiment that I carried out during a four-year teaching period with a
group of 15 candidates from the Istanbul Psychoanalytical Association: a meeting
with a small group of analysts-in-training over three weekends that encouraged
exchanges between analysts-in-training and two training analysts.

The value this brings to our exchanges between analysts, both within our society
and with colleagues from other societies, has always made me give priority to attending our scientific meetings, but also to writing, as can be seen from the book
Reading French Psychoanalysis, undertaken on the initiative of Dana Birksted-
Breen and co-authored with Sara Flanders, both members of the British Psychoanalytical Society (Birksted-Breen, Flanders & Gibeault, 2010). During my exchanges
over four years with my two British colleagues, we were able to assess the differences between the Anglo-Saxon approach to psychoanalysis and the French approach, in particular the constant reference in France to Freudian metapsychology.
Lacan contributed to this with his call for a "return to Freud", implying a return to
Freud's meaning. But André Green (2005/2002) later argued, quite rightly that the
meaning of a return to Freud was a return to Lacan's meaning. While working on
this book, the discussion of the concept of representation revealed the differences
with the Anglo-Saxon approach, as shown by the difficulties in translating the concepts of *Vorstellung* (*représentation* in French and idea in English) and *Darstellung*
(*figuration* in French and representation in English (Green 2005/2002, 269).

This psychoanalytical journey continued with research into the origins of symbolization, based on the remains of prehistoric art: parietal paintings bear witness
to a representation of absence, and negative stencil-painted hands show that *Homo
sapiens* demonstrated for the first time their ability to become a subject of themselves and a spectator of the world. These reflections are part of interdisciplinary
research between psychoanalysts, prehistorians, ethnologists and art historians
over more than 30 years, which has led to the publication of several books, the most
recent of which is both a scientific book and an art book (Sacco & Robert 2016).

My experience of psychoanalysis is thus one of belonging to the French psychoanalytic tradition and culture, while adopting Freud's recommendations, in 1932,

to the presidents of the IPA: "The analyst should not wish to be English, French, American or German before becoming a follower of analysis; he should place the common interests of analysis above national interests" Mijolla (1982, p 31).

References

Birksted-Breen D., Flanders, S., Gibeault, A. (Eds.) (2010). *Reading French Psychoanalysis*, trans. D. Alcorn, S. Leighton, A. Weller. London and New York: Routledge.

Chiland, C. (2003). *Transexualism: Illusion and Reality*. Middletown, CT: Weysleyan University Press.

Gibeault, A. (1981). "Jugement et négation. De la théorie du jugement chez Kant et Freud". In: *Les Cahiers du Centre de Psychanalyse et de Psychothérapie*. Association de Santé Mentale du 13e arrondissement de Paris, pp. 91–131; reprinted in *Psychanalyse et psychose*, 21: 77–106 (Cheminements en pays psychotiques), Centre de Psychanalyse et de Psychothérapie Evelyne et Jean Kestemberg.

Gibeault, A. (2000). "In response to Otto F. Kernberg's 'Psychoanalysis, psychoanalytic psychotherapy and supportive psychotherapy: contemporary controversies'". *International Journal of Psychoanalysis*, 81: 379–383.

Gibeault, A. (2001). "Problèmes et enjeux de l'API à l'aube du XXè siècle". *Le Carnet Psy*, 66: 18–21.

Gibeault, A. (2010). *Chemins de la symbolisation*. Paris: Presses Universitaires de France. (To be published in English under the title *Paths of Symbolization*.)

Gibeault, A. (2015). "René Diatkine et le psychodrame. Réflexions sur l'approche psychanalytique de la psychose" (followed by a previously unpublished text by René Diatkine: "Dépression et culpabilité, au sujet du psychodrame"). In: *L'héritage vivant de René Diatkine*, ed. F. Quartier and A. Casanova. Paris, Presses Universitaires de France, 2015, pp. 103–136.

Green, A. (2005/2002). *Key Ideas for a Contemporary Psychoanalysis*, trans. A. Weller. London and New York: Routledge.

Kestemberg, E. (2001/1957). "Quelques considérations à propos de la fin du traitement des malades à structure psychotique". In: *La psychose froide*. Paris: Presses Universitaires de France, pp. 15–54.

Kestemberg, E. (2001/1981). "Le personnage tiers: sa nature, sa fonction". In: *La psychose froide*. Paris: Presses Universitaires de France, pp. 145–177.

Laplanche, J. & Pontalis J.-B. (1973/1967). *The Language of Psychoanalysis*, trans. D. Nicolson-Smith. London: Hogarth Press.

Mijolla, A. de (1982). "La Psychanalyse en France (1893–1965)". In: *Histoire de la psychanalyse* (Vol. 2), ed. R. Jacard. Paris: Hachette, pp. 9–105.

M'Uzan, M. de & Donnet, J.-L., (1998). "La rencontre analytique". *Revue française de psychanalyse*, 62(1): 189–208.

M'Uzan, M. de (2019/2015). "Introduction to the theory of the preliminary interview". In: *Permanent Disquiet: Psychoanalysis and the Transitional Subject*, trans. A. Weller. London: Routledge, pp. 52–56.

Reith, B., Lagerlöf, S., Crick, P., Moller, M., & Skale E. (Eds.) (2012). *Initiating Psychoanalysis. Perspectives*. London: Routledge.

Reith, B., Moller, M., Boots, J., Crick, P., Gibeault, A., Jaffe, R., Lagerlöf, S., & Vermote, R. (2018). *Beginning Analysis. On the Processes of Initiating Psychoanalysis*. London: Routledge.

Ricoeur, P. (1965). *De l'interprétation. Essai sur Freud*. Paris: Seuil.

Sacco, F. & Robert, E. (2016). *L'Origine des représentations. Regards croisés sur l'art préhistorique*. Paris: d'Ithaque.

Chapter 9

Conversation with René Kaës

Abstract

René Kaës, who is interested in group psychology as a treatment model, sets out his theory of transitional psychoanalysis as an intermediary space between the intrapsychic and intersubjectivity.

• Could you describe the intellectual and personal journey that led you to psychoanalysis?

I was born in 1936 to a mother from Lorraine and a father from Alsace, in an agricultural village located in the heart of the Moselle steel basin, in a border region between France and Germany.

The personal path that led me to psychoanalysis has several elements to it. One of them is the way that I experienced the conflict of loyalty between my social background (very working class) and the milieu to which my studies at university and my academic career led me. My parents supported me in this process, and so I was fulfilling "the wishful dreams they never carried out", as Freud puts it (1914c, 91); but, on the other hand, this support came with some reproaches, the most difficult of which was that I had become a stranger to them, that I no longer spoke the same language as they did, and that I no longer had the same way of life as them and my brothers and sisters. I was trying to repay my debt to them. My doctoral thesis in psychology on the representation of culture and school among French workers was one way of doing this. But this meant postponing the analysis of what constituted this debt; thinking that I could get rid of it in this way spared me from getting in touch with my guilt for surpassing my father, when he had supported my career, but also from taking into account his own rivalry with me, his eldest son of a large sibling group and the first of my generation to go to university.

Another element that led me to psychoanalysis was my place in my sibling group: a place that was certainly envied, and from which I derived many benefits, but which in return required me to shoulder many responsibilities. The personal analyses that I underwent and then those that I conducted and, as an important part of my practice, the psychoanalytical work with groups and psychiatric care institutions were other reasons for finding, in psychoanalysis, a way of freeing myself

DOI: 10.4324/9781003342502-9

from these conflicts and from the difficulty of being both the subject of one's own destiny and the link in a chain of which I was, at the same time, the servant, the beneficiary and the heir (according to Freud's formulation of 1914c). Later, I found in the thought of Piera Castoriadis-Aulagnier (1975, 71–127), the idea that psychoanalysis reconstitutes this "space where the I can come about".

A third path led me to analysis: the pain caused by the death of two of our children, the unbearable break in the chain of generations, the unspeakable traces it leaves with their enigma locked in tombs of silence when such a bereavement had already been imposed on the generations that preceded me, that of my parents and my grandparents.

It was at the end of the 1960s that I began psychoanalytic treatment with Jeanne Latil, a psychoanalyst trained by Loewenstein within the framework of the first French Psychoanalytic Society. I started practising analysis in the early 1970s, and continued to do psychoanalytic work with groups and also psychoanalytic group psychodrama. A little later, I came into contact with the Fourth Group, which emerged from the 1969 split with the Paris Freudian School [L'École freudienne de Paris (EFP)][1] and was founded by Piera Castoriadis-Aulagnier, J.-P. Valabrega and F. Perrier.

In this institution, I found resonances with what I basically expected from a psychoanalytic institution: a fourth analysis, multireferentiality, reinstituting sessions.[2] However, despite this attraction and the contributions of a long fourth analysis with Nathalie Zaltzman, I did not become a full member of this institution, or of any of the other psychoanalytic institutions. The Fourth Group at that time did not tolerate speaking about psychoanalytic work with groups. I decided that I would not be a full member of an institution that would impose a ban on thinking and limits to my research in the field of psychoanalysis.

I did a further analysis with Jacques Poujol in the early 1980s. This enabled me to free myself from my imaginary debts and to understand how my work on the boundaries of psychoanalysis was a work inherent to all creation.

• Could you comment on any opportune encounters you had in training?

It was a rhizome-like development in several spaces of knowledge. I was curious about everything and each discipline brought me its own questions and those it could not answer. I was not so much seeking to increase my knowledge indefinitely as to contrast their singularities and their boundaries with the "remainder to be known" that they all encounter and the way they deal with it, with the crises that arise in the delimitation of their field when it is expanding. I was also interested in the migration of concepts and models of intelligibility from one discipline to another. Later, when I was about 70 years old, I questioned these intellectual and personal journeys and their links with my relationship to psychoanalysis.

The question of boundaries has always intrigued me. I came from several spaces, and the question of the "between" and the "trans" has been at the centre of my personal and intellectual journey, at the heart of my work and my psychoanalytical research.

At the University of Strasbourg, I obtained a degree in psychology, specializing in psychopathology and social psychology, but also in philosophy and sociology. My first job at the University in 1958 was as a psychology assistant at the *Institut National du Travail*, which was part of the Faculty of Law and Economics in Strasbourg. This institute had the task of training the senior managers of the workers' unions. I was in charge of developing research on the French workers' movement, and more specifically, on the social representations of school, culture and leisure among French workers. I gladly accepted this proposal and discovered the reasons for doing so later.

I used this research as the subject for my doctoral thesis in social psychology in 1966. I posed a theoretical question concerning the relations between psychology and sociology and another on the methodology of access to social representations, on the process of their formation. I was not satisfied because the methodology was not able to account for the manifestation of the effects of the unconscious in the process of the formation of individual and collective representations. That was what interested me. I had to take this question up again on different bases.

I found them in the teaching of Didier Anzieu, whom I studied under at the University of Strasbourg in the years 1955–1957, but, above all, I found them by undergoing a personal analysis, and I had more than one reason for doing so. I understood that this thesis served several purposes, including the one I mentioned about my debt to my family.

The meeting with Didier Anzieu was for me the most important one during my years of study at the University. It remained so for 40 years. We became colleagues, friends and the editors of two collections of psychoanalytical works.

I joined him at the Cercle d'Études Françaises pour la Formation et la Recherche Active en Psychologie,[3] which he had just founded in 1962 with some psychoanalysts (J.-B. Pontalis, Ch. Melman, G. Testemale, P. Dubuisson, A. Bejarano and some psychosociologists). It was in this small group that I found the support and the space of freedom for my psychoanalytical research on groups.

The great upheaval of 1968, and the calling into question on many levels of sexual, political and intellectual behaviour, authority, institutions and established knowledge, was an intense experience for me. Psychoanalysis, its practice, its knowledge and its institutions were debated. Dreamy utopias were budding, but also neuroses that had long been kept under wraps by repression. I began to get to know my own.

My 1974 doctoral thesis in letters and human sciences was entitled "Group Process and Social Representations. Psychoanalytical Studies on Training Groups".

• What is the cornerstone of your theoretical and clinical work?

In 1965–1966, I started to develop a psychoanalytical group work setting with D. Anzieu. My initial research had led me to suppose that, in groups, we are not dealing with a single space of unconscious psychic reality but with at least three. First, in the intrapsychic space of each subject, I thought that there were formations whose structure and functioning can be described as internal groups, the main ones being fantasies, the networks of object relations and identifications, while psychic groups are formed by the relationship between the primal unconscious and the repressed contents. Then, in the space constituted by the links between each subject and another subject there are formations and processes that characterize intersubjectivity; among these are identifications and what I call unconscious alliances. Finally, there are formations in the group space as a whole forming a specific entity and containing the other two spaces.

I think that each of these spaces has an unconscious psychic reality. The setting of individual psychoanalytic treatment has brought to light a space of unconscious psychic reality (Freud 1900a): that of the singular subject. This space is defined by its specific contents, energy, processes and resistance: those of unconscious psychic matter, irreducible and opposable to any other order of reality, material, social, economic, etc. This is the constitutive statement of psychoanalysis. The prevalence given to unconscious wishes and the conflicts they generate specify unconscious psychic reality, which is identifiable through its effects: drives, fantasies, dreams, symptoms, complexes and defence mechanisms.

My major hypothesis is that unconscious psychic reality extends in specific ways beyond the psychic space of the subject: it extends to the space of intersubjective links and to the space of groups that bring together several subjects.

At the end of the 1960s, I built a first theoretical/practical model of the articulation and interference between the three spaces of unconscious psychic reality. I described a combinatory arrangement (an assemblage) between certain properties of the psyches of subjects, in particular those of their internal groups, and the same properties in other subjects. I have called this operative fiction of a linking apparatus that is also an apparatus of transformation a "group psychic apparatus". Such a model is transformable and revisable.

In 1976, I published my research in a book with this title (Kaës 1976). The following editions were an opportunity to develop this matrix model which formed, in a way, the cornerstone of my theoretical and clinical work on psychoanalytical work in groups.

This model became more complex with the introduction of two issues: that of unconscious alliances (Kaës 2009) and that of a malaise in contemporary culture (Kaës 2012, reviewed in the *Journal of the American Psychoanalytic Association* [Widawsky 2013]).

Unconscious alliances are one of the main formations of psychic reality. They are two-sided. On the one hand, they organize and characterize the consistency of the links that are formed between several subjects. On the other hand, alliances support what each person, for their own sake, must repress, deny or reject in order to form ties and constitute a group (a couple, a family, an institution). I have differentiated between several types of unconscious alliances: structuring alliances (the alliance of the Brothers, the symbolic alliance with the Father, the contract of renouncing the direct fulfilment of instinctual drive aims), defensive alliances (the pact of denial), alienating and pathological alliances (the narcissistic pact, the pact of shared denial, the perverse pact) and offensive alliances.

They thus participate in the structuring of the unconscious psychic reality of each subject. By virtue of their structure and function, unconscious alliances are destined to produce the unconscious and to remain unconscious.

The question of malaise is at the junction of the three spaces of psychic reality and of sociocultural, political and economic structures. The malaise that I analyse is both an extension of Freud's work on the discontents in culture and introduces three new phenomena: the prevalence of processes without a subject and the society of individuals; the absence of the respondent and the flaws in the symbolic functions; and the dissolution of structuring alliances and guarantor functions.

These emergences are not without consequences for the structuring of psychic life and the early pathologies of the processes of symbolization and subjectivation, disorders in the constitution of internal and external limits, the constitution of psychic envelopes, thought containers and the transmission of psychic life between generations.

The foundational propositions of my theory of unconscious psychic spaces were developed in "applications" to institutions (Kaës 1987; 1996; 2008a), transitional analysis (Kaës 1979), the transmission of psychic life and death between generations (Kaës 1993), psychodrama (Kaës 1999), the polyphony of dreams (Kaës 2002), the sibling complex (Kaës 2008b), ideology (Kaës 1980) and the malaise in contemporary culture (Kaës 2012).

In most of these applications, I pay particular attention to the interferences between psychic spaces, for instance by examining the polyphony of dreams in the space of the psychoanalytic treatment and in that of groups.

Such a theoretical and clinical approach requires the construction of another metapsychology, different from the one to which we primarily refer when we work only with the analytic setting. It must take into account the fact that the unconscious extends to psychic spaces other than the one it occupies in the individual psyche, that it manifests itself in several places, to ensembles such as groups, couples or families, and, consequently, that the subject of the unconscious is at one and the same time the subject of their own intrapsychic processes, the subject of intersubjective links and the subject of the group that contains them. This extension has necessarily led to transformations in psychoanalytic theory (Kaës 2015).

- **What is your theoretical approach to psychoanalytic practice (the couch, frequency, the setting, teletherapy, interpretation and silence)?**

My approach integrates several influences. There is one that has been a common thread for me. It is related to D. Anzieu's position on psychoanalytical practice. He wrote in 1975:

> The question is not to repeat what Freud found when faced with the Victorian crisis, but rather to find a psychoanalytical response to the malaise of modern

man in our present civilization; psychoanalytical work has to be done wherever the unconscious arises, whether standing, sitting or lying down, individually, in a group or in a family, wherever a subject can let himself speak about his anxieties and fantasies to someone who is supposed to listen to them and who is capable of giving him an account of them.

(Anzieu 1975, 135–136)

This opening up of the field of practice develops Freud's (1926) suggestion that analytic treatment is but one of the applications of psychoanalysis.

It is still necessary to draw the consequences of these practices for psychoanalytic theory; and on this question it is not possible to stick to the classical position of the problem of the relationship between psychoanalytic theory and practice, as Freud conceived it with regard to analytic treatment where the practice of psychoanalysis consists in bringing back to consciousness, by means of the transference and resistances, the repressed (and unrepressed) elements that constitute the analysand's unconscious.

In the course of my practice and my theoretical elaborations, I have referred to other positions, such as that of S. Ferenczi and, more modernly, of W. Baranger, J. Bleger and J. Lacan. I agree with the view that the practice of psychoanalysis is not an application of psychoanalytic theory, but that the latter should be available as a latent background (what P. Aulagnier called the analyst's floating theory) and that it always needs to be recognized and re-elaborated, because an analyst is and must remain what Reik called a "surprised psychologist". There is always a necessary gap between practice and theory; there is no perfect coincidence between theory and psychoanalytic practice.

I attach great importance to the stability and regularity of the psychoanalytic setting (frequency and duration of sessions) as an element of the frame and its containing and symboligenic functions, but I think that the frame must be pliable in order to suit the psychoanalytic process of each singular subject.

I would like to make room for the concept of transitional analysis (Kaës 1979). Inspired by Winnicott, transitional analysis is a method for treating the effects of traumatic ruptures in intrapsychic and intersubjective spaces. It emphasizes the re-establishment of the transitional area and processes of symbolization. It is also a general theory for investigating the effects of experiences of traumatic rupture in the internal space and, more precisely, in the intermediate processes and formations that are shaken by these experiences.

Anzieu (1979, 201) applied the principles of transitional analysis to the treatment of borderline adults whose skin-ego is

insufficiently consistent or ill-adjusted or discontinuous or undifferentiated and which does not fulfil its triple function as a containing and gathering envelope, as a protective barrier against the quantitative excess of stimuli, and as a filter discriminating between the various categories of sensitive qualities.

• What is your conception of the transmission of psychoanalysis?

Psychoanalysis is transmitted first of all through experience: necessarily through the experience of psychoanalytic treatment and, I would add and recommend, through the experience of psychoanalytic work with multisubjective groups. Psychoanalysts have always built their practice and theoretical acquisitions both through their experience as practitioners of analysis and through their participation in multisubjective groups: not only in seminars, work groups or supervision, but also in institutions. These three spaces interfere with, and contribute to, the formation of their identity as psychoanalysts and their conduct of psychoanalytic work.

• In your opinion, what are the points of divergence between French psychoanalysis and English-speaking psychoanalysis?

Rather than divergences, I would stress the important influence of Anglo-Saxon psychoanalysis on French psychoanalysis. There was a real liberation among French analysts in their ways of thinking about psychoanalysis (turned towards theory, and often without detailed clinical presentation) when the work of Bion, Winnicott and Meltzer were finally translated into French. Lacan was the first to write, in *L'Évolution psychiatrique*, in 1947, about Bion's early work. Pontalis was one of those who enthusiastically supported the dissemination of Winnicott's and Masud Khan's work. Meltzer's work was translated in 1967, notably by Jean and F. Bégoin, G. and M. Haag and D. Alcorn. The research of Esther Bick, H. Rosenfeld, Hanna Segal and a few others, and their approaches to autism and psychosis, have been a source of inspiration for many French psychoanalysts, as has the interest that most of these analysts have in the analysis of children and practice, along with the remarkable quality of their clinical observations.

For French group analysts, the contributions of W. R. Bion, S. H. Foulkes, R. Hinshelwood, M. Pines and D. Brown, were variously integrated or questioned.

• What is your psychoanalytic approach to the societal debates on racial, gender identities or/and on the new forms of reproduction and parenting?

I am probably not entirely up to date with these debates, of which I have only partial knowledge. I have some difficulty in imagining what a psychoanalytical approach to these debates could be, as these issues are so complex and controversial, especially as the question of gender is outside the field of psychoanalysis.

The notion of gendered identity, on the other hand, raises questions for psychoanalysis. It calls into question our conception of the difference between the sexes, sexuality and sexuation and their relationship with their biological and socio-cultural anchorage. It is a new clinical challenge: How do we listen to the demand of transgender subjects and respond to the psychic suffering that motivates them in adolescence?

Listening to the demand is the surest way to identify how psychoanalysis can find its specific practical and theoretical approach in this debate.

We must also question our prejudices and our established knowledge concerning the new forms of reproduction and parenthood and trust only what we learn from our practice. And we must always bear in mind: What can psychoanalysis do and what can it not do?

Perhaps the attacks on Anglo-Saxon psychoanalysis are a reminder that Psychoanalytic Societies have not always been receptive to various sexual orientations. The recent apology by the President of APsaA [in a statement at the group's 109th annual meeting in San Diego in 2019] attests to this by referring to "our role in the discrimination and trauma caused by our profession".

The time has passed when homosexuality was considered by the majority of psychoanalysts as a perversion. On this point, Freud's position fluctuated; sometimes it was open and liberal, sometimes it was closed, adhering to a conception of homosexuality as deviant and perverse. Today, one can hardly find any psychoanalysts for whom homosexuality is considered a contraindication to the practice of psychoanalysis.

Notes

1 Then directed by Jacques Lacan. Theoretical disagreements on the training of psychoanalysts and on the practice of analysis were at the origin of this split.
2 Editor's note: *Multireferentiality* refers to the possibility of thinking psychoanalytically with the integration of different schools of thought and with different disciplines. *Reinstituting sessions* are sessions which relate and include the role(s) of the institution as part of the psychoanalytic process.
3 This became the Cercle d'Études Françaises pour la Formation et la Recherche: Approche Psychanalytique du groupe, du psychodrame, de l'institution.

References

Anzieu, D. (1975). "La psychanalyse encore!". *Revue Française de psychanalyse*, 39(12): 135–146.
Anzieu, D. (1979). "La démarche de l'analyse transitionnelle en psychanalyse individuelle". In: *Crise, rupture et dépassement. L'analyse transitionnelle en psychanalyse individuelle et groupale*, ed. R. Kaës, A. Missenard, R. Kaspi, D Anzieu, J. Guillaumin, J. Bleger, E. Jacques. Paris: Dunod, pp. 186–221.
Aulagnier, P. (1975). *The Violence of interpretation: From Pictogram to Statement*, trans. A. Sheridan. London: Routledge.
Freud, S. (1900a). *The Interpretation of Dreams*. *S. E.* 4–5. London: Hogarth.
Freud, S. (1912–13). *Totem and Taboo*. *S. E.* 13. London: Hogarth, pp. 1–161.
Freud, S. (1914c). "On narcissism: An introduction". *S. E.* 14. London: Hogarth, pp. 69–102.
Freud, S. (1926e). "The question of lay analysis". *S. E.* 20. London: Hogarth, pp. 183–258.
Kaës, R. (1976). *L'Appareil psychique groupal. Constructions du groupe*. Paris: Dunod.

Kaës R. (1979). "Introduction à l'analyse transitionnelle". In: *Crise, rupture et dépassement. L'analyse transitionnelle en psychanalyse individuelle et groupale*, ed. R. Kaës, A. Missenard R. Kaspi, D Anzieu, J. Guillaumin, J. Bleger, E. Jacques. Paris: Dunod, pp. 1–83.

Kaës, R. (1980). *L'idéologie, études psychanalytiques. Mentalité de l'idéal et esprit de corps*. Paris: Dunod. Revised and expanded edition, *L'idéologie. L'idée, l'Idéal, l'Idole*, Paris: Dunod, 2016.

Kaës, R. (1987). "Réalité psychique et souffrance dans les institutions". In: *L'institution et les institutions. Études psychanalytiques*, ed. R. Kaës, J. Bleger, E. Enriquez, F. Fornari, P. Fustier, R. Roussillon, J.-P. Vidal. Paris: Dunod, pp. 1–46.

Kaës, R. (1993). *Le groupe et le sujet du groupe*, Paris: Dunod.

Kaës, R. (1996). "Souffrance et psychopathologie des liens institués. Une introduction". In: *Souffrance et psychopathologie des liens institutionnels*, ed. R. Kaës, J.-P. Pinel, O. Kernberg, A Correale, E. Diet, B. Duez. Paris: Dunod, pp. 1–47.

Kaës, R. (1999). *Les théories psychanalytiques du groupe*. Paris: Presses Universitaires de France.

Kaës, R. (2002). *La polyphonie du rêve. L'espace onirique commun et partagé*, Paris, Dunod.

Kaës, R. (2008a). "Le deuil des fondateurs dans les institutions: travail de l'originaire et passage de génération". In: O. Nicolle, R. Kaës, A.-M. Blanchard, F. Giust-Desprairies, A. Missenard, J.-P. Pinel, M. Claquin, L. Michel, M. Pichon & J. Viller, *L'institution en héritage. Mythes de fondation, transmissions, transformations*. Paris: Dunod, pp. 45–74.

Kaës R. (2008b). *Le complexe fraternel*. Paris: Dunod.

Kaës, R. (2009). *Les alliances inconscientes*. Paris: Dunod.

Kaës, R. (2012). *Le malêtre*. Paris: Dunod.

Kaës, R. (2015). *L'Extension de la psychanalyse. Pour une métapsychologie de troisième type*. Paris: Dunod.

Widawsky, R. (2013) "Book review: *Le Malêtre* (*The Malaise*)", *Journal of the American Psychoanalytic Association*, 60(6): 1256–1259.

Chapter 10

Conversation with Laurence Kahn

Abstract

Laurence Kahn highlights the interest and importance of metapsychology as an indispensable model of thought for any clinical approach. In this way, she deplores psychologizing tendencies linked, in her view, to the reduction of the treatment to emotion and affect, to the detriment of unconscious processes.

- **Could you describe the intellectual and personal journey that led you to psychoanalysis?**

How is the intellectual journey to be distinguished from the personal journey? I made an appointment with a psychoanalyst to undertake an analysis when I was very young and struggling with great personal difficulties. So I went into analysis for private reasons and not at all to become an analyst. But we know what surprises analysis holds in terms of reactualizations and retroactive revisions (après-coups). In my case, in the very first sessions, I had a vivid memory of my meeting with a literature teacher in my Year 9 class (*quatrième* in France) who, no doubt, had to prepare the syllabus, which included the Romantic soul and dreams or some such subjects, for a competitive examination. He made us read Gérard de Nerval, the Surrealists and Baudelaire. And he asked us to write a dream. I began by composing a false dream that was literary, fiendishly cultured and steeped in classical tragedy; in short, everything that a dream is not. The problem was that I found it very boring trying to keep up this façade, until, that is, I decided to note down one of my real dreams. And I was very surprised at how difficult it was to write it down because weird details kept coming up in the account. I didn't know why … and I didn't know what to do about it. I was 12 and a half years old. To this day, I still remember the "false dream"—which obviously contained its share of fantasy-based ramifications, which are very interesting in retrospect—and I can also remember the real dream, perhaps because I had written it down and this helped it to resist repression.

So my first encounter, one I had forgotten, was rediscovered at the beginning of my analysis and associated with the experience I had when I was 15 years old of reading Freud for the first time. I was very passionate about psychoanalysis, but nevertheless I wanted to study history, which I did, eventually turning to the

DOI: 10.4324/9781003342502-10

anthropology of archaic Greece. It was in this field—and specifically on Greek mythology—that I did my thesis, on Hermes.

However, it was in the course of this personal analysis that my choice of psychoanalysis as a profession was made. In the meantime, I had become an assistant in the research centre of the École des hautes études en sciences sociales (EHESS) directed by Jean-Pierre Vernant (Vernant 1974), who had become a professor at the Collège de France as the chair of Comparative Studies of Ancient Religions. He was a researcher—a maestro I should say—a remarkable researcher who revolutionized the approach to ancient Greece thanks to the interweaving of disciplines such as philosophy, social anthropology, history and philology. However, my inclination was becoming increasingly clear. I therefore went back to study psychology and psychopathology, doing many clinical placements, if only to assure myself that this keen interest was not just the result of an intense transference relationship. After completing five years of studies, and with my university diploma in my pocket, I decided to resign from the EHESS and apply for a post as a psychotherapist in two clinical settings.

Why did I resign? I thought at the time, and I still agree with this decision, that if I continued to attend Vernant's laboratory regularly, given the demanding requirements of the relationship to knowledge in that team, I would not succeed in modifying a certain relationship to the understanding of the world and of words, which is what analytical practice fundamentally requires. That is to say, as J.-B. Pontalis wrote very well, a relationship to not-knowing (Pontalis 1963).

• Could you comment on any opportune encounters you had in your journey and training?

Well, as a matter of fact, I had been reading Pontalis since 1968. For ten years, I had read the *Nouvelle revue de psychanalyse*, of which he was the managing editor, through the eyes of an anthropologist. I was very interested in the approach of this publication, the mixture of genres, styles, objects and references, Machiavelli and the Greeks, "Fetishes without fetishism", Jean-Pierre Peter (1971) and his history of medicine, and Starobinski (1970), a literary critic, the list is really long. It was a mixture that refused to surrender to the ordering of the "sectors" of competence and that rebelled against the fate of analysis to be a "piece of knowledge within a positive body of knowledge" (Pontalis 1968, 99). In short, professionals in the field were being asked to revise their conception of boundaries, and this had already guided my approach as a Hellenist when I wrote *Hermès passe* (Kahn 1978).

It was certainly for this reason that I applied to the French Psychoanalytical Association (APF) to train in psychoanalysis. This is an institution where I found the same openness, with paths of transition from one field to another and a great deal of autonomy offered to analysts-in-training concerning the avenues they can follow. There is no preorganised curriculum each year, and candidates choose the seminars they want to follow according to their centres of interest and the interlocutors that mobilise their interest and curiosity.

Yes, it was a very important encounter. [Pontalis] was my supervisor for five years. I can say that in some ways he taught me my craft as a psychoanalyst. He was a subtle man, a remarkable clinician, with a very great analytical culture. It was he who introduced Winnicott to France. Above all, he was a man capable of offering great freedom of thought to others, but precisely because he was rigorous, I should even say severe and determined, underneath a charming exterior. But it was his quality of being, in the end, without indulgence, which is a good way of helping a young analyst to be controversial, to sustain disagreement. I came to experience this rigour in a different light when, during the last five years of the *Nouvelle revue de psychanalyse*, he invited me to work on the editorial team. The requirements were no less stringent. I might even say that they were exactly the same as the ones I had experienced in supervision—just seen from another angle.

But training is made up of a multitude of identificatory borrowings. Among the people who helped me in my training, I must also count my second supervisor, a woman, Christiane Guillemet (1967), a training member of the APF. She could not have been more different from Pontalis, and that is why I chose her. From her journey with Lacan, she had retained a more visible legacy than Pontalis—it is worth recalling here that the APF was founded in 1964 after a split with the Société française de psychanalyse (SFP) created ten years earlier by Jacques Lacan. Christiane Guillemet worked with a conception of the use of language in analysis where the brief, the unexpected and the elliptical predominated, with keen attention to the analysand's words. She also had a great deal of experience in child analysis, which marked her style of intervention, even in adult analyses. Here too I found the mixture of genres and experiences extremely valuable.

But many other analysts had a decisive influence on me as well: I attended, for instance, Didier Anzieu's seminar and his theory of the skin-ego, as well as Annie Anzieu's seminar—she was a great child analyst and fought a lot within the APF so that this practice could be established. Daniel Widlöcher (Widlöcher 1985, 1986, 2006), president of the IPA from 2000 to 2004 and author of an in-depth reflection on the psychic act as a manifest trace of the action of unconscious phantasy also influenced me a lot as I continued my work on the action of form—which is the subject of *L'écoute de l'analyste* (Kahn 2012). He was a great clinician, notably with a practice of listening in terms of cothinking. But he was a very original theorist within the French psychoanalytical landscape. As a reader of Wittgenstein, von Wright and Searle, he undoubtedly enabled me to approach what was one of the axes of my subsequent research. And others, more distant from the APF, also counted a great deal: For example Jean-Luc Donnet (2009/2005), a member of the Paris Psychoanalytical Society (SPP), whose work on *Agieren* in the transference was one of my starting points.

• What is the cornerstone of your theoretical and clinical work?

It is difficult to answer in one word, but undoubtedly, the reference to Freud. I think that, like Aristotle's work (and I am thinking of what Bertrand Russell does with his reading of Aristotle), we can return to Freud's work for a long time and be nourished by discussing him. The question is rather: Why Freud and not the representatives of the "new" psychoanalysis? In fact, I have slowly come to realise that a "practical" federation of theories—through, for example, the search for common ground such as that advocated by Robert Wallerstein (1988), in his presidential address to the 1987 IPA Congress, "One psychoanalysis or many?". Was there not simply a risk of reducing the common points of the different theories to the lowest common denominator? Were transference and resistance really the only theoretical "pillars" that could be retained? Apart from the fact that these two notions presuppose a solid reference to the intrapsychic forces that play a role in producing repression and displacement—and here we are confronted with the critique of Freudian energetics, whose rout has taken with it not only the drive but also metapsychology in its power of creativity—Wallerstein (1990) argued in his next paper, presented in Rome in 1989, "Psychoanalysis: the common ground", that the analysts who had then presented clinical cases had, despite their different theoretical backgrounds, responded clinically in a way that was similar to their patients' distress. But responding to the patient's distress is perhaps not a universal and universalizable purposive idea of psychoanalysis! I will come back to this further on. Furthermore, leaving metapsychological theories on the sidelines by relying only on clinical theories entails the risk of reducing psychic complexity to the point of rendering it bloodless. As it happens, along with the notion of distress appears the prevalence of trauma, with the danger of a simplification of psychic events. The notion of being in direct contact with facts that can be immediately grasped in the session certainly makes a federation of "practical languages" possible. But does this not, above all, produce a formidable erosion of the key issues that concern us?

There are several reasons for speaking of erosion. The first is clinical and concerns the tools of the method. The second concerns the scope of the contribution of psychoanalysis to the understanding of cultural facts—and by cultural facts I obviously mean political facts.

First of all, the method. My book *Le psychanalyste apathique et le patient postmoderne* (Kahn 2014) had as its starting point the French translation of the Freudian word *Indifferenz* by "neutrality" accompanied by the adjective "benevolent" as if to round off Freud's rather radical position yet a little more. In truth, "indifference" shocks the good intentions that analysts claim to have and seems at first sight to clash with the ideals of treatment. Just like the "objectivity" advocated by Freud, for example, in his letter to Jung dated 31 December 1911, where he tells his correspondent that, like Pfister, he lacks "the necessary objectivity in [his] practice". He then adds the very interesting remark: "You still get involved, giving a good deal of yourselves and expecting the patient to give you something in return" (Freud & Jung 1974, 476).

His response is commensurate with his concern about an aspect that is extremely difficult to deal with in analytic treatments: the narcissistic part of the analyst's relationship with the patient. Now any departure from the principle of reserve will nourish the patient's unconscious fantasy without allowing for its elaboration. Not only does what the analyst communicates of their expectations, personal inclinations and emotions necessarily function as an attractor for the analysand, but it also blurs the analyst's view of the scenario of desire that the patient is trying to embody in their relationship with the analyst.

It is true that Freud speaks of the analyst's abstinence in terms of countertransference control. But behind that, he is questioning the analyst's pride. If the analyst presents themselves as someone whose infinite benevolence is able to make up for the multiple deficiencies inflicted on the patient by their infantile history, there is a risk of the analyst taking themselves for a saviour—which makes it very difficult to grasp the impulses of hate that are covered over by the transference love. By refusing to maintain the asymmetry of the analytic situation strictly, the analyst spares themselves the potential violence of conflicts. Yet the refusal of leniency is probably one of the conditions for flushing out the internalized object relations that are at the source of unconscious guilt. The issues at stake here are the resistance to recovery, the role of masochism and the eroticization of pain. If the analyst does not firmly hold the double position of being both the object whose love the patient fantasizes about and the object whose rejection the patient fantasizes about, they will not succeed in bringing to the fore within the transference the totally antagonistic positions of the superego, a major agent in the treatment: as the spokesperson for Oedipal prohibitions, this agency is constituted by the internalisation of the ties to Oedipal objects that the subject has renounced. In other words, the superego is the bearer of all the internal constraints resulting from the identification with the figures that dominated childhood, especially the fate of the omnipotence that was attributed to the parents and of the ambivalent feelings that one had for them. In my view, the analyst cannot overlook this process by referring only to distress or deficiencies. They have to take violence into account, and to reckon with the ferocity of the internal authority that was fed by the violence that, as children, we would have liked to exercise against the parental figure and its power, as described by Freud (1930a) in *Civilization and Its Discontents*.

Basically, the analyst's abstinence is a narcissistic abstinence. This implies that the analyst must ask him or herself questions about the extremely ambiguous notion of the patient's "good": the conscious good or the good that consists, on the contrary, in lifting the storm of unconscious intrapsychic conflicts?

I think that I have just told you something about one of the cornerstones of my clinical work. You can see how silence plays an important role in it, but this silence obviously has nothing to do with a "leaden silence".

On the theoretical level, I would say the cornerstone is undoubtedly the pair hallucinatory fulfilment/distortion, which I tried to develop in *L'écoute de l'analyste* (Kahn 2012). This implies referring to the drive as the motor of the psychic act and according a fundamental place to transference as repetition.

• What is your theoretical approach to psychoanalytic practice (couch, frequency, teleanalysis, interpretation, silence)?

I would like to say how difficult it is to distinguish between clinical practice and theory! Let us consider the reflections on the effects of the analytic setting and the repercussions of its possible modification. We can see that this dimension is central when it is a matter of evaluating the capacity of the two protagonists of the analytic situation to tolerate not only the sum of excitation mobilised in the transference but also the suspension of meaning that leads to regression and the possibility of gaining access to the unconscious. The process of unbinding solidly secondarized symbolic relations, thereby inaugurating the regressive movement that permits archaic positions in the transference to be worked through, implies renouncing any hopes for a swift emergence of meaning and being able to tolerate the invasion of the psychic field by movements that disconcert the systems of representation. In other words, it is the patient's capacity to tolerate delay—which is also their capacity for putting psychic contents into a state of latency—that decides which form of analytical setting I choose. The advantage and the great defect of face-to-face treatment is that it allows for the rapid semantization of innumerable perceptual signs. It allows for the translation into meaning of elements that would otherwise be deployed without resolution, in a very unstable way for a long time. Does not our sense that one setting is more containing than another stem in particular from the fact that it shortens the time spent in a state of formlessness? As we know, if interpretation excites, its function is also to de-excite.

For this reason, I have the greatest theoretical reservations about empathy, which is currently in vogue, although it does little to explain the processes at work in its mechanism. On the one hand, its close ties with relationalism and intersubjectivism give primacy to the "inescapable mutuality" of the analytic "dialogue" to the detriment of the method of associativity for both patient and analyst alike. And, on the other hand, empathy coexists very well with a knowledge of the "internal world" that has little to do with the unconscious and a great deal to do with the hermeneutics of the self.

Not only is this empathy far removed from what Freud developed in relation to [Theodor] Lipps and his theory of apperception; but, above all, in this interactive space, affect is more or less stripped of its *intra*psychic function, notably its role as a marker of unconscious conflicts. It becomes a territory of sharing. When Freud (1910d, 144) describes countertransference as the result of the patient's influence on the analyst's "unconscious feelings", he is referring to the capacity of the analyst's unconscious to pick up the patient's unconscious from the derivatives that reach it. But, in his eyes, the two scenes remain separate. Moreover, the analyst is urged to seek to understand what is being done to them on the *unconscious* level, not directly on the conscious level of their *feelings*.

The analytical setting that I offer therefore depends entirely on what I perceive in the first interviews. If the patient and I opt for analysis, it is a minimum of three sessions per week when it is the first time the patient has been in analysis and has not had the experience of transference before. It takes time—the most precious commodity there is today—for the process to get underway. And within this setting, of course, there is no question of glossing over or obliterating absences. All absences, whatever the reason, are more or less the embodiment of absence in the deepest sense, that is to say, the territory where loss, amputation and disappearance are played out, with their attendant cohort of ambivalent affects, with the potentially melancholic or triumphant dimension and with masochistic activations—all things that should not, in my opinion, be avoided. And I would add: Under no circumstances, obviously, should a session be replaced by a telephone or video session.

To be quite frank, I don't think much of it at all. A thousand things can be done online: coaching, assistance of all kinds, education, etc. But I have not yet understood how analysts can reconcile themselves with a system where the screen is really a screen between the analyst and the patient, a filter that actually hinders any fine perception of the patient's feelings. Unless one considers that they adapt themselves so well to it precisely because this separating filter protects them! Teleanalysis is, in my opinion, a real bonus for resistance. No more danger of real seduction, no more danger of experiencing despair in the session with a demand for immediate reparation. Analyst and patient are safe.

There is a heavy price to pay, especially as physical distance is compensated for by a constant over-semantization of contents. One interprets to maintain contact. Instead of having a sense of the patient, one launches into hermeneutic overkill. What would Bion have thought of such conditions of listening which, fundamentally, corrupt the basic tissue of the possibility of transforming beta-elements into alpha-elements? And, moreover, how can analysts, and a fortiori those who are responsible at the international level for our practical and ethical criteria, imagine that a training analysis worthy of the name can take place in this way in countries where the authorities relentlessly monitor the internet, where connections can be cut off at any time at their whim, where patients are de facto unable to turn on their superiors or the political authorities? What kind of freedom are we talking about in such conditions?

For a very long time, psychoanalysis endorsed the quasi-false self-analyses of homosexual candidates (Roughton 2002; Feldman 2002), in spite of the fact that Freud never spoke out against the possibility of psychoanalysts being homosexual (Spiers & Lynch 1977). In this case, the puritanical norm prevailed where psychic freedom was Freud's first compass. It was as if a new norm, communicational, had appeared with the idea of a technical development promising supposed progress. But the communicational norm has nothing to do with the conditions that allow for the emergence of an unconscious psychic life!

- **What is your psychoanalytic approach to the societal debates on racial, gender identities or/and on the new forms of reproduction and parenting?**

For the moment, I avoid above all having ready-made ideas. I recall the French debates on the future destiny of children of homosexual couples, who were promised the worst psychic disorganisations due to the absence of a mother or father figure. What I saw in my practice was absolutely contrary to these prophecies: they were very much loved, very well brought-up children, whose extremely attentive parents were worried as soon as something seemed to be going wrong. One would have liked to see the same in many perfectly conformist families! I think human psychic plasticity is an amazing thing. In other words, the problem lies elsewhere: Will these demands for freedom not in turn become the shackles of a new normativity? The worst thing is the prohibition of thinking that is imposed under the guise of freedom of thought. Freud (1933a) describes this very well in his *New Introductory Lectures on Psycho-Analysis* in relation to the Bolsheviks.

Here we are at the crossroads of political and analytical questions with, for me, the collective processes leading to the formation of masses in sight. How does psychoanalysis account for the narrow straight between "idealistic misunderstanding" and the ability to break with reality?

The notion of "mass delusion"—a term that Freud and Einstein as well as psychoanalysts such as Wälder and Simmel used from the 1930s onwards—must be taken literally: It is really a delusion, with its hallucinatory dimension. It is therefore necessary to go back to the drawing board in order to grasp the motive forces of such "negativity" (Kahn 2023/2018). The question is: What is the profound nature of the alliance between progress and barbarity?

I wonder to what extent the attraction of psychoanalysis to problems of individual identity is not a symptom of the deflagration of the inconceivable annihilation that was the Shoah—which undermined the very notion of identity. Identity, claims to identity, ideals, purity: the problem is still topical, and it requires relatively refined metapsychological tools to be dealt with analytically. Confronted with the instrument of a whirlwind of emotions aimed at misleading the masses, or confronted with a relativism openly exploited by the powers that be—for example in the form of "alternative facts"—we are now obliged to ask ourselves what might be the concrete plan capable of stopping the construction of a reality disassociated from the truth? In what way, between fantasy and dogma, could the new horde of brothers—the one that commonly speaks fake news—stumble upon the data of the world? This political dimension, which is particularly active now that there is war in Ukraine, is an aspect of psychoanalysis that interests me greatly.

References

Donnet, J.-L. (2009/2005). *The Analyzing Situation*. London: Routledge.

Feldman, M. (2002). "Panel report: Being gay and becoming a psychoanalyst—Three generations". *Journal of the American Psychoanalytic Association*, 50(3): 973–987.

Freud, S. (1910d). "The future prospects of psycho-analytic therapy". *S. E.* 11. London: Hogarth, pp. 141–151.

Freud, S. (1930a). *Civilization and Its Discontents*. *S. E.* 21. London: Hogarth, pp. 57–146.

Freud, S. (1933a). *New Introductory Lectures on Psycho-Analysis*. *S. E.* 22. London: Hogarth, pp. 1–182.

Freud, S. & Jung, C. J. (1974). *The Freud/Jung Letters: The Correspondence between Sigmund Freud and C. J. Jung*, ed. W. McGuire, trans. R. Mannheim, R. F. C. Hull. Princeton, NJ: Princeton University Press.

Guillemet, Ch. (1967). "Effets de miroirs". *Lettres de l'École Freudienne*, n°2. Avril–Mai, 1967: 65–70. (https://ecole-lacanienne. net/wp-content/uploads/2016/04/EFP-N2-1967. pdf)

Kahn, L. (1978). *Hermès passe ou les ambiguïtés de la communication*. Paris: Maspero.

Kahn, L. (2012). *L'écoute de l'analyste. De l'acte à la forme*. Paris: Presses Universitaires de France.

Kahn, L. (2014). *Le psychanalyste apathique et le patient postmoderne*. Paris: Éditions de l'Olivier.

Kahn, L. (2023/2018). *What Nazism Did to Psychoanalysis*, trans. A. Weller. London: Routledge.

Peter, J.-P. (1971). *Les mots et les objets de la maladie*. Paris: Éditions de la Sorbonne.

Pontalis, J.-B. (1963). "Du vocabulaire de la psychanalyse au langage du psychanalyste". In: *Après Freud*. Paris: Gallimard, 1993, pp. 120–156.

Pontalis, J.-B. (1968). "L'utopie freudienne". In: *Après Freud*, Paris: Gallimard, 1993, pp. 98–113.

Roughton, R. E (2002). "Being gay and becoming a psychoanalyst: Across three generations", *Journal of Gay & Lesbian Psychotherapy*, 6(1): 31–43.

Spiers, H. & Lynch, M. (1977). "The gay rights Freud". *Body Politic*, May 1977: 8–10; 25. (https://archive. org/details/bodypolitic33toro)

Starobinski, J. (1970). *La relation critique*. Paris: Gallimard.

Vernant, J. P. (1974). *Myth and Society in Ancient Greece*. Cambridge, MA: MIT Press, Reprinted 1990.

Wallerstein, R. (1988). "One psychoanalysis or many?". *International Journal of Psychoanalysis*, 69: 5–21.

Wallerstein, R. (1990). "Psychoanalysis: The common ground". *International Journal of Psychoanalysis*, 71: 3–20.

Widlöcher, D. (1985). "The wish for identification and structural effects in the work of Freud". *International Journal of Psychoanalysis*, 66: 31–46.

Widlöcher, D. (1986). *Métapsychologie du sens*. Paris: Presses Universitaires de France.

Widlöcher, D. (2006). "Psychic reality: Belief or illusion?" *American Imago*, 63: 315–329.

Chapter 11

Conversation with
Vassilis Kapsambelis

Abstract

Vassilis Kapsambelis offers some considerations on negative hallucination as constitutive of the encounter between the ego and the object, with reference to his study of pleasure and unpleasure. He identifies three modes of encounter with the object: recognition, knowledge and misrecognition.

- **Could you describe the intellectual and personal journey that led you to psychoanalysis?**

I studied at the School of Medicine at the University of Athens from 1973 to 1980 during what was a very turbulent time. Greece was still under a military dictatorship. Before and after its fall (in 1974), there was a huge movement of political commitment, particularly among students. Working as part of a group, sharing common values and making a collective effort marked my late teens and early adulthood. In a way, these years determined my future choices: In parallel with my work as a psychoanalyst, I have always worked in psychiatric institutions informed by an ideal of humanistic and dynamic psychiatry, and I have taken on various management roles from time to time. I am currently the director of a psychoanalytic centre specializing in psychotic and borderline pathologies within a community psychiatric organization, the Mental Health Association in the 13th district of Paris (ASM 13), which deals with the psychological and psychiatric disorders of children and adults in this Parisian district of 180,000 inhabitants (Kapsambelis 2022).

During my medical studies, I became very interested in the various aspects of brain function. I worked as a student in a neurochemistry laboratory at the University of Athens, and in 1976, I did an internship at the National Institute of Mental Health (NIMH) in Bethesda, Maryland. At the time, I was considering the possibility of going to the United States to do research after finishing medical school, like most of my coworkers in the laboratory.

However, I was also very interested in mental pathologies and madness despite the disappointing situation in the psychiatric hospitals that I had experienced during my studies. I was fortunate enough to meet a psychiatrist and psychoanalyst, Takis Sakellaropoulos. He had trained partly in Greece after the Second World War,

DOI: 10.4324/9781003342502-11

then moved to France in the mid 1950s, where he received psychoanalytical training, while at the same time taking part in the adventure of discovering the first neuroleptics (antipsychotics). This encounter played a part in changing my plans, and, when I finished medical school in 1980, I moved to Paris to specialize in psychiatry and train in psychoanalysis. France has a highly effective public system of community psychiatry that is strongly influenced by psychoanalytic thinking as a theory and practice of the interhuman encounter. The aim is not to provide "psychoanalytic psychotherapy" to all patients who turn to the public psychiatric system but to approach pathologies by looking at mental functioning, internal conflicts, the history of the subject, the transference dimension of therapeutic relationships with all those involved and the dynamics of groups in care institutions (therapy environment).

• Could you comment on opportune encounters in your journey and in your training?

Sakellaropoulos had invented a system of home hospitalization for schizophrenic patients in crisis, on a totally private basis. His reputation meant that families with a family member (son, daughter, husband, wife, etc.) suffering from a relapse of schizophrenia came to him to try and obtain treatment that would avoid hospitalization. He set up a small team of three carers (medical students like myself, psychologists and other mental health workers) who took turns being with the patient 24 hours a day (each working eight hours). We gave the patient medication, talked to them and slept in a cot next to their room, all under the supervision of Dr. Sakellaropoulos. This system would remain in place for a few weeks, and then we would gradually reduce our hours of presence as the patient improved. Everything I learnt about how to make contact with a severely disorganized and paranoid schizophrenic patient, how to maintain a dialogue with them, how to gradually deal with massive projective and identificatory manifestations, I learnt thanks to this unique experience in which I participated for a few years.

Once in France, I was influenced by the thinking of another psychiatrist, René Angelergues, who developed an understanding of psychoanalysis as the only theory of the mind that sets out in biological terms the laws that govern it. For him, psychoanalysis is biological, not because its knowledge can be based on this or that cerebral mechanism, but because it has discovered that phenomena in the order of pleasure/unpleasure (which are sensations and therefore, by definition, of a bodily, biological nature) play a decisive role in the formation and growth of the specifically human mind. In Freud's elaborations, mental representations and human thought in general appear as cathexes that are mobilized by the pleasure principle and that concern traces of satisfaction saved by another system, the neuronal system and its tools (perception and memory layers). Primitive hallucination, an act of the birth of psychic life, is the encounter between a perception (or its trace) and a cathexis guided by the pleasure/unpleasure principle, and it is from this conjunction that a new, specific and relatively autonomous system emerges, which we call the mind or mental apparatus. The "biology" of the mind—Freud (1940b/1938, 282) says: "Psychology, too, is a natural science. What else can it be?"—is defined not by its relationship to the brain but by the fact that the human mind emerges from the organism's experiences of pleasure and unpleasure and from its capacity to relive these experiences by transforming their traces into mental representations.

• What is the cornerstone of your theoretical and clinical work?

The combination of the above approach to metapsychology and my interest in psychotic states led me to take a particular interest in the relationship between the mind and so-called external reality, going beyond expressions such as "external object" and "internal object", which do not seem to me to give a sufficient account of ordinary mental functioning (Kapsambelis 2020b).

We know that Freud's position never varied on the fact that psychoses are defined by a break with reality. However, work with psychoses shows major discrepancies between individuals in terms of what is commonly called "reality", and this is also true for non-psychotics. It therefore seemed important to me to consider that the reality in question in the psychotic break with reality is that embodied by the object: In psychosis, there is a break with that part of reality that is likely to become an "object" for the patient. What does this break consist of? We can consider that our approach to reality (and to the object) is the conjunction, as I said earlier, of a perceptual movement and a hallucinatory movement. The perceptual movement consists in presenting for cathexis by the ego something "outside the infant's own body" (Freud 1905d, 222). The hallucinatory movement consists in cathecting this perception according to the pleasure principle and on the basis of previous experiences of satisfaction—as Freud says, "the finding of an object is in fact a refinding of it" (ibid.) I think Winnicott describes the same movement with the transitional object: finding (i.e., perception)–creating (i.e., hallucination).

However, cathecting the object (as defined above) also means being cathected by it, which is true not only for those objects that are, moreover, human beings, but also for nonhuman objects: we are invaded by our work; we are subjugated by a work of art; we are passionate about a leisure activity; or whatever. Mythologies (and religions) bear witness to this anthropomorphism, which means that the cathexis we make in the outside world seems to cathect us in turn, as if endowed with drive impulses, and even intentionality, similar to our own, which is directed at us. Thus, from the point of view of our mental life, the movement by which we cathect an object leads to an equivalent movement on the part of the object, even when the latter is an inanimate thing, or an idea, or an activity: cathecting an object leads us by definition to become an "object of the object".

It is this movement of being cathected by the object (and by the other) that appears to be highly problematic in psychotic states (and in schizophrenia, in particular). This gives rise to the twofold movement described by Freud (1914c) in "On Narcissism: An Introduction": Initially there is a movement of withdrawal and self-protective defence, "autism" (in the first sense of the term), and then—and because of the need to cathect an object "outside the infant's own body"—a reality (hallucinations, delusions) is created that allows relations with objects to resume to some extent.

Following on from these reflections, I was led to take a particular interest in negative hallucination as a central modulator of the encounter between self and object. Our relationship with the world seems to me to be characterized by three movements: recognition, knowledge and misrecognition. Recognition is our capacity to recognize in any new object, any new encounter, some aspect of a previous object: an object, therefore that is not only found, but also refound. This aspect of the movement is sustained by our hallucinatory capacity (in the sense of primitive hallucination). Knowledge is openness to cathect the object and the acceptance of the fact that, in cathecting an object, we receive not only what we expected of it, but also what we did not expect, which is nevertheless part of it. The raw material for this movement is provided by the perceptual function, and this knowledge is the basis of what we call otherness. Misrecognition is, I believe, the main mechanism by which the shock between recognition and knowledge (between hallucination and perception) is attenuated and modulated, thereby limiting its traumatic impact. It makes us capable, not only of seeing (hearing, feeling …) what we want to see and hear (hallucination), not only of seeing and hearing what comes from the object and which we had not foreseen (perception), but also of not seeing and not hearing what is nonetheless there. This capacity for negative hallucination (which I think can be detected in any love relationship) is, it seems to me, the condition that allows the ego-object encounter to unfold more or less harmoniously.

I think it is possible to describe psychotic states, acute or chronic, as anomalies of this negative hallucination function: It is omnipresent in acute psychotic states, and very defective in chronic psychotic states (Kapsambelis 2020a).

• What is your view of the transmission of psychoanalysis?

I think it is important to bear in mind that Freud, in his project "to furnish a psychology that shall be a natural science" (Freud 1950/1895, 295), introduced a continuity/break in continuity dialectic between man and the animal world. We need to retain this dual polarity in our theorizing. In other words, we need to retain both the notion of drive (which carries the echo of instinct, common to mammals) and its "object" ("object of the drive"), but at the same time, we need to consider that the object, when it is human, is the creator of the psychic life of the human infant, starting from its own psyche. Psychoanalysis is a general conception of the human being, in continuity/discontinuity with the animal world, particularly the mammalian world.

• What is your theoretical approach to psychoanalytical practice (the couch, frequency, framework, teletherapy, interpretation, silence)?

I practise in a fairly traditional way for the French context, i.e., analyses three times a week, for three quarters of an hour, using the couch-armchair setting, and psychotherapy once or twice a week face-to-face, lasting 45 minutes per session.

I am not very interested in technical debates. Of course, I understand that a method of investigation and therapy (as Freud defined psychoanalysis) has its share of technique, like any method. But the ultimate objective is the development, in the patient, of psychic work, associativity and the analytical process; and as no one in reality speaks and thinks in a vacuum, the person who is being addressed inevitably acquires the status of an object (in the object-related sense of the term), which is a valuable tool for guiding our interventions and interpretations, the aim of which is to encourage the process to unfold. And there are silences that encourage this process, and others that do not.

In my work with non-neurotic patients and in institutions, I have come to practise psychodrama a great deal (Kestemberg & Jeammet 1987). In its classic form, psychodrama involves a patient, a group leader and five to seven psychodramatists, for weekly half-hour sessions. The process is as follows: The group leader accompanies the patient into a room where the psychodramatists are seated in a semicircle. The group leader and the patient sit facing the group. The group leader asks the patient to suggest a scene. This could be a dream, a recent or distant memory, a recent incident, a discussion with someone close to the patient, a daydream … in short, any situation that comes to the patient's mind. The group leader helps the patient to specify the characters in the scene and the patient designates the psychodramatist(s) who will take on a particular role. Deceased people, a pet, an inanimate object or a concept ("duty", "shame", etc.) can also be used as characters. The patient can keep their own role or take on another, in which case they designate the psychodramatist who will play their own role. Once the scene has been defined, patients and psychodramatists stand up and play. The group leader may interrupt the role-playing at any time with an intervention, an interpretation, a link with a previous session or with elements of the patient's problem, etc. There are usually two to four scenes per session.

From my point of view, psychodrama is a genuine experimental model, in the same way as the standard treatment. The latter is appropriate for exploring the ego-drive axis, whereas psychodrama explores the ego-object axis. The transformation of objects (the psychodramatists are free to play the role assigned to them, as described by the patient, or not), the discovery of unexpected aspects of the patient's relationship with them, the enactment of thoughts and phantasies unknown to the subject and the internal conflictuality in the patient's relationship with the world are some of the elements that appear in psychodrama. The existence of several psychodramatists enables the transference to be diffracted in patients where the dual relationship could mobilize situations of dependence or hatred that are too extreme to be elaborated. Play, and the involvement of psychomotricity, are suitable for patients who are too inhibited or withdrawn in a psychotic sense.

- **In your opinion, what are the points of divergence between French psychoanalysis and English-speaking psychoanalysis?**

I am not sure I can answer that question. I have the impression that the main differences are no longer national, but doctrinal: in every country, and in every language, there are colleagues who define themselves as Kleinian, Winnicottian, Bionian, Lacanian ... Personally, I think it's a bit of a shame but, at the same time, unavoidable: Freud's work goes back more than a century, and like any fertile theory, it has given rise to multiple and sometimes divergent developments. It is undoubtedly characteristic of French psychoanalysis that it remains attached to the reading of Freud as a prerequisite and matrix for all other developments. But this does not apply to all French psychoanalysts. For example, it is striking to see Lacanians laying claim to a "return to Freud", when in their articles there are only references to Lacan! (It's the same with the Kleinians, except that at least they don't claim to have discovered the real Freud). And, moreover, there are many non-French psychoanalysts, especially German-speaking ones, who still read Freud carefully.

- **What is your psychoanalytic approach to the societal debates on racial, gender identities or/and on the new forms of reproduction and parenting?**

My experience in this field is limited, and it may be considered that the Paris Psychoanalytical Society (SPP), to which I belong, has not engaged in any systematic and collective reflection on these subjects. I will therefore confine myself to four remarks.

The first is that the terms "dysphoria", "psychic suffering", etc. refer, above all, to a *feeling*, which is therefore *subjective* (like any feeling), which means that it may or may not exist independently of any objectively observed situation. People can be "dysphoric" about their obesity or not, just as there are anorexics who are dysphoric about putting on weight even though they are extremely thin. The psychoanalyst's task is to be open to the subjective nature of "suffering" and "dysphoria", and we do not have to worry about, or pass judgement on, the "objectivity" of such suffering or dysphoria. And so, conversely, we have no judgement to make about situations that diverge from the statistical majority but are not accompanied by suffering or dysphoria (or, in any case, by a dysphoria which chooses us as interlocutors). Psychoanalysis is not a "worldview" (*Weltanschauung*) (Freud 1933a) and it does not define norms. If some psychoanalysts think they can establish norms, the LGBTQIA+ movements are right to attack them, and Joyce McDougall (1978), a very influential psychoanalyst in France, published a *Plea for a Measure of Abnormality*, which is still very relevant to psychoanalytical thought and practice. Our task is to study the multiple manifestations of the pleasure principle in a species—the human species—where pleasure has emancipated itself considerably from the satisfaction of its two fundamental mammalian needs: to feed (and more generally to protect and care for oneself) and to reproduce. And with the knowledge that "things that have to do with love are incommensurable with everything else; they are, as it were, written on a special page on which no other writing is tolerated" (Freud 1915a, 160).

My second comment is as follows: Some people believe that if there are people who suffer from a discrepancy between their anatomical sex and gender, biological identity and psychic and mental identity, it is because of the way society views them and rejects them or because of social gender identities that have long been confused with anatomical identities. This may be true. But when a doctor sees someone who was walking down the street and has been shot in a gunfight, they treat their patient's injuries and do not go off to take part in an antigun demonstration. And as Green (2006, 241) said: "If it's in me, it's me, even if the object seems to have put it there". Now, if there are people who think they have no need to think about the fact that they are LGBTQIA+ and that the whole issue is to do with their acceptance in the world, we can calmly state that as psychoanalysts we think it is useful for human beings to exercise this unique faculty of thinking about themselves. And we don't just think this for LGBTQIA+ people! We believe that it is useful for *every* man to think about the fact that he thinks he is a man, and for *every* woman to think about the fact that she thinks she is a woman, which is why psychic bisexuality occupies an important place in our theory and practice. As Freud (1911c, 46) puts it: "Generally speaking, every human being oscillates all through his life between heterosexual and homosexual feelings, and any frustration or disappointment in the one direction is apt to drive him over into the other." The opposition between anatomical identity and gender identity could boil down to an analogous "pair of opposites", and it would be illusory to think we could escape the psychic conflict by eliminating one or the other of the two terms.

A third remark concerns the fact that some psychoanalysts publicly take a stand against the various hormonal and surgical interventions designed to change an individual's biological sex and denounce the impoverishment at both the psychic and fantasy levels associated with these interventions and amputations. They are not wrong in doing so, but it's important to bear in mind that every new technology does a lot of damage in its early days, and this in no way foreshadows what it will become, or what it will achieve as it evolves. In Greek mythology, Icarus paid with his life for the "unnatural" desire to have wings and to fly like a bird, but this did not dissuade human beings from the desire to go beyond the limits of their anatomy and biology, and a few millennia later, humanity invented a number of ways to fly (while still *fantasizing* about having wings, as we see in film and literature).

My fourth comment: Today, LGBTQIA+ people feel that they must fight to secure their place in the world, free from persecution and discrimination, and to have their identity recognized. Freud (1914c, 85) wrote, "A strong egoism is a protection against falling ill, but in the last resort we must begin to love in order not to fall ill, and we are bound to fall ill if [...] we are unable to love". Bearing in mind that "egoism", in this context, refers to the "ego drives" of the first drive theory and their subsequent evolution, thus including the need to ensure survival, but also the consolidation of narcissistic foundations and the establishment of an identity, one may consider that once the goal of recognition has been achieved, psychoanalysis will have to explore, with those LGTBQIA+ people who wish to do so, the new forms of object cathexis that these identities and practices bring to our understanding of the human mind.

Finally, at the level of psychoanalytic institutions, I note that women are now in a large majority and that, for example, of the 26 societies that make up the Congress of French-Speaking Psychoanalysts, 19 have a woman as president. I can only hope, therefore, that the women in our psychoanalytic societies will not do as the men who preceded them did, and they will respect the rights of the male minority … which perhaps, thanks to this cohabitation, will learn to work better with the female part of its psychic bisexuality.

References

Freud, S. (1905d). *Three Essays on the Theory of Sexuality*. *S. E.* 7. London: Hogarth, pp. 123–246.

Freud, S. (1911c). "Psycho-analytic notes on an autobiographical account of a case of paranoia". *S. E.* 12, London: Hogarth, pp. 1–82.

Freud, S. (1914c). "On narcissism. An introduction". *S. E.* 14. London: Hogarth, pp. 67–102.

Freud, S. (1915a). "Observations on transference-love". *S. E.* 12: 157–171.

Freud, S. (1933a). *New Introductory Lectures on Psycho-Analysis* (Lecture XXXV: "The Question of a *Weltanschauung*"). *S. E.* 22. London: Hogarth, pp. 158–182.

Freud, S. (1940b/1938). "Some elementary lessons in psycho-analysis". *S. E.* 23. London: Hogarth, pp. 279–286.

Freud, S. (1950/1895). Project for a scientific psychology. *S. E.* 1. London: Hogarth, pp. 281–391.

Green, A. (2006). "Le tournant des années 2000". In: *Unité et diversité des pratiques du psychanalyste*, ed. A. Green. Paris: Presses Universitaires de France, pp. 229–247.

Kapsambelis, V. (2020a). "Les deux versants de l'hallucination clinique". *Topique* 149: 7–19.

Kapsambelis, V. (2020b). *Le schizophrène en mal d'objet*. Paris: Presses Universitaires de France.

Kapsambelis, V. (2022). "Psychoanalysis in the community in France". *International Journal of Psychoanalysis*, 103(1): 191–210.

Kestemberg, E. & Jammet, P. (1987). *Le psychodrame psychanalytique*. Paris: Presses Universitaires de France.

McDougall, J. (1978). *Plea for a Measure of Abnormality*. London: Free Association Books. Reprinted, 1990.

Chapter 12

Conversation with Julia Kristeva[1]

Abstract

Julia Kristeva explains how psychoanalysis is one of the human sciences that can still propose a renewed model of humanism which includes, among other aspects, an ethics of the feminine.

• Personal and linguistic journey

The place of language in my research took shape through my participation in the journal *Tel quel*,[2] which saw language as a revolutionary possibility. But the role of language in my life is also in unison with the place Freud gave language as an instrument of speech that enables us not just to communicate but to question ourselves, our identities and those of others and to rebuild ourselves. Bion speaks of transformation; in 1968, we called it revolution. Language as a possible transformation of human subjectivity is a notion found in Judaism under the term *Teshuvah*, return, response, anamnesis and rebuilding.

I have made these concepts my own in the light of my biography. When you are a psychoanalyst, you know how much you owe to the memory you have of your life. I wrote *Je me voyage: A Journey Across Borders and Through Identities* (Kristeva 2016), an intellectual autobiography in the form of interviews with a psychologist, Samuel Dock. In this book, I talk about the journey within oneself, while travelling across all disciplines.

Perhaps something was triggered in me when I was a child in Bulgaria, where I was born, two days after the Nazis declared war on the USSR, on 24 June 1941.

I think of myself as someone who survived, not in the morose sense of surviving distress and death but in terms of the energy it takes to get through the ordeals. There was the war, the bombing, the economic difficulties, Stalingrad, Berlin, the Red Army, Yalta and Bulgaria, which was initially allied with the Germans but then turned communist. My parents were not communists, my father was a believer and my mother a Darwinian biologist. My parents taught us that memory can be appropriated through books and knowledge, that one can survive irrespective of the regime. My openness to books and languages, French, Russian and English, meant that language was not a schema, a grid, an ego ideal, but a possible life that

DOI: 10.4324/9781003342502-12

involved the body. I copied page after page of Voltaire's philosophical dictionary, Rousseau's *[Du] contrat social*, Diderot's texts, etc. The French literary language was particularly in tune with 18th century philosophy, to which I had been exposed before arriving in Paris, and at the same time, with the Russian and French surrealist and formalist movements that used language as a means of transforming social ties, targeting not only the class struggle but also the way of thinking.

I did my doctoral thesis on the 19th century avant-garde, on Mallarmé and Lautréamont, in order to interpret the difficult, hermetic French language of these authors who wanted to use language to explode conventional codes—"books are bombs", as Mallarmé put it. This whole transformation of the human order and social ties through language was the subject of my doctoral thesis, *La Révolution du langage poétique*.

At that time, around 1968, Derrida, Barthes and Goldmann took post-Hegel, in other words phenomenology, as their starting point. On the horizon of phenomenology, conception implied an upheaval of language. Husserl, with the transcendental ego, alongside the Cartesian ego, or logical ego, considers that there is an antepredicative sphere, made up of passions, drives and sensations that underlie reasoning, conception.

Thanks to Sollers too, I read Nietzsche, attended Lacan's seminar and discovered Freud. So my thesis on poetic language led to Husserl but also to psychoanalysis, Freud and Melanie Klein, to the unconscious and the drives.

From then on, I had an entire philosophical and linguistic conceptual framework that brought me closer to Freud. It was at that point that I decided to undergo psychoanalysis and become a psychoanalyst. This is the path I started on, based on the idea of the social role of language and therefore of psychoanalysis.

• Psychoanalysis and humanism

Since the Enlightenment, we have broken with the religious tradition, and this has been called secularization or *laïcité* in France. Freud's work is part of this break, but although he was an atheist, he never forgot the role of religious experience, as his anthropological texts show. Freud's approach teaches us that probing the unconscious does not mean denying religious and spiritual experience, but it can offer a kind of elucidation of it. And the experience of transference may be seen as a way of rebuilding the inner self in all its complexity, which, in my opinion, is the only way of resisting today's robotization and transhumanism. Faced with the crises we are going through—industrial, health, economic, climatological—the rebuilding of humanism is a necessity, not as a denial of religious experience, which remains what people cling to in times of crisis, but as an elucidation of inner suffering.

Psychoanalysis and human sciences are all actors that can and must play a role in rebuilding humanism, to help human beings get through the crisis and go beyond the programmatic approach.

In *The Philosophy of Julia Kristeva* (Beardsworth 2020), a major American book on my work written by 36 researchers in different disciplines, several authors, including psychoanalysts,[3] examined the concept of maternal *reliance* in relationship to *abjection* which I developed in *Powers of Horror* (Kristeva 1982/1980). Abjection refers to the child's separation from the mother in a movement of tension, violence and destructiveness where, as yet, there is no subject or object. But this *reliance* also permits the emergence of language with the negative force that Freud (1925h), in his article "Negation", recognized as being fundamental to psychic development because it makes representation possible. "It's Mummy and yet it is not her. I can name her but it's not her. I love Mummy and yet I don't love her". In this movement of tension between presence and absence, the naming arises under the pressure of the negative or destructive drive.

In this book, *The Philosophy of Julia Kristeva*, it was also noted that this type of notion, the *abject* in maternal *reliance*, helps to build a bridge between biology and behaviourism on the one hand—which are interested in the foundations of language at the biological and neuronal level—and the philosophical or linguistic study of language on the other. But we do not have the dynamics of the construction of subjectivity between the two, neuronal biology and philosophical thought. Now some authors and analysts[4] see my work on abjection, which follows in the footsteps of Freud, Klein and others, as a way of moving beyond this binary approach to the human being, biology versus the human sciences.

Our work as psychoanalysts enables us to think about our humanity in a more sensitive way and to accompany the emotional movements of our patients, who find themselves compressed, confined, repressed, denied, exasperated or even radicalized. This boiling pot of inner sensations, affects and passions challenges the need to understand that which constitutes the effort of *reliance*.

What I mean by *maternal reliance* is not the promotion of an idyllic, perfect mother who adapts to everything to satisfy the demands of society. It is also a mother who can be exposed to flaws, violence and inner madness. At the same time, this mother has the role of introducing language into the child's life, making it a mind game that allows the child to be him or herself.

It is this community of researchers and psychoanalysts that we are, with all our differences, that seems to me to be part of a social contribution. Perhaps we don't see it as such because psychoanalysis, as we know, is devalued. But I think that as psychoanalysts we are doing work that is personally useful and socially necessary. And if we don't say so, who will?

• The enigma of the feminine

I think this concept needs to be handled very carefully. I am an atypical feminist. Some feminists see my ideas as essentialist. I believe that the feminine exists, and I explore all its complexity and its aptitude for transformation.

The liberation movements triggered by the French Revolution—proletarians/bourgeois, third world/colonization/decolonization, women/men—are marked by a polarized way of thinking that believes that freedom emerges from a binary confrontation.

Faced with these tendencies, we are also witnessing a fragmentation of the social fabric, and a so-called archipelization of community ties, due in part to the effects of digital technology. Beyond the activist battles for the respect of rights, we need to ask ourselves about the meaning of this dispersal, this crumbling of affirmed identities, where we feel neither male nor female but transgender—and this can also manifest itself in the renunciation of sexuality, in a kind of ego affirmation, where we are completely untouchable and unthinkable. Faced with this, there is the binary thinking of the war of the sexes.

Between binarism and crumbling, the feminine, as I understand it, seeks to slip into psychic bisexuality or gender. This is a very sensitive area. I think that psychoanalysis is precisely the field that has the power to escape binarism on the one hand, and fragmentation on the other, and thus to open up other possibilities for thinking about sexual difference. I would go even further than that: This sexual difference is to be considered as being the essential problem. I developed this question in the opening speech of the IPA conference on the feminine (Kristeva 2019),[5] in which I concluded that heterosexuality is the problem.

But long before that conference, I had addressed the question of the feminine outside psychoanalysis proper. To avoid confining the feminine to a sexual category, I wanted to approach it from the point of view of singularity. So I worked on the singularized female *genius*, in other words, the singularity of a few women: Klein, Arendt and Colette, a psychoanalyst, a philosopher and a writer.

Then I looked at the question of the feminine from a psychoanalytical point of view, and I worked a lot on the double female Oedipus.

I have developed the notion of the primary feminine Oedipus (Kristeva 2000/1996), partly as Freud describes it, that is the Oedipus of loving attraction, of the libidinization and eroticization of the bond between child and mother, and, in particular, between the little girl and her mother. This Oedipus refers to an intense primary homoeroticism. This can be either an enamoured identification or a violent rejection, or even both at the same time on the part of both partners.

We often hear very violently on the couch about the hysteric's infinite wars with her mother, battles that manifest themselves on different subjects—passion, money, inheritance—where everything is mobilized, ideals and anality, in great violence and anger. It is exhausting for the person who cannot successfully negotiate this first encounter with a first otherness—it is not the only one, but it is the first—which takes place first through the relationship with the mother, the *maternal reliance*.

Then there is an intermediate position, which I have developed (Kristeva 1987/1983, 1987/1985, 1993/1985) although it has not been discussed much, that of the father of individual prehistory which Freud refers to on several occasions in his work (Freud 1912–1913, 1921c, 1923b, 1939a). In *The Ego and the Id* (1923b, 31) in particular, he considers this imaginary father as an *immediate and object-less* primary identification. In his view, this identification is necessary for building the ego ideal. Freud postulates that this preoedipal paternal possesses the qualities of both parents. It is therefore a complex paternity that is also a maternity situated between a dual and a tertiary relationship, an extremely important position for the construction of the feminine, which allows us to recognize the opposition between the invasive maternal dimension and the Oedipal father.

This *father of prehistory* exists as both feminine and masculine. Freud noted that bisexuality is more pronounced in women, probably because of this cathexis of the primary Oedipus with the mother and of this ideal imaginary father with whom *I* identify as the dawn of the ego ideal. Then comes the Oedipal father of the law who says, "No, you're not going to sleep with your mother. You're going to learn the laws of the city and be top of your class."

If a woman masters this process successfully, the result is a subject of great maturity. Negotiating the psychic traversal of the two Oedipuses successfully means not falling into exaggerated hysteria, feverish melancholia or the false self that wreaks havoc. If a woman is capable of doing all this, she will reach a maturity of the feminine that is emerging in the third millennium where women are on all fronts of society, in health, politics, astrophysics. This feminine revolution involves subjectivizing the three stages I have just mentioned. And I would like to cite here Simone de Beauvoir's (1952/1949) famous phrase, "One is not born a woman, one becomes one." One becomes one if society is willing to recognize us, but also if one is able to complete this whole journey in three stages. That's why I think that one is not born a woman, but *I* become one, because when you make this journey, you can say *I. I* can be this transformative singularity.

The feminine is like the quantum notion of the Higgs boson. Just as the latter is elusive but indispensable for the existence of matter, so the feminine is elusive but indispensable for the psychic life of both sexes. There is the transformative feminine through three stages, which I have just explained, and there is the feminine of both sexes. In a heterosexual couple, there are at least four components. There can be no subject without otherness. Singularity only exists in coexistence with the other.

This brings me back to heterosexuality as a recent invention. Of course, there have always been couples, but not in the modern sense of the term, namely, the loving encounter of two individuals of either sex. As Lévi-Strauss (1969/1949) has shown, women have always been an object of exchange for men, not a "*hetero*sexual" object that is different and faces someone else. Benveniste (2016/1969) has also clearly shown that marriage between men and women is a late institution in Latin legislation in which the woman is considered as the mother. It was not until the troubadours of the Middle Ages that it was considered socially possible for a woman and a man to fall in love. In the 19th century, Romanticism recognized women as sexual objects and desiring objects, not just objects of pleasure for men. Finally, in the 20th century, thanks to the existentialist movement, we arrive at *The Second Sex* (de Beauvoir 1952/1949), where women could claim their rights and try to achieve parity. Here again, the recognition of *hetero*sexuality as an encounter with the other was the fruit of a long and fragile journey. I often quote this phrase by Alfred de Vigny (1963/1864), taken up by Proust, "The two sexes will die estranged from one other." I hope that Freud will preserve us from this early death and that there will be varieties with multiple, creative identities.

With the notion of psychic bisexuality, the late Freud (1930a, 1931b, 1933a) tried to combine this discovery with the theory of drives. He opened up the question that the 21st century would take up. But he was already wondering about the social place that this bisexuality might take when he asked Marie Bonaparte the question, "What does a woman want?" In asking this question, he was not concerned with female sexuality or the sexual particularity of the feminine, but rather with what women wanted in the social sphere and what they wanted to contribute to the symbolic and political spheres. Freud sketched out avenues that we must continue to develop if we are to understand all the sexual uncertainties and questions of today.

Notes

1 This text is a written transcription of excerpts from an oral interview conducted in 2021 by Marianne Persinne for the Paris Psychoanalytical Society (SPP). https://www.spp. asso.fr/vimeo-video/julia-kristeva
2 An avant-garde journal founded by Philippe Sollers in 1960 in which the French intellectual and literary elite published contributions.
3 B. Brusset, J. L Baldacci, R. Balsam, R. Boué-Widawsky.
4 See the articles by B. Brusset and J.-L. Baldacci in *The Philosophy of Julia Kristeva* (Beardsworth 2020).
5 51st IPA Congress, London, 2019, "Prelude to an Ethics of the Feminine".

References

Beardsworth, S. (Ed.) (2020) *The Philosophy of Julia Kristeva. The Library of Living Philosophy*, Vol. 26. Chicago, IL: Open Court Books.
Benveniste, E. (2016/1969). *Dictionary of Indo-European Concepts and Society*. Chicago: HAU Books.
Beauvoir, S. de (1952/1949). *The Second Sex*. New York, NY: Knopf.
Freud, S. (1912–1913). *Totem and Taboo. S. E.*, 13. London: Hogarth, pp 1–161.
Freud, S. (1921c). *Group Psychology and the Analysis of the Ego. S. E.*, 18, pp. 69–143.
Freud, S. (1923b). *The Ego and the Id. S. E.,* 19. London: Hogarth, pp. 3–66.
Freud, S. (1925h). "Negation". *S. E.*, 19. London: Hogarth, pp. 235–239.
Freud, S. (1930a). *Civilization and Its Discontents. S. E.*, 21. London: Hogarth, pp. 57–146.
Freud, S. (1931b). "Female sexuality". *S. E.*, 22. London: Hogarth, pp. 112–135.
Freud, S. (1933a). *New Introductory Lectures on Psycho-Analysis* (Lecture XXXIII: "Femininity"). *S. E.*, 22. London: Hogarth, pp. 112–135.
Freud, S. (1939a). *Moses and Monotheism. S. E.*, 23, London: Hogarth, pp. 1–138.
Kristeva, J. (1982/1980). *Powers of Horror*. New York: Columbia University Press.
Kristeva, J. (1987/1983). *Tales of Love*, New York: Columbia University Press.
Kristeva, J. (1987/1985) *In the Beginning was Love, Psychoanalysis and Faith*. New York: Columbia University Press.
Kristeva, J. (1993/1985). *New Maladies of the Soul*. New York: Columbia University Press.
Kristeva, J. (2000/1996). *The Sense and Non-Sense of Revolt*. New York: Columbia University Press.
Kristeva, J. (2016). *Je me voyage*. Paris: Fayard. [Translated as: "Je me voyage: A journey across borders and through identities". In: *The Philosophy of Julia Kristeva*, ed. S. Beardsworth. Chicago, IL: Open Court Publishing (2020), pp. 1–151.]
Kristeva, J. (2019). *Prelude to an Ethics of the Feminine*, Plenary Speech at the IPA Congress, London 2019. (www.kristeva.fr/prelude-to-an-ethics-of-the-feminine.html)
Levi-Strauss, C. (1969/1949). *The Elementary Structures of Kinship*. Boston, MA: Beacon Press.
Vigny, A. de (1963/1864). "La colère de Samson". In: *Les Destinées*. Paris: Minard.

Chapter 13

Conversation with Laurie Laufer

Abstract

Laurie Laufer addresses the questions of power that the LGBTQIA+ community raises for psychoanalysis inasmuch as they call into question the relevance of psychoanalytic rules as possible sources of discrimination or domination.

• Could you describe the intellectual and personal journey that led you to psychoanalysis?

Literature was one of my first loves. I studied literature and I would have liked to teach literature, but one does not always decide on the course one's life takes. I came across psychoanalysis at a time of family bereavement, when I was going through painful experiences. Today, I don't know what I would have done without this adventure, without this encounter. And yet, I am still an avid reader of fiction and poetry. I have tried fiction and I ventured to write a few children's books; the attempt was amusing but not conclusive. Then I started an analysis when my father died, which echoed the death of my brother ten years before. This analysis was one of the greatest adventures of my life. A few years later I resumed my studies in clinical psychology at what was then the University of Paris 7, now Paris City University. I presented my doctoral thesis "From the enigma of mourning to the work of burial: the psychopathology of loss". Pierre Fédida was my supervisor. This doctoral thesis was my way of saying something about the bereavements I had experienced.

My training is therefore that of a clinical psychologist and an analysand. When I was studying psychology at the University of Paris 7, what triggered my clinical reflections on exclusion, discrimination and oppression was above all the question of AIDS, of the social and subjective treatment of AIDS. At university, I was often surprised, and even offended, by the normative, moralizing remarks I heard from certain teachers. Text commentaries seemed to me to be nothing more than refrains, conventional discourses, almost automatic, without any real critique or historicization of the concepts being possible; a sort of permanent self-reference. Psychoanalysis was repeated and commented on using its own vocabulary. In my academic career, I had the opportunity of doing a two-year placement at the Salpêtrière

DOI: 10.4324/9781003342502-13

hospital, in Professor Bricaire's infectious diseases department. At the time there was no tritherapy. It was the 1990s, and tritherapy appeared in France in 1992. So I worked in a department where there were people who were homosexuals and drug addicts. There were also many African women. All of them had contracted AIDS, and at the time, this epidemic was very stigmatized and stigmatizing. I then became aware of something quite strange: There was a gap, almost a dissociation, between what I was learning at university and the clinical reality. I asked myself this question: "But what are we talking about?" On the one hand, there was the academic point of view, and on the other, the clinical reality, the clinical "real" (*réel*). Every day, when I arrived at the Salpêtrière, this "real" jumped out at me and made me read on the doors of the patients' rooms: "deceased ... deceased ...". Sometimes there were just three letters: "DCD".

It was extremely violent. The way that some patients were able to talk about what was happening to them was overdetermined by problems of social violence, discrimination and homophobia. Sometimes they talked about rejection by their families and the impossibility of having the fact that they had had a partner for a long time recognized. The African women I met did not understand what was happening to them. They were excluded and stigmatized by those around them. I therefore asked myself the question: How can psychoanalysis survive in the social sphere if it is totally disconnected theoretically from what is happening in this reality?

• **Could you comment on any opportune encounters you had in your journey and training?**

One of the turning points in my academic career was my meeting with Pierre Fédida, a French psychoanalyst who was a figure in psychoanalytic phenomenology and who wrote books on absence, mourning and depression. Without his support and encouragement, my academic path would have taken a different course. My first encounter with his work was when I read *L'Absence* (Fédida 1978). I was a master's student at the time. I had never attended one of his lectures; I had only read lecture notes or heard recorded tapes. I was studying his texts and lectures in a work group that we had formed with several students. His research themes on mourning and his theoretical advances concerning analytic practice and technique gradually became essential echoes for me in my research and for my clinical practice. I then said to myself that an encounter with a research supervisor is also a matter of how it resonates, how it helps one to think. A research supervisor does not only allow one to direct or transmit knowledge but also to *become acquainted* with the knowledge that is being acquired. Pierre Fédida's thinking and writing made me associate and elaborate both in my clinical work and in my research. There are several authors who supported me during my research, with whom I was able to form, deform and transform my thoughts, always working on them again, keeping them ticking over. I learned from him that dreaming, thinking and writing are works of burial. I understood with him the importance of ghosts and survival. I dedicated my work to him when I presented my thesis on mourning and loss.

Then there was my meeting with Jean Allouch, who was analysed by Lacan and was one of the founders of the École lacanienne de psychanalyse (ELP) as well as of the EPEL book series, *Les grands classiques de l'érotologie moderne* (which publishes, among others, American queer authors such as David Halperin, Judith Butler, Lee Edelman, Leo Bersani, Gayle Rubin, etc.). These theoretical interconnections between Foucault and psychoanalysis were very innovative in the analytical field. Jean Allouch has been a friend for more than 15 years and his work has had a decisive influence on me, not only in my training but also in my way of practising psychoanalysis. I came across his book *Érotique du deuil au temps de la mort sèche* (Allouch 1995) when I was writing my thesis, which became the book, *L'énigme du deuil* (Laufer 2006). I discovered in it another psychoanalytical music, sensitive to the tones of historicization, critical of the authoritative effects of psychopathology, of intimidating psychiatrization, of normalizations and universal discourses. This music was familiar to me without my really knowing it and I encountered the tone I was looking for in psychoanalytical books. This tone and this music have accompanied me since then along with the joy of our friendship. It was he who, as early as 1998, said: "Either psychoanalysis will be Foucauldian or it will not" (Allouch 1998). If I have been able to highlight some points of interconnection between Foucault and psychoanalysis in the academic and university field, it is first of all to Jean Allouch that we owe the dialogue between Foucault and psychoanalysis, starting from the Freudian field itself, from psychoanalysis.

These are my epistemological and theoretical sources of inspiration, filiations, I daresay: Freud, Lacan, Foucault, Deleuze, Derrida, Allouch and, on the American side, Halperin, Rubin, Butler, de Lauretis, Bersani, Edelman, and Joan W. Scott. It is with these authors that I try to conceive of a certain form of psychoanalysis, freed from normalizing discourses or, at least, that knows how to recognize them and to shake them up. Among my encounters, I must of course mention Sandra Boehringer—without whom many things would not have been possible—who is deeply inspired by Greek and Roman antiquity and, in particular, one of the recognized specialists on sexuality in antiquity.

All these authors have been a source of inspiration in the way I practise clinically, from a critical perspective. I myself was analysed by a Lacanian analyst who was open to a reflexive epistemological approach to psychoanalysis.

• What is the cornerstone of your theoretical and clinical work?

I think that a certain form of psychoanalysis can support forms of emancipation, and the authors I have quoted help me to think about this question and are a cornerstone for me. The psychoanalysis that woke me up (from my dogmatic slumber, as the expression goes, and its melancholic byproducts) is neither ordered by a given meaning, nor by a hermeneutic, and even less an ontology or an anthropology, but by a certain joy of subjective invention. Joy is not the antonym of sadness. Joy is a certain dynamic of desire, an insurrection, as Georges Didi-Huberman (2019) would say in *Désirer désobéir. Ce qui nous soulève, 1*, or as Jean Allouch (2017) develops it. I also like to talk about reversal. With psychoanalysis there is a dimension of joy, wit and freedom that I think is not developed enough. Emancipation, in the Kantian sense of exit: "out of the state of tutelage". The possibility of emancipating oneself (with reflexivity as well), this is what Foucault and psychoanalysis have given me, including from any idea of liberation. This is how Foucault (1978/1976) ends *The Will to Knowledge.*

In *Studies on Hysteria*, Sigmund Freud (1895d, 305) replied to patients' objections: "[Y]ou will be able to convince yourself that much will be gained if we succeed in turning your hysterical misery into common unhappiness." This sentence has been used to give a romantic reading of the ordinary melancholia of existence. Accepting the commonness of our unhappy existence—such would have been the aim (is there one?) of analysis according to Freud. Yet in the last sentence of the *Studies on Hysteria*, Freud (ibid.) also writes: "With a mental life that has been restored to health, you will be better armed against that unhappiness." Freud calls for struggle, insurrection and emancipation from this "common unhappiness." For me, this is also what the analytic experience is about, what Jean Allouch or George Didi-Huberman call "insurrection", Jacques Rancière "emancipation", Judith Butler "trouble" and Michel Foucault "an aesthetic of existence"; in short, various forms of invention. It is a matter of "not letting oneself be governed so much", Foucault said of *dispositifs* (or apparatuses)—and I would like to draw inspiration from this: Don't let yourself be subjected by your own melancholia. Freud invites us, encourages us to struggle, to resist (*Wehr*). It is in this sense that I wanted to develop all this in my latest book *Vers une psychanalyse émancipée. Renouer avec la subversion* (Laufer 2022).

- **What is your theoretical approach to psychoanalytic practice (the couch, frequency, the setting, teletherapy, interpretation, silence)?**

My theoretical approach to practice is based on transference and the fundamental rule of free association.

- **What are your views on the transmission of psychoanalysis?**

Lacan (1979, 219–220) said, "As I am now coming to think of it, psychoanalysis is untransmissible. It's very tiresome. It is very tiresome that each psychoanalyst is forced—since he has to be forced—to reinvent psychoanalysis." It is undoubtedly through the invention of a certain style that escapes all normalization that psychoanalysis can find the paths of its transmission.

The question of teaching psychoanalysis and of research at the university is a vast and difficult one. Freud (1919j) had already written a text titled: "On the Teaching of Psycho-Analysis in Universities". He doubted that psychoanalysis could expect anything from universities (in my opinion, he was not entirely wrong!), but he did think that universities would gain (at the time, he was thinking in particular of the training of doctors who were reluctant to be taught anything but anatomy) from the contribution of psychoanalysis. Speaking of the medical student, Sigmund Freud said: "[F]or the purposes we have in view it will be enough if he learns something *about* psychoanalysis and something *from* it" (1919j, 173). "About" psychoanalysis and "from" it. This is why I think that all epistemological, critical and historical research on psychoanalysis and stemming from psychoanalysis can bring something to students, in short, a "psychoanalysis in extension" as Jacques Lacan said, or "open to revision" as Freud said. Universities do not train psychoanalysts, but a certain form of psychoanalysis at universities can train academics to be intellectuals. The specificity in France, contrary to other countries, is that psychoanalysis is taught in psychology departments.

Jacques Lacan (1965) offered this analysis:

A subject is a psychoanalyst, not a scholar who is tucked away behind categories in the midst of which he tries to make drawers in which he will have to arrange the symptoms that he registers of his patient, whether psychotic, neurotic or other, but insofar as he enters into the play of signifiers.

In short, the clinician's task is one of paying attention to the signifying chains, of hearing the associations, the echoes and the correspondences.

What does the clinician do with his or her knowledge, his or her supposed knowledge? Of course, the training that one receives in psychopathology, nosography and psychiatric semiology is necessary; I am not saying that we do not need this academic training, but it is not designed for clinical use with patients, or rather it is a language for use between ourselves that is not useful when one is listening to a speaking subject. I know that many would not agree with me: I believe that the meaning effects of diagnoses serve to reduce the anxiety of the practitioner, who is enveloped in knowledge that contains him or her when faced with the "reality of clinical practice" as it is customary today to say a little quickly. As Georges Lantéri-Laura (2012/1979) writes in his essential work on the historicization of the medical appropriation of the term perversion and its use, these discourses belong to "an imaginary construction in which science would be able to say everything about sexual behaviour". Yet, he writes, "there is no global science of sexual behaviour [...]. Culture wants to force knowledge to provide norms" (2012/1979, 180). All forms of universalization or globalization of knowledge about a particular form of behaviour or conduct are more related to the current knowledge of clinical sociology than to psychoanalysis. It is not a hierarchy of knowledge that I am advocating here, it is simply not the same practice.

- **What is your psychoanalytic approach to the societal debates on racial, gender identities or/and on the new forms of reproduction and parenting?**

There has been a lot of hurt and theoretical humiliation inflicted on people who did not have the right to speak and who were reduced to being an object of study or a clinical case. I am thinking of women, homosexuals, transgender people, intersex people and "the rest of us". As Gayle Rubin (1975, 47) has analysed so well, "[t]he battle between psychoanalysis and the women's and gay movements has become legendary". For Sigmund Freud (1905d), homosexuality is not a distinct category, but a variation of sexual function, which Gayle Rubin (1975) takes up in a new way by adding that there is an excess of significance given to sexuality and an obsession with sexual aetiology. From this perspective, she is Foucauldian. Freud constantly wanted to distance himself from any kind of orthosexuality; today, we would say from any kind of heteronormativity of desire or sexuality. As he points out, with the words of his time and the conceptual tools of his era, in a famous page of his monograph on Leonardo da Vinci: "[E]veryone, even the most normal person, is capable of making a homosexual object-choice, and has done so at some time in his life" (Freud 1910c, 99). For Freud (1905, 134), the question is that of "the Eros of the divine Plato", as he writes.

This is why Jacques Lacan was to speak of erotology to evoke analytical practice. It was a matter of conceiving of psychoanalysis freed from *scientia sexualis*.

The LGBTQIA+ community has been particularly stigmatized by the authoritarian theoretical deviations of certain psychoanalysts who combined the domination of discourses with the discrimination of subjectivities and sexualities. The analysis of power relations, of social relations of sex and gender, has facilitated the emergence of a critical field concerning the domination and oppression of populations, classes, racialized groups and minorities. The analysis of norms and discourses has made it possible to work on questions relating to discrimination against subjectivities, identities and sexualities. I believe that the practice of psychoanalysis cannot avoid the suffering caused by domination and discrimination. Of course, it is impossible to conceive of a world without domination, and power will always have a place. But here again I remain Foucauldian. Power will inevitably be in a certain place. The question is therefore how to deal with this power, how to resist it so that it becomes a capacity for action for the subject.

The way in which we can apprehend the problem of norms is then a matter of a position, of perspective, depending on whether we apprehend them as power or as potential, as a subjugating agent or as a transforming agent. I am delighted today to see a young generation of psychoanalysts, academics and researchers, such as Beatriz Santos, Thamy Ayouch (2018), Fabrice Bourlez (2018), Nicolas Evzonas, Sophie Mendelsohn (Mendelsohn & Boni 2021), Stéphane Habib (2020), Lionel Le Corre (2017), Silvia Lippi and others probably whom I do not know, who are working on a critical epistemology of analytic theory from within its practice and who are perhaps making dialogue possible between gender studies, queer studies, critical theory, postcolonial studies and the epistemology of the bodies of knowledge they address in their work.

A psychoanalyst does not stand above the era he or she is living in, and I do not believe in illusory forms of neutrality. In my opinion, it is a question of returning to what Jacques Lacan said when he spoke of a certain renunciation of analytical practice: "Let whoever cannot meet at its horizon the subjectivity of his time give it up then" (Lacan 2006/1966, 264).

One of the interests of gender studies is to have politicised the question of psychoanalysis by putting back into perspective the importance of a denaturalization of "human nature" and, in its wake, of woman or man. The interest of the method is to think about categories that appear immutable and ahistorical, to demystify essentialism. Gender makes it possible to restore conflict, instability, hesitation and disquiet to the ways of apprehending male/female differences, feminine/masculine polarities, social hierarchies, fixed identities, so-called "natural" facts or even the uses and norms of disciplinary approaches, by means of a discursive analysis that questions imaginary boundaries. Linked to Jacques Derrida's notion of "undecidability", Judith Butler's notion of "trouble", Michel Foucault's "discursive analysis of disciplinary *dispositifs*", Joan W. Scott's notion of "insoluble dilemma" or Françoise Collin's "praxis of the unrepresentable", gender and sexual difference have a heuristic and epistemological function.

In short, by blurring the disciplinary and epistemological dividing lines that freeze knowledge, and by analysing the productions of discourse, this deconstruction of discourses cannot fail to have political effects. Since my training at Paris 7, I have always been sensitive to the discourses of authority that seemed to tell the truth about a particular form of behaviour and pathologized a particular form of behaviour. This seemed to me to run counter to what the field of analysis was for me. There were teachers when I was a student, who later became colleagues, who had written articles against the PACS (The Civil Solidarity Pact is a domestic partnership contract concluded between two adult persons, of different sex or the same sex), making it sound like the end of civilisation, who spoke of women or homosexuals or transsexuals in terms that I found inappropriate, sexist, devaluing, stigmatizing under the guise of theory and protected by supposedly authoritative discourses. Is a therapist a scientist or a police chief, a prosecutor? What are the dividing lines and categories that they draw through and in within their practice?

I have learned to think through, and in, my analytical experience. It seems to me that I have been through the anxieties that are necessary for thinking, the trials of doubt and sometimes of depersonalization, which undo the illusions of identity, which make one experience lures and deflate the inflation of the ego; I have been exposed to the tremors of transference love. I have experienced and become familiar with my areas of fragility and vulnerability and shed my ideals to some extent, while trying to discover what is possible for me. It is in and through my analytical experience that I have learned to hear better the stigmatizing and discriminating words that could be those of the public prosecutor or the police commissioner.

References

Allouch, J. (1995). *Érotique du deuil au temps de la mort sèche*. Paris: Epel.

Allouch, J. (1998). *La Psychanalyse, une érotologie de passage*. Paris: Epel/Cahiers de l'Unebévue.

Allouch, J. (2017). *La Scène lacanienne et son cercle magique. Des fous se soulèvent*. Paris: Epel.

Ayouch, T. (2018). *Psychanalyse et hybridité: Genre, colonialité, subjectivations*. Louvain: Leuven University Press.

Bourlez, F. (2018). *Queer psychanalyse. Clinique mineure et déconstruction du genre*. Paris: Hermann.

Didi-Huberman, G. (2019). *Désobéir, Désirer. Ce qui nous soulève*. Paris: Éditions de Minuit.

Fédida, P. (1978). *L'absence*. Paris: Gallimard.

Foucault, M. (1978/1976). *The History of Sexuality. Vol. 1, The Will to Knowledge*, trans. R. Hurley. London: Random House.

Freud, S. (1895d). *Studies on Hysteria. S. E.* 2. London: Hogarth.

Freud, S. (1905d). *Three Essays on the Theory of Sexuality. S. E.* 7. London: Hogarth, pp. 123–243.

Freud, S. (1910c). *Leonardo da Vinci and a Memory of his Childhood. S. E.* 11. London: Hogarth, pp. 57–137.

Freud, S. (1919j). "On the teaching of psycho-analysis in universities". *S. E.* 17. London: Hogarth, pp. 171–173.

Habib, S. (2020). *Faire avec l'impossible. Pour une relance du politique*. Paris: Agora.

Lacan, J. (1965). *Book XII: Crucial Problems for Psychoanalysis*. Unpublished seminar book.

Lacan, J. (2006/1966). "The function and field of speech and language in psychoanalysis". In: *Écrits*, trans. Bruce Fink. New York: W. W. Norton, pp. 197–268.

Lacan, J. (1979). "9th Congress of the École freudienne de Paris on 'Transmission'", *Lettres de l'École*, 25 (2), pp. 219–220.

Lantéri-Laura, G. (2012/1979). *Lecture des perversions. Histoire de leur appropriation médicale*. Paris: Economica.

Laufer, L. (2006). *L'énigme du deuil*. Paris: Presses Universitaires de France.

Laufer, L. (2022). *Vers une psychanalyse émancipée. Renouer avec la subversion*. Paris: La Découverte.

Laufer, L. (2022). *Vers une psychanalyse émancipée. Renouer avec la subversion*. Paris: La Découverte.

Le Corre, L. (2017). *L'Homosexualité de Freud*. Paris: Presses Universitaires de France.

Mendelsohn, S. & Boni, L. (2021). *La vie psychique du racisme*. Paris: La Découverte.

Rubin, G. (1975). "The traffic in women: Notes on the 'political economy' of sex". In: *Deviations*, ed. G. Rubin. Durham & London: Duke University Press, 2011, pp. 33–65.

Chapter 14

Conversation with Clotilde Leguil

Abstract

Clotilde Leguil, who trained as a Lacanian, reaffirms the role of interpretation in the treatment as a search for the truth of the enigma of desire. Based on this conception of enigmatic desire, and a critique of norms, she takes a nuanced approach to the complex notions of consent and gender.

- **Could you describe the intellectual and personal journey that led you to psychoanalysis?**

I was fortunate enough to encounter psychoanalysis at the age of 25, when I was finishing my philosophy studies in Paris. My intellectual curiosity had already been awakened by my philosophy teachers because references to Freud are present in the philosophy classes of the final year of high school in France. It is often the moment when one has the opportunity of hearing about Freud for the first time, and this can leave traces. For my part, I will never forget my first reading of Freud at the age of 17. I immersed myself in *The Interpretation of Dreams* (Freud 1900a). I had the impression that the key to the world was in this book. I asked myself: "But what is this psychic reality that Freud is talking about?" I wanted to know in what way it was something real. Then, Lacan's *Seminar, Book II* on the ego (Lacan 1991/1978) was the first one I read at the age of 18, following a course given by my teacher in preparatory classes for the grandes écoles on Pascal's ego, reread by Lacan. These were the first small pebbles placed on my path, which initiated something in me. And then it is also true that some works by Freud, and also by Bruno Bettelheim, were in my mother's library.

But the real encounter was that of the analytical experience itself, at the age of 25, at a time when I was going through a life ordeal in the face of which I felt I was capsizing. Mourning a parent is an ordeal that makes one lose one's footing and faces one with the experience of lack, not only with one's own lack, but with the lack of the place that one occupies in the desire of another person. As Lacan (2014/2004, 141) says, one is in mourning for another of whom one can say, "I was his lack." This sentence gradually took root in me during my analysis. It was the question of symbolic heritage that led me to analysis—the question of the obscure legacy

DOI: 10.4324/9781003342502-14

("*legs*" (Lacan 2021, 75)) left by the words, the misunderstandings, the aborted desires, the "censored chapter" (Lacan 2006/1953, 215) of history, the "mumbling" (Lacan 2021, 75) of our ancestors. This ordeal of life—experienced as a moment when there is a "trespassing of death on life" as Lacan (1992/1986, 194) says—was transmuted into a desire to speak, a desire to experience speech in analysis.

I had also reached a point in my life when my philosophical training—after the *agrégation* in philosophy and the École normale supérieure (ENS)[1]—was no longer sufficient to answer the question of my desire. I had a strong taste for concepts, for 20th century French philosophy in particular—the philosophy of Sartre and of Merleau-Ponty—but I also felt uneasy about the powerlessness of this knowledge to orient me in matters of love and the relationship to loss. I met my first analyst, who was a Freudian. Then I came up against what was no longer a matter of asphyxiated speech but of repetition. I could not get rid of this legacy, the mark of which was on my body. The "*legs*" is an expression of Lacan's that I am taking up today from what psychoanalysis has taught me. Lacan (2021, 74) says of our body that "it is the fruit of a lineage, and a large part of your misfortunes lies in the fact that your lineage was swimming in misunderstanding as long as it could". What is bequeathed to us is always, in short, a misunderstanding of our being.

When I encountered Lacanian psychoanalysis, I realized that, through the reading of signifiers and the cut, it offered a different practice that touched on another dimension of the symptom. I then undertook a long analysis with a Lacanian psychoanalyst from the École de la Cause freudienne (ECF), who had himself completed his analysis with a psychoanalyst analysed by Lacan. It was an unforgettable experience, full of surprises and also ethical rigour. A desire—one that had always been there—was finally able to emerge and my life took on a completely different turn. It was a real breath of fresh air! This inevitably had consequences for my relationship with knowledge, the taste for which had been renewed in me thanks to this new impetus. It was at this point in my life that my first book, *Les Amoureuses* (Leguil 2008), was published. In this book, I was able to bring together two dimensions of what I had inherited: a questioning of femininity and love, and a passion for cinema. I took three film heroines, Lux Lisbon in Sofia Coppola's 1999 film *The Virgin Suicides*, Christa-Maria Sieland in Florian Henckel von Donnersmarck's 2006 film *The Lives of Others* and Diane Selwyn in David Lynch's 2001 film *Mulholland Drive*, and tried to interpret their journeys from the angle of the question of love. Writing this book was a step forward for me. It was about intimate matters, but I also found, through writing, a way of saying, by working on language, what was enigmatic for me. I made room for what had remained silent up until then. Through psychoanalysis and with Lacan, I found my own way of shedding light on what Freud (1926e, 212) called the "dark continent". I was moving into this continent, taking as my starting point the question of Lux's loss of virginity, the question of love in a totalitarian regime with Christa and the question of dreams and nightmares through Diane's confrontation with her fascination for Camilla Rhodes.

That was also when Lacan's (1992/1986, 319) famous aphorism took its place in my life: "Don't give ground relative to your desire". My commitment to the psychoanalytical movement was affirmed. I became a member of the ECF. My family history was marked by the emigration of my father, who had fled Hungary after the 1956 revolution, and this experience left its stamp on me in the form of an engaged or committed style. I began to write about the function of psychoanalysis in its time, that is, "here and now", affirming the breath of fresh air that the analytical interpretation of suffering brings in comparison with the cognitivist or scientistic reading. My first engaged articles (Leguil 2006) appeared in *L'Anti-Livre noir de la psychanalyse,* edited by Jacques-Alain Miller. I had been invited by my editor Monique Labrune to preface the new translations of Freud published by Le Seuil (Leguil 2010a, 2010b, 2010c, 2010d). At the same time as my desire was letting go of what was blocking it—symbolic conflicts and imaginary fixations—the movement of life accelerated. I continued my analysis beyond this emergence of desire because the question of the end of the analysis was an enigma that I wanted to decipher. And then, I'm not the kind of person to stop before the end of the journey. There was a moment of disarray. Something wasn't getting through, and yet it could no longer be told through history. I experienced this through a dream that I called "the dream of the severed tongue", a dream that I talk about in my essay *Céder n'est pas consentir* ("Giving in is not consenting") (Leguil 2021). The last two years with a third analyst condensed the long analysis I had done, and I was able to touch the umbilical point that remained. It was a matter of coming to terms with a loss, but this time it no longer involved an event in my history but a relationship to saying and the body. The outcome was a happy event!

The end of my analytical journey also had an impact on my way of reading Lacan, of being sensitive to his remarks on language and the letter, on the real and the body, which had remained foreign to me for a long time. I taught differently, by becoming even more engaged in my enunciation. I could allow myself to interpret Lacan, his formulations, his theses and his obscure phrases; thanks to the thread that analysis had enabled me to draw on, I could now stumble too and still not know. This also transformed my practice. Thanks to the analysis, a new and more assertive style, informed by sensitivity to the language of the other, gradually emerged in me; and above all, desire freed from anxiety.

• Could you comment on any opportune encounters you had in your journey and training?

Psychoanalysis is indeed a story of encounters, of *kairos*, of chance events that push us here and there and end up forming a web. While I was doing my analysis, I met professors at the Department of Psychoanalysis at the University of Paris 8 Vincennes-Saint-Denis—where I have been teaching for ten years now as a professor—who introduced me to Lacan's work. It was a place of encounters with a discourse and a style, driven by the desire to transmit Lacan. I acquired clinical experience by following the clinical conversations of Éric Laurent at the Sainte-Anne Hospital; he himself had been analysed by Lacan and had followed his presentations. The encounter with madness being a matter of speech and language opened my eyes to the distinction between the symbolic, the imaginary and the real. And then a decisive encounter in my life occurred in 1999: I started to attend Jacques-Alain Miller's seminar, *The Lacanian Orientation*, in the Department of Psychoanalysis at Paris 8, and continued to do so until 2011. This conceptual training was crucial. Links between desire and the relationship to knowledge were forged there. I then did a doctorate on Lacan's little-known relationship with existentialism, supervised by my professor at ENS, Pierre-François Moreau—an eminent specialist in Spinoza, but also in epistemology and the history of ideas. An indication by Jacques-Alain Miller, in his course during the year 1999, distinguishing between the Sartrean subject of the *lack of being* and the subject divided by the Lacanian Other, sowed a seed of desire in me. It was actually a sentence he uttered in his lecture of 17 March 1999 that was the starting point for my doctoral work:

> In other words, when in 1966, in the *Écrits*, Lacan celebrates his 1953 text, "The function and field of speech and language" as introducing the question of the subject in psychoanalysis, this subject is founded in existentialism and at the same time it is a break with any kind of philosophy of consciousness.
>
> (Miller 1998–1999)

It fascinated me to read Lacan from the standpoint of this paradox of being able to borrow the concept of the subject from existentialist philosophy while reinvesting it in the service of the unconscious. It was this thread, which was related to my own long-standing question concerning the subject, that I explored in my research. After my doctorate, I was invited to give a public talk at Jacques-Alain Miller's last course, in May 2011, on the question of being in Lacan's work.[2] This was a great honour for me. My doctorate on Lacan, which became a book, published under the title *Sartre with Lacan* (Leguil 2012) deals with the way Lacan read Sartre, used him, and put his existential concepts such as those of subject, lack and desire, in the service of psychoanalysis. It is a Lacan beyond Sartre.

I would add that the art dimension is also very important to me. I am the daughter of a filmmaker. I have been immersed in the language of film since my early childhood. This is also a story of encounters. At the very beginning of my analysis, I discovered in Rome, in the gardens of the Villa Medici, the netted statues by the French artist Annette Messager—I had the feeling that I was thus caught in nets, prevented from moving, like these statues that seemed to want to break free of these ties. I was able to grasp for the first time what Lacan meant by the *non-sexual relationship* after seeing David Lynch's 2001 film *Mulholland Drive*. After a performance of Visconti's 1969 film *The Damned,* adapted by Ivo van Hove at the Comédie-Française in 2016, in a post-traumatic moment following the 2015 attacks in Paris, I was able to open my eyes to a blind spot in my speech. At the very end of my analytical journey, a painting appeared in a dream that I named *The Night Watch* after Rembrandt. I have an unconscious that is very much in love with art.

• What is the cornerstone of your theoretical and clinical work?

The question of interpretation is at the heart of Lacanian practice and therefore of my practice. A word, a silence or a cut are different modalities of interpretation, relating to the enigma of truth and the inexpressible dimension of the real. Interpretation introduces an enigma into the heart of saying and awakens the subject's desire to decipher what they say. The cornerstone of my theoretical and clinical work is therefore interpretation and its change of regime in the course of the analysis: interpretation of the truth of desire, as the first regime, and then interpretation that makes the dimension of the real visible and allows the traces of trauma to be read, as the second regime. Involvement in supervision with two psychoanalysts from the ECF is fundamental here. The logic of the case is extracted from the supervision, based on the singularity of the subject encountered, from the always unprecedented character of his suffering and his utterances. I began to receive my first patients after about ten years of analysis at a breakthrough moment in my analytical journey—although my training as a philosopher had already been completed by training as a clinical psychologist. I felt that I had arrived at a point where my relationship to speech, listening and silence had been transformed.

I also think of my teaching activity as a process of working-through, a crossing that takes a question that I consider to be a crucial problem for psychoanalysis in the 21st century as its starting point. In 2021, I wanted to work on feminine jouissance because this Lacanian approach is relevant to contemporary gender issues. I gave my seminar the title "Feminine jouissance, between obedience and disobedience", and I tried to respond from Lacan's perspective to the Simone de Beauvoir of the second volume of *The Second Sex*, which deals with "the lover". I believe that this was a truly innovative year of work for me and for my students on the question of consent. How far can consent go in the name of love? What is the forcing that can lead someone to letting themselves be pushed around to the point of mistreating their desire? These are contemporary issues, both in clinical work and in civilization.

I also gave a course following the end of my analysis that I entitled "Untying the knots of destiny", because it appeared to me that destiny was too often considered as being reduced to anatomy. However, in psychoanalysis, destiny, with Lacan, takes on different meanings, which can be explored in the experience of analysis from the standpoint of the interpretation of saying (*dire*), in order to better free ourselves from this *obscure legacy*. This presupposes a practice of interpretation that leads to something initially said that marked the subject without him knowing it. This question of destiny affects each of us. In the "here and now" in which we find ourselves, in a world weakened by the pandemic, in a Europe where war has returned, it is crucial to make room for psychic destiny, for the traces of the great migrations and the waves of history in our personal lives.

- **What is your theoretical approach to psychoanalytic practice (the couch, frequency, the frame, teletherapy, interpretation, silence)?**

Psychoanalytical practice is, first of all, an experience of speech within which *empty speech* and *full speech* are distinguished (Lacan 2006/1956, 206). This is a first orientation. In my opinion, it is more important than the couch/face-to-face distinction. Conversing is not enough, it is a matter of making one's way towards a particular way of speaking, of speaking in one's own name, of saying what one did not know. This speech then has a dimension of revelation through interpretation. One must know how to let the empty speech that comes from the ego, nourishing narcissism, anxiety and aggressiveness, die out. This distinction implies being interested in the place "where speech comes from" (Lacan 2006b, 386). I like Lacan's formula very much, because today we are concerned with the question of "where we speak from", but from the angle of a logic of identity assignment. But with Lacan, the place "where I speak from" is to do with "where speech comes from". This leads us to interest ourselves in another place of origin of speech than identity with oneself. This implies listening that is situated at the very level of the signifiers, listening that is capable of picking up on slips of the tongue and equivocations. The performative aspect in analysis is the speech that I utter insofar as it comes from another place, insofar as it makes me other to myself. It is this speech that realises being.

The guiding thread of the analytical experience is therefore the unconscious as experience. This is what distinguishes psychoanalysis from psychotherapy and of course from all psychology. I am always happy to note that the interpretation of dreams remains the "royal road" (Freud 1900a, 608) to the unconscious. Dreams, slips of the tongue and stumbling blocks in speech trip up the discourse of the ego, which is narcissistic and rationalizing, and always introduce a new dimension, that of a subject who speaks from another place. It is marvellous, this field of dreams that survives in the 21st century, "here and now", in spite of the domination of science over the body and intimacy, in spite of the virtual world that offers another path of escape but often locks the subject into a mass narcissism.

Weekly frequency, regularity and commitment to the analysis are essential conditions. Once the transference has allowed interpretation to operate, the process has begun. Analysands who do analytic work two or three times a week also progress more quickly. The pandemic and the lockdowns to which we were subjected led me to offer consultations by telephone. The work was able to continue in a genuine way with the voice as the point of address of speech. During telephone sessions, I noticed that analysands had had dreams, that thoughts were emerging, and that there was a pressing urge to talk about them to the analyst. Personally, I do not do Skype consultations. Whatever happens, physical presence is necessary at some point, and remote practice deserves to be circumscribed.

• What is your conception of the transmission of psychoanalysis?

Transmission is at the heart of my commitment to psychoanalysis. This requires encounters that also involve bodies and not just the virtual world. Psychoanalysis will be lost if there are no more real encounters. I like teaching, and in particular immersing myself with my students in the paths of analysis based on reading Lacan. Psychoanalysis is not transmitted as a tradition, a discipline or a technique, but as a desire. The dimension of contingency, of *tuché*, of the encounter, is at the heart of the transmission of psychoanalysis. "Do as I do, don't imitate me", Lacan said. Psychoanalysis is not transmitted by imitation, but through a singular desire. The signifier of "light" stood out in my analytical journey as being central. Lighting was my father's profession in the cinema. I think that my analysis has allowed me to find my own way of shedding light on psychoanalysis based on my sensitivity and my intellectual rigour which comes from philosophy.

To hear another person speaking in a way that resonates with this experience, who knows how to read to the point of agreeing not to know, and who examines his own knowledge thoroughly in the light of Lacan's teaching is what constitutes transmission. The transmission of theory also involves the exigency of demonstration, clinical precision, the exploration of concepts, with regard to the experience itself. Jacques-Alain Miller's course, which I followed for ten years, had this effect of transmission on me. And of course, transmission also passes through the psychoanalytical association to which one belongs, which elicits a transference. As far as I am concerned, it is through my involvement with the ECF, by organizing study days, by participating in congresses and by directing reviews that I also work on transmitting what has been transmitted to me. Transmission has both a very singular and a very collective dimension.

• What, in your view, are the points of divergence between French psychoanalysis and English-speaking psychoanalysis?

By way of a response, I could start by referring to Lacan's own criticism in the 1950s of a kind of deviation of psychoanalysis under the effect of the requirements of adaptation specific to the American state of mind. English-speaking psychoanalysis was marked by the legacy of Anna Freud, who emphasized the analysis of defence mechanisms instead of the interpretation of speech. The reference to the ego replaced the reference to the unconscious. For my part, I wrote a short essay on the 2008 American series *In Treatment*, which I entitled *Lost in Therapy* (Leguil 2013), where I had fun showing how the practice of psychoanalysis depicted in this series was the antithesis of that advocated by Lacan. Moreover, the cognitive-behavioural approach seems to me to be predominant in the English-speaking world.

It comes back to us through language itself. We no longer speak of war trauma, as in Freud's time, but of PTSD, or post-traumatic stress disorder. The substitution of "stress" for anxiety is entirely symptomatic of an approach to symptoms in terms of disorder and dysfunction. This stifles the discourse of psychoanalysis. Lacan said that anxiety was "an affect of the subject". As long as we take the subject into consideration, the one who speaks, we can consider that the perspective of the unconscious is saved.

But there is another side which led Lacan to pay tribute to the English psychoanalysts of the 1950s in various seminars, for their clinical sense. Thanks to Lacan, I discovered and worked on Ella Sharpe, Joan Riviere, Margaret Little and Lucia Tower. There is a lot to learn from these women psychoanalysts, who have an extremely concrete approach to clinical practice, which I personally appreciate very much. Lacan said of them that, as women, they show a freer relationship to desire in their practice and that they are truer and more real. To come back to the "here and now", I was very sensitive to the reception given to my essay on consent, *Céder n'est pas consentir* (Leguil 2021), in the United States, within the framework of the Rutgers University in New York. I was able to appreciate the value of the Lacanian perspective on consent, which is a burning issue, highly topical, and too often approached from a purely contractualist perspective. There are also many schools of Lacanian psychoanalysis in Anglo-Saxon countries, such as the New Lacanian School. So I am certain that, provided Lacan's contribution is made to resonate in a nondogmatic way, the Lacanian approach to psychoanalysis can and must be transmitted there too, and that it will also do so thanks to this book.

- **What is your psychoanalytic approach to the societal debates on racial, gender identities or/and on the new forms of reproduction and parenting?**

I am passionate about the "here and now", about the times in which I live, about words that express subjective questioning in a new way, about what emerges here and now to express the discontents in civilisation. The question of consent[3] is at the heart of my work on love, trauma and female jouissance.

If I have worked on gender (Leguil 2015), it is because I have asked myself what distinguishes gender trouble in Judith Butler's work from the enigma of sexuality in Lacan's work. This led me to try to find a way out of the stereotypes concerning psychoanalysis. The critique of gender norms is perfectly legitimate, politically and socially. But it is also crucial to maintain the possibility of thinking about sexual identification, the relationship to the enigma of sex, as something other than a relationship to gender norms. Lacan said in the 1970s that there are "social norms for want of any sexual norm" (Lacan 1974, 7), that is to say that in matters of sexual life, desire, love and jouissance, no norm will make anxiety disappear. No norm will give an intimate meaning to the experience I may have of being confronted with a lack of knowledge. Just as becoming a mother does not depend on any knowledge, any method, any norm, but on a desire, which cannot be separated from the dimension of anxiety, encountering sexuality is to experience something that does not refer to any prior knowledge. I can, of course, cling to the discourses of my time, but I will not be able to do without invention. Each subject invents his way of identifying himself on the male side, on the female side and even of refusing these two sides.

Calling oneself gender-fluid can be a way of responding to anxiety, but also a way of separating oneself, a way of recognising oneself or a way of naming an enigma. What counts is to identify the function that a discourse may have for a subject.

Similarly, in terms of wanting a child, it is not the case that science can respond to new demands that the enigma of this desire, the enigma of becoming a father or mother, so the enigma does not remain. It remains an extraordinary, subjective event. Giving birth, giving life, adopting, recognizing and naming are acts that touch on the symbolic, imaginary and real dimensions at the same time. It transforms a person to occupy a new place with a child to whom he or she wishes to transmit. Here, we are in the performative dimension which involves a symbolic breakthrough. What we must not lose sight of is the dimension of desire as the foundation of the place from which a human being comes. A child does not come so much from a medically assisted procreation method as from a desire, the desire of those who wanted that child to come into the world. And this desire is not without misunderstanding. I always inherit an obscure legacy, which is "the misunderstanding which I come from" as Lacan said in 1980 (Lacan 2021, 75). Science will not change anything in this respect.

• What is your psychoanalytic approach to the current debates on gender identities or/and on the new forms of reproduction and parenting?

I am very interested in these questions because a few years ago I wrote an essay that I chose to call *L'être et le genre, homme/femme après Lacan* (Leguil 2015). But approaching these questions from the standpoint of analytical clinical practice implies ditching the belief in identity assignment or in the possibility of defining oneself in all transparency from a position of performative self-assertion. I would say that it is a discourse that can have different functions depending on the subject and that what matters is to preserve a place in a subject for questioning, for the enigma that they can become for themselves when they encounter a particular form of suffering. Defining oneself in terms of a gender identity can occupy a certain place in existence, but in analysis this is specifically traversed by interpretation. As soon as it is a matter of agreeing not to know what one thinks, of discovering also that one does not know what one is saying and basically of discovering through the practice of interpretation that one is different from what one thought one was, it is a case of letting go of the moorings of identity. This is also what I wanted to show in my essay *« Je », une traversée des identités* (Leguil 2018). Finally, another dimension of the performative is encountered in analysis, that of the assertion that escapes us and comes to signify something other than what we thought we were saying. In 1954, Lacan called this the *creative function of speech* (Lacan 1988/1975, 237), thus going beyond, and in advance of, Austin's notion of performative utterances defined in his book *How to Do Things with Words* (Austin 1962). This "saying" in analysis is the product of a process of speech that involves the deciphering of its history and in particular of the *censored chapter* of its history.

• Is there any other question that you would like to discuss?

Today, the critique of patriarchy, the question of gender fluidity, the transition from heterosexuality to homosexuality, or the change of object-choice, are part of the movement of the era and of mainstream discourse. But where it becomes interesting in analysis is when a subject is confronted with paradoxes, with contradictions, leading them to see that what they thought was clear and fluid is in reality confused for them. It is this dimension that Lacan called in 1980 "the obscurantism proper to speech" (Lacan 2021, 75). I believe that a place must be preserved for the obscurantism of speech, the enigma of destiny as a psychic destiny involving the relationship to desire and jouissance, the relationship to truth and the real, and the value of interpretation. While the psychoanalyst must be aware of "his function as interpreter in the strife of languages", as Lacan (2006/1953, 264) wrote, he (or she) is the one who can hear beyond the strife of languages a singular desire. There is therefore no question of turning one's back on the language spoken by an era. The practice of psychoanalysis has a place in its epoch, and we could also say that the epoch is part of psychoanalysis, insofar as it speaks a language that is always reinvented. But at the same time, psychoanalysis only survives if the place of the subject, of the enigma, and therefore of interpretation, is preserved. To seal off any enigma is to make the discourse on existence unbreathable.

Notes

1 *Agrégation* is a highly selective and competitive examination for teachers in France. The École normale supérieure (ENS) is one of the leading higher education institutions in France.
2 Available online: https://disparates.org/lun/2011/06/jam-15-juin/#more-2099
3 See https://abcpenser.com/notions/consentement/

References

Austin D. (1962). *How to Do Things with Words*, ed. J. M. Urmson, M. Sbisà. Oxford: Clarendon Press.
Freud, S. (1900a). *The Interpretation of Dreams*. S. E. 4–5. London: Hogarth.
Freud, S. (1926e). "A question of lay analysis". S. E. 20. London: Hogarth, pp. 183–258.
Lacan J. (1974). "Declaration to France Culture concerning the 28th Congress of The International Psychoanalytical Association". *Le Coq Héron*, 46/47: 3–8.
Lacan J. (1988/1975). *The Seminar of Jacques Lacan, Book I, Freud's Papers on Technique*, ed. J.-A. Miller, trans. J. Forrester. New York, NY: Norton & Co.
Lacan, J. (1991/1978). *The Seminar of Jacques Lacan, Book II. The Ego in Freud's Theory and in the Technique of Psychoanalysis, 1954–1955*, ed. J.-A. Miller, trans. S. Tomaselli. New York, NY: W. W. Norton & Co.

Lacan J. (2014/2004). *The Seminar of Jacques Lacan, Book X. Anxiety*, ed. J.-A. Miller, trans. A. R. Price. London: Cambridge: Polity Press.

Lacan, J. (2006/1953). "The function and field of speech and language in psychoanalysis". In: *Écrits*, trans. B. Fink. New York, NY: Norton & Co., pp. 197–268.

Lacan, J. (2006/1956). "The situation of psychoanalysis and the training of psychoanalysts in 1956". In: *Écrits*, trans. Bruce Fink. New York, NY: Norton & Co., pp. 384–411.

Lacan, J. (1992/1986). *The Seminar of Jacques Lacan, Book VII, The Ethics of psychoanalysis, 1959–1960*, ed. J.-A. Miller, trans. D. Porter. New York, NY: Norton & Co.

Lacan J. (2021). "Dissolution". In: *Aux confins du Séminaire*, ed. J.-A. Miller. Paris: La Divina, Navarin, pp. 44–77.

Leguil, C. (2006). "Être ou ne plus être, le sujet du XXIe siècle face à l'empire des neurosciences", and "Sur le cognitivisme, ou le langage de l'homme sans qualités". In: *L'Anti-livre noir de la psychanalyse*, ed. J.-A. Miller, Paris: Seuil, pp. 241–278.

Leguil, C. (2008). *Les Amoureuses, voyage au bout de la féminité*. Paris: Seuil.

Leguil, C. (2010a). "Du mal au malheur, la civilisation et ses impasses". Preface to S. Freud, *Le Malaise dans la civilisation*, trans. B. Lortholary. Paris: Points Seuil.

Leguil, C. (2010b). "Désir et désarroi, la religion au miroir de la psychanalyse". Preface to S. Freud, *L'Avenir d'une illusion*, trans. B. Lortholary Paris: Points Seuil.

Leguil, C. (2010c). "Du totem au symptôme, la civilisation et ses racines". Preface to S. Freud, *Totem et Tabou*, trans. D. Tassel. Paris: Points Seuil.

Leguil, C. (2010d). "Le symptôme de Léonard". Preface to S. Freud, *Un souvenir d'enfance de Léonard de Vinci*, trans. D. Tassel. Paris: Points Seuil.

Leguil C. (2012). *Sartre avec Lacan, corrélation antinomique, liaison dangereuse*. Paris: Navarin Le Champ freudien.

Leguil, C. (2013). *In Treatment, Lost in Therapy*. Paris: Presses Universitaires de France.

Leguil, C. (2015). *L'être et le genre, homme/femme après Lacan*. Paris: Presses Universitaires de France. Reviewed in 2017: R. Boué-Widawsky (2017) "Book Review: L'être et le genre: homme/femme après Lacan (Being and gender, man/woman after Lacan)". *Journal of the American Psychoanalytical Association* 65(3): 568–571.

Leguil C. (2018). *« Je », une traversée des identités*. Paris: Presses Universitaires de France. (https://abcpenser.com/auteur/clotilde-leguil/)

Leguil C. (2021). *Céder n'est pas consentir, une approche clinique et politique du consentement*. Paris: Presses Universitaires de France.

Miller, J.-A., (1998–1999) "L'expérience du réel dans la cure analytique". *L'Orientation lacanienne*. Course of the year 1998–1999, lecture of 17 March 1999, teaching given at the Department of Psychoanalysis, Paris 8, CNAM. (https://jonathanleroy.be/wp-content/uploads/2016/02/1998-1999-Le-reel-dans-l-experience-psychanalytique-JA-Miller.pdf)

Chapter 15

Conversation with Sophie Mendelsohn

Abstract

Sophie Mendelsohn, who trained as a Lacanian, explores the clinical repercussions of colonial and postcolonial racism in her research and practice. As a researcher and psychoanalyst, she returns to the historical sources of this subject by comparing the writings of Frantz Fanon with those of the psychoanalyst Octave Mannoni—one of the first psychoanalysts to take an interest in the psychology of colonization (1950).

• Could you describe the intellectual and personal journey that led you to psychoanalysis?

The world I come from, which has largely contributed to shaping my way of thinking in general and my relationship to psychoanalysis in particular, is a paradoxical world. Permeated by fault lines that have given it its own conflictual dynamics, it obliges those who see themselves as its heirs to play out its possibilities in a different way and to avoid its pitfalls. This was the world of the assimilated Jewish liberal bourgeoisie, which believed in the political emancipation of European Jews and the promise of a future, if not radiant, then at least free of the many constraints and restrictions that had hitherto weighed upon European Jewish ways of life. But the murderous violence that had swept through the first half of the 20th century made it clear that their inclusion in that society remained uncertain and gave rise to the constitution of a hitherto unprecedented existential category, what I call the "Jews/non-Jews". As Jews, it was now clear that they would never be French enough, never truly French; but as Jews who had aspired to be French for at least a century, it was also now quite clear that they had to be as non-Jewish as possible. Maintaining oneself in this position of being neither one nor the other is a perilous exercise which produced lives that are fragile, as if on hold. In this context, Freud and psychoanalysis were important, but again in a paradoxical way: not as witnesses to what a secularized Jewish culture could build to the maximum degree of its refinement, since it had been necessary to reject this affiliation, but as a privileged space for negotiating the sometimes inextricable psychological conflicts that arose from it.

DOI: 10.4324/9781003342502-15

This impeded Jewishness nonetheless produced a form of cryptotransmission—in the same way that Freud (1920b) spoke of cryptomnesia to refer to knowledge that we think we have discovered, when in fact we already had it but could not remember it. The value placed on thought, in the form of interminable questioning exploring the space of a relationship to knowledge largely put in the service of self-reflexivity, associated with the fetishization of books as objects, subterraneously kept alive the Jewish diasporic experience and the exegetical tradition by which it was sustained. It was as if, to use the famous Freudian phrase differently,[1] where it is not possible to be, we must at least try to know. It took another diversion in my journey, involving a stay in the United States, for the two lines outlined here to intersect: that of a relationship to knowledge determined by an impeded Jewishness, and that of psychoanalysis as a commitment to knowledge that modifies being.

The intersection occurred during a stay in Chicago, where I was a teaching assistant at the University of Illinois for a year in the mid-1990s, in my early twenties. At the time, I was working on a pre-doctoral dissertation under the supervision of Julia Kristeva on the work of Edmond Jabès, an Egyptian Jewish writer related to my paternal family, whose *The Book of Questions* (Jabès 1976/1963) bears poetic witness to a literature of exile at a time of postcolonial reorganization.[2]

• Could you comment on any opportune encounters you had in your journey and training?

In order to go to Chicago, I had interrupted a first analysis that I had begun at a very young age, which had opened up questions about transference and the end of analysis (at least as a horizon, if not as an actualization) that I felt powerless to answer. These questions were unexpectedly clarified thanks to the formidable American university libraries, which gave me access to Lacan's seminars (in French). At the time, I was studying humanities and literature, and I had never had the opportunity to take a close interest in psychoanalytic literature, apart from a few of Freud's so-called cultural texts. Coming across the 1953–1954 seminar devoted to *Freud's Papers on Technique* (Lacan 1988/1975), which although it subsequently appeared to me to be necessary, at the time seemed entirely contingent, even improbable, enabled me to identify the difficulty that I had come up against in my first analysis, drawing on Lacan's critique of the theory of the end of analysis proposed by a psychoanalyst of the Budapest school, Michael Balint, whose great clinical finesse, moreover, he acknowledged. The variant of the standard theory that Balint proposed, which he called "two-body psychology", was of interest to Lacan at a time when he himself was reconsidering intersubjectivity; but the French psychoanalyst also pointed out the pitfall represented by the conception of transference that went with Balint's clinical approach: conceived as a dual relationship that reproduces the supposed reciprocity of the initial mother–child relationship (Balint 1952), the transference is limited to the imaginary dimension that fosters identification with the analyst and makes it particularly difficult to think about how it can be resolved and lead to the termination of an analysis. The interpretations that made explicit the patient's supposed thoughts, the attention to "body language" and the verbalization of what was conceived as non-verbal communication that I had experienced in my own analysis appeared to me to be a form of imaginary alienation from the person of the analyst and an obstacle to the very process of analysis. In contrast to this way of practising psychoanalysis, Lacan posited a way of handling transference that was based not on the real presence of individuals, but on the function of the Other that the analyst embodies by occupying the place of the subject who is supposed to know, from which the analysand can disentangle their desire from their demand. I found an opening in this, allowing me to imagine the possibility of becoming disentangled from the relational imaginary projections nourished by the transference in which I felt trapped. This was a major factor in my decision to return to France rather than stay in the United States and, at the same time, to do a Lacanian psychoanalysis and follow a university course in clinical psychology and psychoanalysis in the Doctoral Training Department of Fundamental Psychopathology and Psychoanalysis at the University of Paris 7.

• What is your view of the transmission of psychoanalysis?

At the end of the 1990s, this department, which had been created by Jean Laplanche in 1975, was run by Pierre Fédida, whose relationship with psychoanalysis was strongly influenced by phenomenology, particularly that of Binswanger. The spirit in which Laplanche had sought to support university research in psychoanalysis remained in place but was weakened: the aim was "not to provide technical teaching of psychoanalysis", that is, not to turn it into a mere engineering of the mind, but at the same time, "not to propagate the theory as a dogmatically constituted body of doctrine" (Laplanche 1975). This was made possible by the concern to place psychoanalysis within the field of the human and clinical sciences and thus to build an active interdisciplinarity. The teaching of psychoanalysis included a clinical component, which made it compulsory to do several placements in institutions or associations where patients were received, and a very European-centred theoretical component; but the presence of a large number of international master's students, particularly from Latin America, counteracted this Eurocentrism, thereby pluralizing references and perspectives. Lacan's influence was very noticeable, whether it was recognized as such or not—it seemed to me that he was indeed the leading figure, studied more outside the university than within it—but did not always avoid, far from it, the pitfall of dogmatism of which Laplanche was wary.

The dispute over succession that began in 1981 after Lacan's death, and which is still going on, has had a paradoxical twofold effect on his disciples, whether they were in analysis with him or trained in his seminar and school, the Paris Freudian School [École freudienne de Paris (EFP)], from 1964 onwards. On the one hand, there has been a tremendous effort to study the transcripts of the seminar held by Lacan between 1953 and 1980 (to date, the publication of the official version by Jacques-Alain Miller in the Seuil publishing house has still not been completed), which has given rise to an abundant literature explaining and interpreting Lacanian concepts and their development; on the other hand, conflicts over the establishment of seminar texts, fuelled by the dispersal of disciples into rival schools and associations, tended to produce a sacralization of Lacan's words which inhibited the creativity and freedom of thought of the Lacanians, often transforming them into exegetes.[3] This situation has undoubtedly been reinforced by one particularity: the practice of psychoanalysis is not authorized by a diploma in France. From the early 1950s onwards, emphasis was placed on the importance of lay analysis [*Laienanalyse*] practised by nonmedical practitioners, as encouraged by Freud; but this was also a strategic position: to support lay analysis was to reject the criteria for standardizing analytic practice promoted by the IPA. Nevertheless, a persistent desire for guarantees found satisfaction in referring to a theory that was tending to be transformed into dogma; the challenge became to validate the "real" Lacan over and against readings of his work that supposedly betrayed him.

This internal power struggle within the Lacanian field was crystallized in particular around the question of the transmission of psychoanalysis, through the mechanism proposed by Lacan in 1967 known as "*la passe*", which was an immediate source of reticence: Lacan's intention was to continue to actively promote a relationship with the analytic institution that would not be determined by ordinary forms of recognition (diploma, certificate, co-option by peers, etc.), nor by hierarchical norms, but rather based on the disturbing effects of the formations of the unconscious as they can be experienced and shared when we are still in the process of discovering the psychoanalytic process. It was also a question of shifting the relationship to knowledge by placing the results of individual analysis at the service of the analytic institution, counting on the fact that analysis produced a different kind of knowledge for the analysand, linked to the real of the unconscious, that which is not symbolized but is active. This was the knowledge on which the analytic institution was to be nourished. However, this ambitious and a priori seductive proposal, which was the "pass", effectively implemented in a large number of Lacanian groups, turned into a dead end and gave rise to a kind of "psychoanalytic nepotism".

• What is the cornerstone of your theoretical and clinical work?

It may seem astonishing that the psychoanalytic asceticism of the "orthodox" Lacanian analysis could constitute a space of emancipation, but that was exactly what I experienced when I undertook a second analysis with a Lacanian analyst in Paris on my return from my stay in the United States. I had specifically chosen an analyst, Jean-Jacques Rassial, whose book that had just been published at the time (Rassial 1999) concerned the question of borderline states, an issue that was subject to a sort of thought-taboo among Lacanians. This category was all the more criticized because, on the one hand, it had been better integrated on the other side of the Atlantic (via Heinz Hartmann and ego psychology in particular) than in Europe, where it had initially been developed in the 1930s, and because it was of interest to eminent French Freudian psychoanalysts (in particular André Green and Didier Anzieu). As it referred to a personality disorder, it could be suspected of psychologism or associated with a behavioural approach: the clinical phenomenology of borderline states involving a characterological analysis seemed incompatible with a dynamic theory of the modes of psychic structuring inherited from Freud (neurosis, psychosis, perversion) based on the Freudian defence processes (repression, foreclosure, disavowal/denial) and oriented towards the productions of the unconscious (symptoms and phantasies in particular). What interested me especially was that a Lacanian analyst had overcome this prohibition and was ready to look at a clinical category that had returned from the United States, while seeking a Lacanian source of inspiration for thinking about and understanding clinically what might create resistance to the analytic process in this kind of treatment, based on the latest advances in Lacan's teaching around the sinthome. This late concept modifies the function of symptoms, which cease to be something we have to get rid of and instead become the knot of singularity with which we can finally identify. In the course of my career, I have continued to seek out and draw on the work of psychoanalysts whose concern is to confront the conflicting theoretical knots and blind spots of clinical practice, extending Lacanian proposals in creative and personal ways: I am thinking here in particular—though this is by no means exhaustive—of the writings of Geneviève Morel (2008) and Colette Soler (2009) on the concept of the sinthome and the category of the Real, the work of Jean Allouch (1995; 2009) on bereavement and love, and Solal Rabinovitch's interest in "transference madness" (Rabinovitch 2007).

This second analysis therefore took place in parallel with my university course in clinical psychopathology. The sessions were short (sometimes 15 minutes, often 10 or less), with two or three sessions a week over a period of eight years. The analyst was silent most of the time, with only the scansion serving as interpretation. The absence of projections on his part, or at least that is how I perceived it, contrasted sharply with the style of my first analysis, effectively producing the feeling that I could freely say "everything"—even if this analytical rule is obviously an ideal, albeit a necessary one. It was only in the last year that the dryness of this technique produced a certain exhaustion of speech, leading me to envisage, in agreement with the analyst, the end of an analysis that had given me direction in my love life and intellectual life. An event during the last session nevertheless relaunched the analytical process just when I least expected it, inaugurating the search for a third analyst: I sometimes paid for sessions by cheque (all orthodoxy has its limits …), which I did that day, but instead of making the cheque out in the analyst's name, I made it out in my own name. The analyst interpreted this slip of the pen as a sign that the analysis had been a self-analysis. In the months that followed, I was subject to unusual anxieties, bungled actions and somatic symptoms that I could not ignore: this interpretation had acted as a retroactive cancellation of the work done in analysis, invalidating the transference. Less than a year after the end of this second analysis, I began a new analysis with Laure Thibaudeau, a Lacanian analyst whose published articles led me to believe that her clinical practice was guided by a particular concern for transference. I had thus experienced successively an invasive hypertransference presence and then a hypotransference presence, which had the effect, as it were, of pulling the carpet from under my feet.

• What is your theoretical approach to psychoanalytic practice (the couch, frequency, the setting, teletherapy, interpretation, silence)?

As a result of these two very contrasting experiences, to say the least, I have paid a great deal of attention to the handling of the transference in my own clinical practice, which developed first in public institutions, from the mid 2000s onwards, and then in my own private practice. Two points are crucial for me: the limits of the use of the short session lie in its standardization, whereas the variable-length session, which was the starting point for this technical innovation, presupposed a clinically fruitful art of cutting because it stimulated the work of the unconscious by manifesting the presence of the analyst, albeit in a hollow way. In my clinical work, therefore, I strive to undo the automatisms that are bound to set in if we are not careful and to modulate the forms of my intervention (interpretation, silence, act, etc.) strictly according to what the patient says—it is the analysand who makes the analyst, not the other way around, and I regularly find that we are not the same analyst for each analysand, as long as we allow ourselves to be affected, to be displaced transferentially. This, moreover, is what makes analytic practice so lively and interesting. The other essential point, in my view, is not to shy away from what Jacques Derrida, at a conference titled "Etats généraux de la psychanalyse" which took place at the Sorbonne in Paris in July 2000, described as the most genuinely psychoanalytic aspect of analysis, namely the use of cruelty (Derrida 2000). Cruelty in analysis manifests itself in several ways: in the experience we have of being the object of our own phantasies (and not their subject); in the encounter with the limits of jouissance and its psychic and physical metabolization; in the final observation of the nonexistence of the Other (in other words, the Lacanian way of saying that the subject is naked, with no guarantees apart from those they give themselves by accepting, and this requires a lot of work, the burden of their autonomy, the responsibility for their own life, as a result of which they are in a position to shoulder responsibility for their destiny). But transference itself is also a cruel experience of the structural inequality of human relationships: because it implies a supposition of knowledge, it is necessarily a place where power is exercised, a place of confrontation with the question of the Other's power. It is not possible for the analyst to shirk their role here, even in the name of progressive ideals promoting social equality, without missing out on what makes the transference so powerful: to be able to free oneself from the weight of the Other, one must first have confronted it. This is what the analytic theatre proposes, insofar as the analyst has taken note of the fact that the power that the transference confers on them is nothing but a sham, which must eventually appear as such. In other words, the transference cannot be virtualized without losing its power to actualize the cruelty on which it is based. The experience of global lockdown has shown that analysis can be practised remotely for a while, if necessary, but the presence, and even the materiality of bodies (that is to say, of drives and affects, in the psychoanalytic sense), is necessary if speech is to venture to traverse those obscure zones where common law is of little recourse.

- **What is your psychoanalytic approach to the societal debates on racial, gender identities or/and on the new forms of reproduction and parenting?**

These internal quarrels within psychoanalytic schools may have elided the external social and cultural challenges that psychoanalysis has constantly been faced with. I am thinking here of the particularly heated public debates surrounding the Civil Solidarity Pact (PACS), marriage for all, assisted reproductive technology (ART) and adoption by homosexual couples. The psychoanalysts who have made their voices heard in these debates have generally defended ideological positions that are socially and legally conservative, rejecting other ways of building society in the name of a psychoanalysis that has built an essentialized conception of the unconscious. Some of my published work concerns gender issues, both in terms of their contribution to the psychoanalytic theory of sexuation and also the way in which they enter into dialogue with psychoanalysis with regard to the identity/identification binomial. My long association with some of these groups—La lettre lacanienne and the Association de psychanalyse Jacques Lacan (APJL) in particular but also others—gave me the feeling that this form of transmission of psychoanalysis consisted essentially in ensuring its own social reproduction by neutralizing, in the process, the enthusiasm of those who belonged to the "third generation", that is, those who had not taken part in the initial adventure of Lacanianism and who were driven, on the one hand, by a genuine interest in the fruitfulness of Lacanian theory and, on the other, by the impetus found in personal analysis.

A few years ago I started to become increasingly sensitive to the cruelty of the situation in which some of my patients found themselves by listening to what was making itself heard as an impasse from the couch, which began to resonate strongly with my own history: the absence of collective work on French colonial history, justified by the universalist ideal inherited from the revolution, produces a subjective conflict in those of us from colonial and postcolonial migrant backgrounds that found no echo in French psychoanalysis. In the name of analytical neutrality, the questions raised by experiences of racism (whether anti-Black racism, Islamophobia or anti-Semitism), giving rise to what the American sociologist W. E. B. Du Bois called "double consciousness" (Du Bois 1990/1903), and the unconscious splits that underlie it could not find a place here. This was also in the name of the fact that psychoanalysis should not be interested in the political orientations of the subjects who turn to it but only in their psychic lives—and the artificiality of this separation needs to be recognized here. While questions of gender had been debated within French psychoanalysis since the late 1990s—thanks in particular to the translations of American texts by the publishing house EPEL—it seemed that racism remained off the agenda. This observation led a few colleagues and I to set up an autonomous collective, the Pantin collective (www.collectifdepantin.org), breaking with the hegemonic ways in which French analytic groups were set up (in the quest for horizontal rather than vertical transmission), where it would be possible to work freely on questions of racism and racialization using the tools of an enlarged psychoanalysis, including all its national and international components, and to encourage points of contact with anthropology, philosophy, sociology and so on. Reference to existing American studies on the intersection between critical race studies and psychoanalysis was decisive (Fuss 1994; Lane 1998; Crooks 2000; George & Hook 2022). But we were also looking for a way to situate our questions in the space of our own practice and with conceptual tools that were not simply an import from Anglophone usage, where melancholia and phantasy in particular are the most widely used conceptual touchstones—from this point of view, it was the work of Octave Mannoni that gave us our impetus.

The work of the collective found its first form in a book written in collaboration with Livio Boni, *La vie psychique du racisme* (Boni & Mendelsohn 2021), in which we analyse one of the first psychoanalytical works on the colonial question, written by Octave Mannoni, *Psychologie de la colonisation* (Mannoni 1950). In the light of the criticisms levelled at it by Frantz Fanon, Livio Boni and I developed the concept of *denial* from different angles in order to analyse the position adopted by Mannoni in the development of his psychology, the erasure of the colonial question in French psychoanalysis and finally the link between this Freudian defence process and the Lacanian theorization of a racism of different forms of jouissance and discourse, that is to say the competition between the various forms of jouissance, their hierarchisation and segregation by discursive devices, which reflects a certain state of the balance of power in culture. The figure of Octave Mannoni was all the more valuable to us because he had the courage to critique his own position, symptomatically in a text first published in English in the journal *Race* (Mannoni 1969/1966), in which he gives an early indication of what is involved in the decolonization of oneself, which begins by rejecting the framework of thought imposed by universalism.

Strikingly for me, this was also how Mannoni returned to the "Jewish question". He writes:

> At the beginning of my analytic practice, I remember being tempted to tell a Jewish patient, who was having difficulties with his own Jewishness, that there really were no Jews, that it was just a word, a label that had been stuck on their backs—an indefensible interpretation, because even if the Jewish race has no scientific (or "objective") existence, the problem raised for each Jew by his relations with non-Jews cannot be resolved, far from it, by this kind of denial.
>
> (Mannoni 1966, 296)

Nor can the problem every Jew faces on account of their relationship with Jewishness, particularly if it has been inhibited. Refusing to give in to the temptation which would have consisted in declaring that being Jewish is null and void so as not to have to take it into account in his listening, he nevertheless notes that he could very well have given in to this if his patient had encouraged him to do so by solving the problem before it even arose—"many Jews try this solution [the universalist solution] themselves, striving to assimilate with non-Jews and often succeed, provided that they pay a price for this negation in the form of anxiety and disorders of all kinds" (ibid.). This observation is an invitation to psychoanalysts to take an interest in the subjective price paid for assimilation, the price paid for using this universalist solution against oneself. In order to appreciate the disorders thus created, we need to be prepared to understand that it is precisely the imperative of assimilation that requires a Black person, Jew or Muslim to assimilate in order to speak about the disorders it causes. Because if we do not speak about the disorders we are affected by, then what is the point of ending up on a psychoanalyst's couch? The extent of what is at stake can no doubt be gauged by considering the alternative that emerges: either psychoanalysis is reserved for those who do not risk undermining the universalist solution, to the exclusion of all others, and it itself becomes a de facto segregating practice; or psychoanalysis must actually be able to accommodate the anxieties and disorders of all kinds faced by all those who are likely to turn to it, and then it has no choice but to stop believing in the universalist solution itself, or at least to stop using it as a ploy to actively ignore the blind spots it has created. And it is very much the ambition of the Pantin collective to seek to shed light on these blind spots. Additionally, our mission is to explore the new venues of postcolonial psychoanalysis (Boni & Mendelsohn 2023).

Notes

1 *"Wo Es war, soll Ich werden"* ("Where id was, there ego shall be") (Freud 1933, 80)
2 After the Suez Canal Crisis in 1956, Egyptian Jews were considered foreigners, even though they had been settled on Egyptian soil since the 8th century, and expelled by Nasser. This largely French-speaking community sought exile in France for the most part.
3 But it should be added here that this relationship to exegesis, which claims to fix meaning, is missing precisely the power of the exegetic tradition as conveyed by the Talmud, where it is a matter of never leaving thought in peace by constantly rekindling the process of meaning.

References

Allouch, J. (1995). *Erotique du deuil au temps de la mort sèche*. Paris: EPEL.
Allouch, J. (2009). *L'amour Lacan*. Paris: EPEL.
Balint, M. (1952). *Primary Love and Psycho-Analytic Technique*. London: Routledge.
Boni, L. & Mendelsohn, S. (2021). *La vie psychique du racisme, 1. L'empire du démenti*. Paris: La Découverte.
Boni, L. & Mendelsohn, S. (2023). *Psychanalyse du reste du monde. Géo-histoire d'une subversion*, Paris: La Découverte.
Crooks, S. (2000). *Desiring Whiteness: A Lacanian Analysis of Race*. London: Routledge.
Derrida, J. (2000). *Etats d'âme de la psychanalyse*. Paris: Galilée.

Du Bois, W. E. B. (1990/1903). *The Souls of Black Folk*. New York: Vintage.

Freud, S. (1920b). "A note on the prehistory of the technique of psychoanalysis". *S. E.* 18. London: Hogarth, pp. 263–265.

Freud, S. (1933a). *New Introductory Lectures on Psycho-Analysis. S. E.* 22. London: Hogarth, pp. 7–182.

Fuss, D. (1994). "Interior colonies: Frantz Fanon and the Politics of Identification". *Diacritics*, 24(2/3): 19–42.

George, S. & Hook, D. (Eds.) (2022). *Lacan and Race, Racism, Identity and Psychoanalytic Theory*. London: Routledge.

Jabès, E. (1976/1963). *The Book of Questions*, trans. R. Walder. Middletown, CT: Wesleyan University Press.

Lacan, J. (1988/1975). *Freud's Papers on Technique (1953–1954). The Seminar of Jacques Lacan, Book 1*, ed. J. A. Miller, trans. J. Forrester. Cambridge: Cambridge University Press.

Lane, C. (Ed.) (1998). *The Psychoanalysis of Race*. New York: Columbia University Press.

Laplanche, J. (1975). "Psychanalyse à l'université: éditorial". In: *Psychanalyse à l'université*, tome 1. Paris: Replique.

Mannoni, O. (1950). *Psychologie de la colonisation*. Paris: Seuil, 2022.

Mannoni, O. (1969/1966). "La décolonisation de soi". In: *Clés pour l'Imaginaire ou l'Autre Scène*. Paris: Seuil.

Morel, G. (2008). *La loi de la mère. Essai sur le sinthome sexuel*. Paris: Anthropos.

Rabinovitch, S. (2007). *La folie du transfert*. Toulouse: Erès.

Rassial, J.-J. (1999). *Le sujet en état limite*. Paris: Denoël.

Soler, C. (2009). *Lacan, l'inconscient réinventé*. Paris: Presses Universitaires de France.

Chapter 16

Conversation with Dominique Scarfone

Abstract

Dominique Scarfone, inspired by Laplanche's work, emphasizes the importance of language as the key to psychological processes that are permeable to the unconscious. From this he derives a "translational model" of psychic functioning that makes transference possible. For the analyst, this implies a non hermeneutic work of interpretation favouring an analysis of the patient's effort to translate.

• Could you describe the intellectual and personal journey that led you to psychoanalysis?

I first studied classics (Latin/sciences) and then health sciences, before going on to study medicine. During my secondary and pre-university education my interest in the humanities and the sciences was equally strong, but one day, when I was 17, I came across a copy of Freud's *The Interpretation of Dreams*, and I then had the feeling that I had encountered something really new. Afterwards, I followed a particularly influential course given by a history of science teacher. His name was Camille Limoges and, while talking to us about science in antiquity, he one day mentioned Freud saying that we had still not fully understood the meaning of his discoveries. This made me even more curious about psychoanalysis. In retrospect, I realized that I had thus found a middle way between medicine and literature!

• Could you comment on any opportune encounters you had in your journey and training?

A first pre-internship in psychiatry had turned me away from psychiatry for all practical purposes. Day after day, I witnessed the distribution of medication to agitated patients in the wards of the inpatient department of a large psychiatric hospital. In the outpatient department, we students watched the psychiatrist briefly enquire about the patients' condition before simply renewing their prescriptions. The following year, during an internship, this time in an institute small

DOI: 10.4324/9781003342502-16

enough to have a more human touch, and where the psychoanalytical orientation was predominant, I was reassured about psychiatry's possibilities of seeking to understand the psychic dynamics at work in psychopathology. I began my training at what was then called the Albert-Prévost Institute and I was fortunate enough to have two psychoanalysts as clinical supervisors who introduced me to analytical listening. The institute regularly received renowned analysts as lecturers: I remember, for example, lectures and seminars given by Serge Leclaire, Gisela Pankow and Piera Aulagnier. Exposure to these prominent figures—whose full importance I did not realise at the time—certainly influenced my theoretical and clinical options.

While training at the Montreal Psychoanalytic Institute, I practised community psychiatry for about ten years, then consultative psychiatry in medicine and obstetrics, before opting for a private psychoanalytic practice. My encounter with the psychoanalyst Jacques Mauger, who was to become a great friend, gave rise to another project: the creation of a French-language psychoanalytic journal in North America. We called the journal *TRANS*, thinking of the prevalence of this prefix in psychoanalytical vocabulary, as in transference, translation, transformation, transitionality, trauma, etc., and also of the fact that "trans" is the Latin version of the Greek prefix "meta". The title had the advantage of not immediately evoking a precise image; it marked our unwillingness to include the journal within a particular psychoanalytical current. The journal only published ten issues, but it had the privilege of welcoming talented Quebec authors, such as Jean Imbeault, as well as renowned French authors: Didier Anzieu, Jean Laplanche, J.-B. Pontalis, Monique Schneider, Jacques André, René Major, to name but a few.[1] Along the way, by chance, I was offered a lecturing post at the University of Montreal to teach basic psychoanalytical concepts to psychology students. This was an important turning point for me and led me to the title of full professor, working to ensure the presence of psychoanalysis in a university environment increasingly dominated by biologism.

The encounter with Laplanche's work, and then with Laplanche himself, was also to have a determining influence on me, as I will explain below.

• What is the cornerstone of your theoretical and clinical work?

Shortly before starting my psychoanalytical training, by chance I came across a volume of Jean Laplanche's *Problématiques*. I was impressed by the clarity of the style and by the fact that Laplanche read Freud and commented on him critically. Until then, I had only had the example of the professors who had provided my psychiatric training, and who either embraced Freudian doctrine without questioning it or rejected it outright. Laplanche's method showed me another way. I also found confirmation of what my former professor of the history of science had said, namely that it was necessary to continue to examine Freud's writings. I was able to join a study group led by a young analyst, Jean-Pierre Bienvenu, in which

Laplanche's work was closely studied. This gave me the opportunity of deepening my knowledge of Laplanche, which also taught me to read Freud with a method that was both critical and respectful, and above all a method that turned, so to speak, the Freudian weapons on Freud's work. With Laplanche, psychoanalysis in fact submits to its own method, becomes a self-critical discipline, untying its own syntheses, questioning its own foundations, and re-examining the acquisitions that one might think are definitive.

It is worth noting that this re-examination is fully in line with another aspect of Laplanche's work, namely the translational model of psychic functioning. In this model, all translation or symbolization has another facet, which is called repression. Here again, Laplanche follows Freudian thought. The translational model is the development of an idea expressed by Freud in a letter to Fliess: the psyche is essentially translational or transcriptive, and what, in clinical terms, is called "repression" consists in a failure of translation or transcription ("Letter from Freud to Fliess dated 6 December 1896", Masson 1985, 208). This is a fundamental metapsychological conception that runs through the whole of Freud's work, although it is not always obvious at first sight. Laplanche uses it to think afresh about the theory of seduction that Freud was to abandon a few months after writing this letter. The theory of generalized seduction that Laplanche proposes is thus also based on Freud, suggesting that repressed sexuality is implanted in the infantile psyche through the partly failed translation of messages emitted by adults—failed because the said messages, which are otherwise quite ordinary, contain, without the emitters being aware of it, a "sexual charge" that the infantile psyche is unable to translate. This conception of seduction has as its corollary a conception of the analytic situation in which the analysand finds themselves in the position of the *infans* exposed to the enigma of the analyst, which excites the patient's translational function, thus provoking the transference. It should be noted that according to this model, it is the patient who is the translator, the analyst's function being essentially to analyse, that is to encourage the detranslation or deconstruction of the translations brought to the session by the patient. This influences the style of the analyst's intervention, which will not be a hermeneutic type of interpretation, since the formation of meaning is essentially left to the patient. The methodological and ethical aspects of psychoanalysis coincide here.

It should be noted in passing that the translational model applies at all levels. It accounts for the formation of the sexual and of the dynamics of the transference, but it also concerns psychoanalytic theorization itself, including Freud's. If well-conceived, it can contribute to making the confrontation between the various psychoanalytical theories productive. Indeed, it is conceivable that provided the proponents of the theories in question adopt the translational model, they can develop a common method of discussion based on this model, that is, on the recognition that any translation or understanding *of the theory of the other* will involve an "untranslated" element which should then become the focus of interest for both parties involved (Scarfone 2017a, 2017b).

• What is your theoretical approach to psychoanalytic practice (the couch, frequency, the setting, teletherapy, interpretation and silence)?

I am classically Freudian in this respect; I believe that one of Freud's most important contributions was the invention of the psychoanalytic method as developed from dream work and perfected over time. In my opinion, what makes a practice psychoanalytic is the implementation of the Freudian method of free associations and free-floating attention. The ways in which this task is carried out obviously vary according to a number of factors: the psychic functioning of the patient (and of the analyst!), the material possibilities that influence the number of sessions or the use of the couch, etc. There is no guarantee that the method can be implemented at all times, and in any case, no session is fully analytic: rather, in each session there are more or less long, more or less frequent, *analytic moments* and *therapeutic moments* (Laplanche 2011/2006). For this reason, although I believe that a high frequency with the use of the couch, when possible and compatible with the patient's capacities, is generally preferable, I do not believe that the number of sessions, the use of the couch, working in each other's presence or at a distance are what decide whether or not analysis is taking place.

My position on the question of silence and interpretation stems from the conception of the method and of psychic functioning in the light of the processes of binding and unbinding. Analytical work, when possible, is a work of unbinding that leaves the patient with the task of making new connections. Silence is not, therefore, a question of personal style or school of thought but stems from the analyst's readiness to make themselves available to a particular kind of listening that respects the patient's psychic autonomy and welcomes their speech, ideally without directing it, simply underlining the inflection points in the patient's discourse that evenly suspended listening has revealed (Scarfone 2018a, 2018b). This is another way of saying that interpretation is not hermeneutic in nature, since it is not the analyst's task to produce meaning; this is left to the patient as much as possible, it being understood that the analyst may be called upon to assist the patient, to varying degrees depending on the case, in the work of elaboration or psychic binding.

• What is your view of the transmission of psychoanalysis?

I believe, though this is not very original, that the transmission of psychoanalysis occurs along at least three channels: the personal experience of analysis, the supervision of the first experiences of practice and the teaching of metapsychology. What is most difficult, I find, is to make people see that, in fact, the three channels are not parallel and that metapsychology permeates the first two. Let me explain: When I say "teaching *of metapsychology*", note that I am not saying "of psychoanalytical theory". Theories can be studied in books, and there are plenty of them. These are only of value in my view insofar as they contain what I would call a "*meta*-disposition". What I mean is that in the word "metapsychology", what matters most is the prefix "meta". Freud used it to make it clear that it is a matter of taking seriously the hypothesis of the unconscious and thus a psychology "beyond" ("meta-") consciousness. Now taking this founding hypothesis into consideration consistently leads to everything else: how one is listened to and how one hears oneself speak during one's personal analysis; how one listens to the patients whom one has in supervision—and how the supervisor listens to the supervisee—and how one becomes aware of and criticizes the theoretical elaborations that circulate among us.

- ## What, in your view, are the points of divergence between French psychoanalysis and English-speaking psychoanalysis?

I do not believe that one can speak of *a* French psychoanalysis, any more than there would be *an* English-speaking psychoanalysis. Nevertheless, it must be acknowledged that, roughly speaking, historical differences can be identified. I am unable to say, however, to what extent they still exist or are diminishing, given that there is a certain dissemination of the work of French-speaking authors in the English-speaking world and, to a lesser extent, of English-speaking authors in the French-speaking world. If I had to point out only one or two major differences, I would say that it is first the relationship to language, and then the relationship to metapsychology, two aspects that are linked. On the question of language, it seems to me that English-speaking analysts—at least those who have not been "contaminated" by French thought—tend to see it only as a means of communication, whereas French psychoanalysis sees it as psychic matter itself, the field where the effects of the unconscious are observed in analysis. In this respect, Lacan's influence on French psychoanalytical thought, whether Lacanian or not, has been decisive. This goes hand in hand, in my opinion, with the importance given to metapsychology, which, precisely, allows us to hear and take into account the effects of the unconscious (of the repressed) on language and interhuman communication.

- ## What is your psychoanalytic approach to the societal debates on racial, gender identities or/and on the new forms of reproduction and parenting?

On the subject of gender, I am once again strongly influenced by the work of Jean Laplanche. He seems to me to have opened up a fruitful avenue of reflection when he suggested that there was operant link between gender, sex and what he called the *Sexual*—a German word taken from Freud and used to remind us that, in psychoanalysis, we are not interested in sexuality in general, but in infantile sexuality, the repressed. Laplanche first suggested that gender is in the nature of a message—a message that also conveys sexuality—which necessarily implies a translation or, if one prefers, a work of symbolization. Now, as we have seen, any translation, any symbolization, any production of meaning also involves, simultaneously, a repression. But if we speak of the translation of the gender message ("It's a boy!", "It's a

girl!"), we must ask ourselves on the one hand if the said message is as transparent as it seems, since, like any message, it is compromised by parental repressions. On the other hand, we must ask ourselves on what basis the receiver of this message makes their translation, their personal interpretation. Laplanche suggests that it is on the basis of the perception of sex, of sexual difference, given that that this is strongly marked by symbolic, mythical elements, etc., provided by the surrounding culture. Laplanche thus argues in conclusion that "[t]he sexual is the unconscious residue of the symbolization-repression of gender by sex" (Laplanche 2011/2003, 167).

This conception seems to me to be liberating, in the sense that it allows us to maintain a strictly psychoanalytical position that does not give in to the effects of fashion, while at the same time being open to the relatively new questions that the notions of gender or the questions of new parental configurations raise for psychoanalysis. As we can see, the translational/repressing model that Laplanche had already extracted from the Freudian text is intact and just as operative. For example, what is called "gender identity" needs to be analysed just as much as any other type of identity. As with everything else, the analytic position is in the nature of analysis; that is to say, it is a matter of dissecting what has been established in the analysand's life that has proved problematic to the point of leading to a request for analysis. I can only insist on the fact that psychoanalysis cannot be normative or prescriptive. I have explained this in more detail in an article about the feminine in Freud (Scarfone 2019), and I can only refer the reader to it. This non-normative and nonprescriptive position also stems from a consistent metapsychological position.

• Is there any other question that you would like to discuss?

Generally speaking, I consider that anyone who wants to practise psychoanalysis must try to satisfy one of Freud's requirements, namely, to be curious about everything. This means developing as much scientific, literary, anthropological, philosophical and artistic culture as possible.

As a general rule, I think of things in terms of a system/environment relationship, which I believe is a general model that is applicable to all fields (Varela 1979; Luhmann 2013/2002). For us psychoanalysts, this implies paying constant attention to what does not fit perfectly into the coherent part of the psychic system (the repressed in relation to the ego), but also, of course, to what defies the coherence of our theories. In other words, it implies taking into account *otherness* in all its aspects if we want to ensure the vibrancy of our discipline. This, moreover, was one of Freud's own ideas, forming part of the biological speculations set out in *Beyond the Pleasure Principle*, where he writes:

[T]he life process of the individual leads for internal reasons to an abolition of chemical tensions, that is to say, to death, whereas union with the living substance of a different individual increases those tensions, introducing what may be described as *fresh "vital differences"* which must then be lived off.

(Freud 1920g, 55, emphasis added)

Note

1 The full text (in French) of the ten issues of *TRANS* can be found at the following web address: http://transvirtuel.com/Revue/Catalogue.html

References

Masson, J. M. (Ed.) (1985). *The Complete Letters of Sigmund Freud to Wilhelm Fliess*. Cambridge, MA: The Belknap Press.

Freud, S. (1920g). *Beyond the Pleasure Principle. S. E.* 18. London: Hogarth, pp. 1–64.

Laplanche, J. (2011/2003). Gender, sex and the sexual. In: *Freud and the Sexual*, ed. J. Fletcher. New York, NY: The Unconscious in Translation, pp. 167–188.

Laplanche, J. (2011/2006). "Psychoanalysis and psychotherapy". In: *Freud and the Sexual*, ed. J. Fletcher. New York, NY: The Unconscious in Translation, pp. 287–292.

Luhmann, N. (2013/2002). *Introduction to Systems Theory*, trans. P. Gilgen. Cambridge: Polity Press.

Scarfone, D. (2017a). "On 'That is not psychoanalysis': Ethics as the main tool for psychoanalytic knowledge and discussion". *Psychoanalytic Dialogues*, 27(4): 392–400. (https://doi.org/10.1080/10481885.2017.1328174)

Scarfone, D. (2017b). "Reaching for the untranslatable: A response to Poland, Puget, and Rozmarin". *Psychoanalytic Dialogues*, 27(4): 423–432. (https://doi.org/10.1080/10481885.2017.1328181)

Scarfone, D. (2018a). "De la disponibilité au transfert. La leçon d'Hamlet". *Revue française de psychosomatique*, 2018/1(53): 5–20.

Scarfone, D. (2018b). "Free association, surprise, trauma and transference". *Psychoanalytic Inquiry*, 38(6): 468–477. (https://doi.org/10.1080/07351690.2018.1480232)

Scarfone, D. (2019). "The feminine, the analyst and the child theorist". *The International Journal of Psychoanalysis*, 100(3): 567–575.

Varela, F. (1979). *Principles of Biological Autonomy*. New York, NY: North Holland.

Chapter 17

Conversation with Alain Vanier

Abstract

Alain Vanier, a Lacanian by training, explains the concept of the object *a*, as bringing together all the objects—partial, lost, and transitional—thus representing the lack that is essential to desire. He also offers an epistemological reflection on the meaning of analytic principles, such as the duration of sessions, the role of interpretation, and the question of transmission.

- **Could you describe the intellectual and personal journey that led you to psychoanalysis?**

What led me to psychoanalysis is linked both to the overdetermination dear to Freud and to contingent factors. Overdetermination, because I come from a family that was shattered by the Second World War which left traces in the whole family history; I tried to cope with them as best as I could, but I always felt that there was a difficulty there. I thought I had found a solution in the events of 1968. I was 20 years old at the time, a student, and I got involved in this movement with the wild dream of creating a society where relations between human beings would suddenly be calm, peaceful and finally happy. In short, like many young men and women of my generation, I had converted the religious messianism that had run out of steam, particularly in France, into a secular messianism, that of the hope of the "*grand soir*" or social upheaval promised by a revolution, and the advent of a better world that would make it possible to avoid the arrangements of an unjust and violent society to which we did not want to contribute. These post-war years were years of war, with the wars in Algeria and Indochina, which extended to Vietnam, that is to say the ravages of colonization and, of course, the unmade history, covered over by a state lie in France, of the Second World War.

For my part, I had obtained a scientific baccalaureate a few years earlier, but I went on to study literature. I studied mainly literature, but also philosophy, ethnology, etc. I also taught French literature for two years in secondary schools. Then, for my master's degree, I turned to linguistics. I focused my research in particular on structural linguistics and work on literary texts in the wake of Roland Barthes. It must be said that at the time the movement known as "structuralism" was very

DOI: 10.4324/9781003342502-17

important but had difficulty finding its place in the university. When the University of Paris splintered into multiple universities, it made it possible to create a department of literary studies with a structuralist orientation. Among the teachers in this department was Julia Kristeva. In the research seminar in linguistics in which I was enrolled, which was led by a philosopher who was a student of Derrida and by a linguist, Lacan's name often came up as something precious but too difficult to talk about. We spoke about him allusively because "he had nonetheless said things about language, about speech, etc.", which intrigued me greatly. Despite the decline of the movement of 1968, it continued for more than four years in the Latin Quarter in Paris, where I lived, with an astonishing atmosphere, a sort of island of solidarity, of unexpected encounters, of exchanges of thoughts. Little by little, a return to "normal" life was on the cards, and I was feeling more and more uneasy in this situation of being an eternal student. I went to consult the University Psychological Aid Office. They were full up, so I was referred privately to a psychoanalyst from the Paris Psychoanalytical Society (SPP) affiliated to the IPA, with whom I started a psychotherapy, which later became a psychoanalysis. Quite quickly, I decided to study psychology, during which I met again someone I had already met during my studies in literature, Félix Guattari, who came to a seminar accompanied by Gilles Deleuze to talk about what they were preparing, which they were to publish, which was *Anti-Oedipus*.

In my psychology studies, work placements were compulsory. I was increasingly interested in Lacan but also in how I had already been interested in the work of "mad" writers during my studies of literature, and I found myself on a placement, which was to become my workplace, at the École expérimentale in Bonneuil-sur-Marne, which Maud Mannoni had founded in 1969. I arrived there as a trainee almost at the beginning and was taken on as an employee when the institution received funding from the public authorities.

Meanwhile, while finishing my studies in psychology, I took up medical studies with the aim of going into psychiatry. I am probably one of the few psychiatrists who started out as an antipsychiatrist. My SPP analyst, with whom I felt I was doing very good work, encouraged me, at the end of my analysis, to start seeing patients at the same time as I was studying medicine. In France, it was not necessary to be a doctor to practice psychoanalysis. My first patient was a very disturbed drug addict who upset the very strict framework of my way of conducting an analysis. He led me to do a supervision and, after a few years, to do a second period of analysis with an analyst from the Paris Freudian School [École freudienne de Paris (EFP)] that Lacan had founded. Indeed, during all those years from 1972 onwards, I attended Lacan's seminar as often as I could, which was an absolutely incredible place.

I continued this process by working at Bonneuil, then by becoming a psychiatric intern and also by starting to work in child psychiatry in the Paris suburbs in the public service. So I did a supervision at Bonneuil with Maud Mannoni for the work I was doing with a schizophrenic adolescent, who was considered dangerous to himself and to others. My second supervisor was Solange Faladé. At the end of my medical studies, I entered a competitive examination to become a hospital psychiatrist, and the outcome was that I was appointed head of liaison psychiatry in a hospital where there was a gynaecology and obstetrics department that received psychotic mothers during their pregnancy and then with their babies for a few months after birth. I then began a third supervision with Françoise Dolto.

Public psychiatry in France was deteriorating, so I left the hospital world in the mid 1990s to teach at the university, where I was a senior lecturer for five years, then a full professor for 22 years, then distinguished professor at the University of Paris 7-Denis Diderot. Moreover, the psychoanalytic association broke up in 1994, and I played a part in the foundation, by Maud Mannoni, of the association to which I belong today, which is called the Espace analytique (AFPRF).

• Could you comment on any opportune encounters in your journey and in your training?

First and foremost, my two analysts and my three supervisors, but also some meetings with Lacan to try to deal with a very complicated relationship with Félix Guattari that was interfering with my personal analysis.

First of all, a word about Maud Mannoni, a psychoanalyst trained in Belgium and a member of the Belgian Society of Psychoanalysis affiliated with the IPA. She had stopped over in Paris on her way to the United States where she planned to continue her training. But in Paris, she met Françoise Dolto and, more particularly, her future husband, Octave Mannoni. She began an analysis with Lacan and he sent her to London to meet Winnicott with whom she undertook supervision. Maud Mannoni had already published two books in France on psychoanalysis with children. She was very critical of the way child psychiatry worked at that time. Winnicott sent her to visit Kingsley Hall where Ronald Laing, David Cooper, Joseph Berke, etc. had created an original place of antipsychiatry. She returned to Paris and founded, in Bonneuil-sur-Marne, in the Parisian suburbs, this experimental school which she called a "place of antipsychiatry", that is to say an institution which retained the antipsychiatric attitude but not the theories. At Bonneuil, I was very impressed by the invention of this absolutely extraordinary place, by the quality of the clinical successes and by Maud Mannoni's clinical attitude, particularly with psychotic children. But my longest supervision, more than ten years, was with Solange Faladé. She was an analyst with a passion for clinical work, but also a fine reader of Lacan. Finally, Françoise Dolto, who was my third supervisor, allowed me to work with babies, with supervision sessions that were like no other because she was extremely imaginative and surprising. I also attended her public consultations with children.

As chance would have it, I had written a commissioned book on Lacan which was translated in the United States (Vanier 2000). I was then invited first by my publisher and then by American colleagues to various colloquia and congresses of the American Psychoanalytic Association (APsA), and then by other associations. Thus, I was able to meet American psychoanalysts of all orientations with whom I could exchange views and work regularly. Today I work very regularly with colleagues from the Après-Coup Psychoanalytic Association in New York.

Furthermore, in France, I found myself in a small working group of five psycho-analysts from different associations, Lacanian and non-Lacanian. We had decided to question our clinical practices, what we were doing with the patients. And I was surprised to see, as with certain Anglo-Saxon colleagues, that with different theo-ries, we could sometimes do things that were quite similar, sometimes more similar than was the case with certain analysts who shared the same theoretical field. This never ceased to intrigue me.

And then, of course, there was the meeting with my wife, Catherine Vanier, who is also a psychoanalyst, and we have accompanied each other in this adventure for many years now.

• What is the cornerstone of your theoretical and clinical work?

Freud above all, of course. This was the message of Lacan's teaching, because Lacan was a formidable reader of Freud, putting himself in a position that aimed to analyse what had not been analysed in Freud. So, Lacan, but also Melanie Klein, D. W. Winnicott and so on. Lacan said that he was an epigone of Freud, recognizing only one invention, the object *a*. With this concept, Lacan tried to bring together the Freudian objects—mainly the *Three Essays* (Freud 1905d) and "Mourning and Melancholia" (1917e), but also the transitional object—on the basis of Freud's very early assertion that the object is fundamentally lost and that every discovery is a rediscovery. This object *a* is embodied in various objects—part-objects, the object of mourning (in the person one is mourning, one does not know what one has lost, says Freud), the transitional object (made to be lost, says Winnicott), etc.—where one believes one can find this object again, but "it is not that!" In fact, it is not so much the object of desire as the person that causes it, because they are missing.

My interests, almost every time, have followed my clinical encounters. Psycho-ses, the child and the first mother–baby relationships led me to take an interest in the question of time in psychoanalysis, which was the subject of my thesis in psy-chopathology and of my authorization to become a full professor.

Now, this picture that we have of the time of development in child psychoa-nalysis is a very problematic question because it is extremely normalizing; for it is modelled on the time of the child's bodily development and does not nec-essarily correspond to what we encounter in our analytic treatments. Equally problematic is the question of origins, of time in analysis, insofar as it concerns remembering and Freud's thesis that the unconscious does not know time, the time of the sessions, their rhythm, in short, this whole temporal dimension regu-lated in analytical practice that I have tried to link precisely to Lacan's object *a*, which is so clinically important. But my various encounters have also led me to take an interest in the clinical domain of adult neuroses and psychoses, in questions relating to art (I taught for about ten years at the École nationale supérieure des Beaux-Arts, now the Beaux-Arts de Paris), as well as in politics and social ties, etc.

• What is your theoretical approach to psychoanalytic practice (the couch, frequency, setting, teletherapy, interpretation, silence)?

Each analysis is unique. But, above all, Freud notes:

> The technical rules which I am putting forward here have been arrived at from my own experience in the course of many years, after unfortunate results had led me to abandon other methods. It will easily be seen that they (or at least many of them) may be summed up in a single precept. I must however make it clear that what I am asserting is that this technique is the only one suited to my individuality. I do not venture to deny that a physician quite differently constituted might find himself driven to adopt a different attitude to his patients and to the task before him.
>
> (Freud 1912e, 111)

This *single precept* is the "fundamental rule of psycho-analysis". The patient is encouraged to say everything that comes to their mind without making any sort of selection. But Freud adds to this fundamental rule another, which has been called the second fundamental rule, which is that the analyst must maintain a position of "evenly-suspended attention". But this position is only possible because the psychoanalyst has undergone a "psychoanalytic purification" [*psychoanalytische Purifizierung*]. From this it can be inferred that all the standards that have presided over analytic practice have ultimately been no more than tools for holding together, as Lacan suggested, a community whose theoretical references are particularly diverse, not to say scattered. These standards have varied enormously here and there and practice teaches us that in the end they are of no use whatsoever. My practice is oriented by two main features, first the frame, that is to say the two fundamental rules which cannot be ignored, and secondly the conviction that the frequency as well as the duration of the sessions can be very variable from one analysand to another.

It would take too long to elaborate on the subject of interpretation here but it has necessarily varied enormously with time, social conditions and, above all, the penetration and dissemination of psychoanalytic ideas in culture. For, in penetrating culture, psychoanalysis itself produces its own resistance. One can imagine the effects of the revelation of an incestuous desire or a murderous desire on a young girl at the end of the 19th century or the beginning of the 20th century in a society such as Viennese society, provoking unquestionable analytical effects. But as one colleague said, patients in the 1950s, especially in the United States, came to the psychoanalyst saying, "I desired my mother and I wanted to kill my father, and so what?" Interpretation cannot be reduced to the communication of knowledge that the psychoanalyst infers from what they hear from the analysand, because this dimension of knowledge must itself be questioned. Lacan listed his modes of interpretation: the enigma, the citation, the equivocation. It is a question of making the analysand hear something that will produce the emergence of knowledge, new material of the unconscious and the eventual collapse of an identification.

We should not forget that Freud himself emphasized that in order to make the right interpretation, it was necessary to wait for the patient to have it practically on the tip of his tongue—in German, for him to come to *sein Wort*. Lacan translated this by saying to the analysand, after a statement where he had said something without really hearing himself say it: "I'm not making you say it." Finally, a good interpretation is marked by the fact that it has produced an effect of surprise that lies in the aspect of reality that has been glimpsed. Similarly, silence: In reality, analysts are not necessarily very silent, but they do not respond where the response is expected, where the analysand may expect to be comforted on the imaginary level. One of the crucial issues of the analytic treatment is what Lacan called the object *a*. Now, precisely, this object *a*—the voice, for example—emerges all the more in silence, just as the cutting of the gaze produced by the couch will make the gaze emerge as an object *a*. For we are constantly enticing this gaze and this voice. We see this, for example, with phobic people who have the radio or television on non-stop.

As for teletherapy, the practice has developed since the COVID epidemic in France. For my part, I find it difficult to conceive of analysis taking place solely by telephone or videoconference. From time to time, a physical presence is necessary because, although psychoanalysis excludes all physical contact, the presence of bodies is important. Nevertheless, judging by what my American colleagues say, some of whom do supervisions with me where the practice of teletherapy is very important, and also a certain number of French colleagues, it can be effective in a certain number of cases. For my part, I mainly do supervisions by videoconference or by telephone, but also some analyses of people I meet occasionally when they can come to Paris or when I go to the country where they live. And I must say that in most cases we do a good job.

• What is your view of the transmission of psychoanalysis?

On this point, I am very marked by the influence of the French school, that is to say I consider that the most important thing in the training of the psychoanalyst is the personal analysis. Freud thought that it was necessary for the future analyst to undergo the experience of the analysis in order to acquire a personal conviction in the existence of the unconscious that no theoretical knowledge can give. Only in this way will the analyst be able to maintain this position of "evenly-suspended attention" and analyse the effects of what has been called countertransference, namely the analyst's prejudices. That said, for psychoanalysis to be transmitted there are three complementary paths, all of which are necessary but none of which is sufficient. The most important is personal analysis, but there are also supervisions or "control" analyses, which are indispensable. Moreover, an analyst cannot be alone, they must belong to a collective grouping in order to be able to have exchanges through seminars, teachings, small working groups, cartels, etc. Indeed, it is the theoretical-clinical tools produced by our elders that allow us to try to articulate what is absolutely singular in each analysis. This is why Lacan's formula, affirming that psychoanalysis is untransmissible and that each analyst must reinvent psychoanalysis, seems to me to be particularly accurate, on the condition that we insist on the "re" of reinventing, because this can only be done by assuming and assimilating the heritage of the history of psychoanalysis, that is to say, the history that fundamentally begins with Freud. From this reinvention, they will be able to try to transmit something that will be useful to their colleagues and to young analysts. Indeed, we must never forget that theory in psychoanalysis—Freud did not like the word "theory"—is at least as much the attempt to articulate solid concepts in order to find one's bearings in the movement of the treatment, in order to try to elaborate a clinical theory, as it is the testimony of the analyst's infinite analysis beyond the end of their analysis. This is what Lacan meant when he said that in his seminar he was in the position of a hysteric, that is to say, tirelessly continuing to analyse what had not yet been analysed, or what still had to be analysed.

- **In your opinion, what are the points of divergence between French psychoanalysis and English-speaking psychoanalysis?**

I will not go back over the debate that pitted Lacan against American psychoanalysts, namely "ego psychology", a current, moreover, to which his own analyst belonged. Let us recall that Freud warned against *furor sanandi*, that is, the desire to cure, which itself is a desire to analyse, but that he thought it necessary to have confidence in truth, as he wrote to Putnam in 1914: "The great ethical element in psychoanalytic work is truth and again truth, and this should suffice for most people. Courage and truth are of what they are mostly deficient" (Hale 1971, 171). In other words, the analyst should have no other intention than to apply the psychoanalytic method in the treatment, that which seeks to bring about the singular truth in its relation to the real for each person. As for American psychoanalysis today, it is so diverse and varied, broken up into numerous currents and original positions of certain practitioners that it is difficult to give a very general opinion. We need to exchange views with these colleagues, which, in my own way, I try to do.

- **What is your psychoanalytic approach to the societal debates on racial, gender identities or/and on the new forms of reproduction and parenting?**

First of all, we have to put these debates into perspective, that is to say they are an attempt to fight against violent segregation and in this sense these struggles and these demands seem to me to be completely legitimate. This movement has taken the form of identity claims and raises the question of why identity has become such an acute issue because it affects not only the whole LGBTQIA+ movement but also everything from the identities of those who have been colonized, to Black identity, to psychiatric diagnoses that can make up identity. This claim to identity is a form today of the struggle of people who have been, or are being, rendered invisible, which, once again, makes it legitimate.

Yet Michel Foucault pointed out that we are in a world, not where we are losing identity but where we are overidentified (Wade 2019). This overidentification in our world is the product of scientific and technical devices, ranging from national insurance numbers to DNA, but it does not tell us anything about our being, it does not ground social ties, it allows surveillance. This is why Foucault said that Bentham's panopticon is the paranoid truth of our world.

But the problem for psychoanalysis is that it is not a practice that aims to ensure an identity, since, for psychoanalysis, identity is a crystallization of identifications which fill the gap in our being, of the question "Who am I?" that remains unanswered. The social system is called upon to constantly provide answers to fill this fundamental gap.

Now, the analytical treatment is a process, to use Octave Mannoni's word, of disidentification. It topples identifications one after the other, because identity is related to the lack of being. Indeed, the subject fixes himself to a point of alienation where he has passed under what Lacan calls the master signifier. Identity as it was inscribed without question in the past is gradually undone by the place that science and technology have taken in our world (multiple demands for assignment), including the movements that the development of capitalism provokes, such as the displacements linked to urbanization, etc. What has always been one of the greatest providers of identity, namely religion, can also be linked to this. Psychoanalysis does not have to take a position on current developments, it can question them analytically. This is all the more true because, in our clinical practice, each treatment is totally unique and, for example, the analysis of a patient with a particular gender or sex characteristic will have nothing to do with that of another patient who has the same characteristics.

I have reservations about the public positions that certain colleagues may take in these debates as "psychoanalysts", placed in the position of experts, a term that should not be one of a corporate name, which does not exempt them from being engaged as citizens. But it is worth remembering that we can find in Freud's work proposals that are close to what all these current movements present. It should be remembered that the first of the *Three Essays*, if we recall the atmosphere at the time concerning homosexuality, which was punishable by law, is extraordinarily progressive. We should also remember that Freud signed Hirschfeld's petition to decriminalize homosexuality, etc. In the same way, a certain number of discoveries made by Freud should give us pause for thought. For instance, the unconscious does not make any difference between the sexes; there is a fundamental psychic bisexuality, we are all polymorphous perverts, etc. As he made additions to the *Three Essays on the Theory of Sexuality* (1905d), and in particular, in the preface to the fourth edition in 1920, Freud indicated that the sexuality he was talking about was an enlarged sexuality, detached from the genitals, which he likened to Plato's *Eros*. Of course, here and there in Freud we can find elements that are quite surprising, and even shocking today, but in keeping with the spirit of his times, such as the idea that women are closer to nature because they are more frustrated, the emphasis placed on the completion of the genital phase, heterosexuality, etc. But we must acknowledge that analytical theory by definition will never be pure. It is, like the patients we receive and like ourselves, linked to the ambient social discourses that shape us, and it is necessary, through the analytical method, to extract what belongs to psychoanalysis and to free it from the current discourses. This task has to be carried out again in each treatment, and for each analyst—and this brings us back to one of the previous questions—this is also the meaning of "reinvention", that is to say, the extraction of the analytic thing from the discourses of the time, knowing that it will never be completely accomplished, and therefore always has to be done again.

Psychoanalysis is not an initiation that leads to integration with a group; on the contrary, analytic treatment leads to what is most singular for each person, and it is then up to them to invent the way in which they will orient themselves among others and in the world.

References

Freud, S. (1905d). *Three Essays on the Theory of Sexuality. S. E.* 7. London: Hogarth, pp. 7–130.

Freud, S. (1912e). "Recommendations to physicians practising psycho-analysis". *S. E.* 12. London: Hogarth, pp. 111–120.

Freud, S. (1917e). "Mourning and melancholia". *S. E.* 14. London: Hogarth, pp. 237–260.

Hale, N. J. (Ed.) (1971) *James Jackson Putnam and Psychoanalysis: Letters Between Putnam and Sigmund Freud, Ernest Jones, William James, Sandor Ferenzi, and Morton Prince.* Cambridge, MA: Harvard University Press.

Vanier, A. (2000). *Lacan*, trans. S. Fairfield. New York, NY: Other Press.

Wade, S. (2019). *Foucault in California.* Berkeley: Heyday.

Index

For Product Safety Concerns and Information please contact our EU
representative GPSR@taylorandfrancis.com
Taylor & Francis Verlag GmbH, Kaufingerstraße 24, 80331 München, Germany